# RACE AND RACISM IN THE WEST

## CRUSADES TO THE PRESENT

*Revised Editon*

Edited by Paul Sweeney
*California State University, San Bernardino*

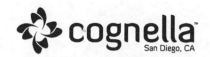
cognella
San Diego, CA

Bassim Hamadeh, CEO and Publisher
Christopher Foster, General Vice President
Michael Simpson, Vice President of Acquisitions
Jessica Knott, Managing Editor
Kevin Fahey, Cognella Marketing Manager
Jess Busch, Senior Graphic Designer
Marissa Applegate, Acquisitions Editor
Stephanie Sandler, Licensing Associate

*Cover credit*: Dave Fuller, copyright © 2011.

First published in the United States of America in 2013 by Cognella, Inc.

Printed in the United States of America

ISBN: 978-1-60927-129-9 (paperback) / 978-1-60927-656-0 (binder-ready)

www.cognella.com   800.200.3908

# Contents

*Handwritten note at top:*

- Federal & International law make it clear that the United States must provide immigrants the opportunity to claim asylum regardless of whether they entered the country legally or illegally

- "The law is clear: People can apply for asylum whether or not they're at a port of entry, & regardless of their immigration status", said Omar Jadwat, the director of the American Civil Liberties Union's Immigrants Rights Project

### Introduction
By Paul Sweeney

Race as a Social Category,
Not a Biological Fact
By Eugenia Shanklin

Holy War Proclaimed
By Thomas Asbridge

The Devastation of the Indies: A Brief Account          29
By Bartolomé de Las Casas

Introduction from *Genealogical Fictions: Limpieza de Sangre, Religion, and Gender in Colonial Mexico*          39
By María Elena Martínez

## Scientific Racism and Nationalism          51

Race and IQ          53
By Alexander Alland, Jr.

Nation and Race from *Mein Kampf*          69
By Adolf Hitler

## Colonialism and Post-Colonialism          79

Discourse on Colonialism          81
By Aimé Césaire

On Violence from *The Wretched of the Earth*          91
By Frantz Fanon

## Color-Blindness and White Privilege 103

The Central Frames of Color-Blind Racism 105
By Eduardo Bonilla-Silva

White Privilege: Unpacking the Invisible Knapsack 127
By Peggy Mcintosh

Defining Racism: "Can We Talk?" 133
By Beverly Daniel Tatum

## Afro-Latin America 143

The Leather Strap 145
By Jorge Amado

A Region in Denial: Racial Discrimination and Racism in Latin America 155
By Ariel E. Dulitzky

## Humor and Culture 173

Freud Goes to *South Park:* Teaching Against Postmodern Prejudices and Equal Opportunity Hatred 175
By Robert Samuels

# Introduction

By Paul Sweeney

●●●●●●●●●●●●●●●●●●●●●●●●●●●●●●●●●●●●●●●●●●●●●●●●

On July 22, 2011, a breaking news story captured the world's attention, albeit for only a short time. What made this particular story exceptional, however, was that it began with reports of a large bomb blast in Oslo, Norway. Within hours, another story emerged about a massacre on an island not too far from the capital. Within a few days more details surfaced, and the focus fell upon the suspect, Anders Behring Breivik. Did he act alone in the violent acts that claimed 77 lives?[1]

Possibly due to association with bomb blasts in public places being the work of Islamist extremists in London and Barcelona, many were quick to jump to that conclusion. When the image of the suspect, Breivik, appeared, there was shock and surprise. Not only was he not an Arab, he looked uncommonly normal: A thirty-two-year-old white Norwegian. The next question asked was "why?" Why did this man commit an atrocity that was admittedly politically motivated? The reasons, however, seemed nebulous at first.

"I acknowledge the acts but I do not plead guilty,"[2] Breivik told the Norwegian court. He also declared himself to be a "military commander in the Norwegian resistance movement and Knights Templar Norway."[3] It is the second statement that puzzled the police, because the Knights Templar were associated with the medieval Crusades that sought the expulsion of Islam from Europe and the Holy Land. The implications of his statement slowly sank in as other details came to light. Breivik also wrote and published on the Internet a massive rambling manifesto that more than a little resembled White Supremist websites such as the Aryan Nation. Quite a bit also came from the treatise written by the Unabomber, Ted Kaczynski.[4]

This last discovery led to another one, equally astonishing. Breivik had traveled to the United States and had cosmetic surgery performed so that he would appear more "Aryan." He also alluded to others sympathetic with his views (removal of Muslims and ending multiculturalism in Norway), and suggested that these "sleeper cells" merely lay in wait throughout Western Europe, biding their time to strike.[5]

If we take the sum of what is currently known about this case at the time of this writing, it points to a disturbing trend in the Western world, and the virulent anti-Islamic feelings that grew not only because of September 11, but also accentuated existing xenophobia and anti-immigrant feelings. For example, Breivik claimed that he is against the Labour Party of Norway's policies of inclusion and multiculturalism that he termed "cultural Marxists," and that is why he committed the atrocity, not against Muslims, but the political party he holds responsible for the societal changes. While Breivik's trial has only begun, he has been declared legally insane, a paranoid schizophrenic.[6]

One of the purposes and aims of this anthology is to guide the reader, student and instructor alike, through a thought process that began a long time ago. What the aforementioned scenario reveals is a long cultural divide still exists between east (oriental) and west (occidental). Another goal in this book is to bridge the gap and examine the causes of racism in all of its manifestations. The reader will be guided through the selections and themes as they occur throughout at the beginning of each excerpt.

Cultural views on race are discussed here, as are varying definitions of racism. The most recent assault, and example of cultural racism in present times, is immigration. Closely related to this topic is the notion that color-blind societies are desirable. Other sections in the anthology look at how concepts of race and nation have evolved, as well as how "scientific racism" still contributes to notions of racial inferiority and white supremacy. The idea that racism is a system of privileges enjoyed by whites also falls into this discussion.

While some of the readings can be taken in chronological order, the instructor, and student alike are encouraged to identify themes and commonalities as they appear. It is also advised to have students engage in discussions on meanings and variations of racism, as well as closely related concepts such as paternalism or "white man's burden." Mating films and support readings is an ongoing challenge, and instructors should go outside the box and employ pop culture as well as tried-and-true classics on this topic.

This is not a "complete" text on the topic of racism, however, the readings can provide insight on when in history people thought what and why in order to appreciate how long the issues have existed in the western hemisphere.

## Notes

1. Gibbs, Walter and Victoria Klesty. "Norway Mass Killer Admits July Massacre," *Reuters*, November 14, 2011, <http://news.yahoo.com/norway-mass-killer-breivik-admits-july-massacre-112110001.html> accessed December 15, 2011.

2. Ibid.

3. Ibid.

4. Ibid.

5. Kulish, Nicholas. "Neo-Nazis Suspected in Long Wave of Crimes, Including Murders, in Germany," *New York Times*, November 13, 2011, <http://www.nytimes.com/2011/11/14/world/europe/neo-nazis-suspected-in-wave-of-crimes-in-germany.html?_r=1&sq=neonazis%20suspected&st=cse&adxnnl=1&scp=1&adxnnlx=1323991518-RbgBSF9xJkaPbv-a8bLKSFQ> accessed December 15, 2011.

6. *BBC World News*, "Norway Massacre: Breivik Declared Insane," November 29, 2011, http://www.bbc.co.uk/news/world-15936276 [accessed December 15, 2011].

# Race as a Social Category, Not a Biological Fact

By Eugenia Shanklin

## Editor's Introduction

In this, the first reading of the anthology, Eugenia Shanklin addresses the concept that race is a social category, not a matter of biology. She immediately introduces the tendency to classify, name, and categorize perceived differences as "a favorite human pastime" (p. v). Her anthropological viewpoint provides a good basis for an interdisciplinary discussion on race, racism, and related maters that will follow in this anthology.

### References

Shanklin, Eugenia. *Anthropology and Race.* Belmont, CA: Wadsworth, 1994.

One of my reasons for writing this book is to put together two ideas of race—as a folk (sociological) concept and as a failed and discarded analytic (biological) concept—into an intelligible, accessible whole, a work that discusses problems with the concept of race on many levels. Another reason is that I have grown weary of explaining to my students that there is no such thing as a scientific concept of race. If, as we will see, Hitler knew this in the 1930s, why are college students in the 1990s so ill-informed on the subject? This then is a book about race for cultural anthropology students, or indeed anyone interested in the social sciences. It is not a technical treatise about populations and clines and other technical terms now used by biologists to describe differences between groups. The emphasis here is on the contrast between folk conceptions of race and what scientists used to consider scientific grounds for defining human races. Banton calls these the "folk" and "analytical" uses of the term and points out that there is "a two-way traffic between the two spheres of discourse" (1987:xiv). He adds that folk concepts change through time:

> Thus people in twentieth-century Europe do not explain misfortune and mental illness in terms of the concepts of witchcraft and madness used by their ancestors. Folk concepts are also modified in line with popular experience: ideas about other peoples change in step with the frequency and character of the

encounters from which that experience is derived. So in the course of time folk concepts acquire additional meanings which increase their serviceability in everyday communication while introducing ambiguities (Banton 1987:xiii).

… In America, folk concepts of race continue to draw credibility from the scientific inconclusiveness about race that so many authors are careful to mention. The distinction between the failed, discarded biological concept of race and the ongoing popular concept of race must be clearly drawn if students are to understand the fallacies of racism.

In the notes to his book, *Strangers in the Land*, John Higham muses that "To a surprising degree the history of race-thinking on both sides of the Atlantic has been neglected, perhaps partly because our sense of guilt makes detachment difficult to achieve, and partly because the subject requires a grasp of both scientific and social thought" (1981:406). Nancy Stepan echoes the sentiment: "Rather surprisingly, considering the long history of social Darwinism and racism, the racial ideas of the founding figures of evolutionism have never been examined systematically and in depth" (1982:48). … I think the reason for the gaps is more convoluted than these authors suggest, but this book is an attempt to bring together several strands in understanding modern anthropological ideas about race, racism, and their effects.

Anthropological consciousness about race has changed considerably since the 1950s and 1960s, when anthropologists, following the lead of Franz Boas and his students, wrote books on the subject, Margaret Mead said that Boas encouraged all his students to participate in major debates of the day. In recent years, however, anthropologists appear to have lost that urge and with it, the inclination to participate in ongoing discussions of racism.

Popular conceptions about race have also changed in the last four or five decades. Think, for example, of the changes in the words used to describe African-Americans in the last few decades: in the 1960s, Negro was the correct phrase; then black or Afro-American became the standard; now African-American is the appropriate phrase. We have moved from a "racial" description to a color description and on to an ethnic-group designation. Perhaps, in the twenty-first century, we will be able to abandon all such designations.

From the beginnings of their disciplines, social scientists have faced the problem of explaining differences among people. One solution, popular until a few decades ago, was the idea of race; but ideas about what constitutes a race, as well as scientific definitions of the word itself, have changed dramatically in the last century. They are still changing. The emphasis of this chapter is, first, on changes in perceptions about what a race is and, second, on the uses that can be and have been made of different understandings of race. Until the mid-twentieth century, many social scientists would have said yes, if asked whether physical differences between people were indicators of other (mental) abilities. Going into the twenty-first century, most social scientists will say no. In the recent past, respected anthropologists appeared on both sides in these debates, but since the 1950s, anthropologists have all but abandoned the concept of race, as well as the belief that other characteristics, such as IQ scores, are associated with apparent physical differences. The recent virtual silence of anthropology on the subject of race, however, may have encouraged students to believe both that physical differences are real and that they have meaningful associations with other nonphysical characteristics.

But if race is not a useful scientific concept, racism—the belief that physical characteristics are inevitably associated with mental or emotional capacities—continues to be a major social problem, and the fuzziness of definitions of race does not help in solving the social ills caused by racism. Racism is a heightened form of ethnocentrism (the belief that one's own people or life-ways are better than all others). Holding racist or ethnocentric ideas is a bit like believing that the stork brings babies—many of us may start out that way, but as we get closer to adulthood we learn that the reality is far more interesting than the myth.

Anthropologists have abandoned the concept of race but not the study of how one group characterizes the differences between themselves and others; in America, physical differences, especially skin color differences, are interpreted according to a "biracial" system of differentiation—there is white and there is nonwhite. These categories are interpreted according to a vague principle of biological descent, a principle perpetuated in social science textbook discussions of race. ...

## Slavery in America

Africans were brought to the colonies as slaves but once there, they "enjoyed the same rights and duties as other Virginians" (Morgan 1972:17) and, until the last quarter of the seventeenth century, were subject to the same laws. Africans could buy their own freedom, own land, cattle, and houses, and sue or be sued in court. But by 1676, there was a new and dangerous group of freedmen in Virginia, men who had come as servants, served their terms, and on their release from service could not find work or land. They were armed, as Virginians had to be at that time, and discontented. Morgan says:

> To be sure, the men at the bottom might have had both land and liberty, as the settlers of some other colonies did, if Virginia's frontier had been safe from Indians, or if the men at the top had been willing to forego some of their profits and to give up some of the lands they had engrossed. The English government itself made efforts to break up the great holdings that had helped to create the problem. But it is unlikely that the policy makers in Whitehall would have contended long against the successful.

> In any case they did not have to. There was another solution, which allowed Virginia's magnates to keep their lands, yet arrested the discontent and the repression of other Englishmen, a

solution which strengthened the rights of Englishmen and nourished that attachment to liberty which came to fruition in the Revolutionary generation of Virginia statesmen.

> ...The rights of Englishmen were preserved by destroying the rights of Africans (1972:24).

Morgan agrees with Winthrop Jordan (1968) that this was not a deliberate move and that slavery probably came to Virginia as an unthinking decision, an automatic result when Virginians bought the cheapest labor they could get. The courts moved to restrict the rights of "Negroes," and by 1690, "slavery began to assume its now familiar character as a complete deprivation of all rights" (Jordan 1968:82). Separate laws were made to govern Negroes and whites. By this means, the problem of the roving freedmen was solved:

> Nor is it surprising that Virginia's freedmen never again posed a threat to society. Though in later years slavery was condemned because it was thought to compete with free labor, in the beginning it reduced by so much the number of freedmen who would otherwise have competed with each other. When the annual increment of freedmen fell off, the number that remained could more easily find an independent place in society.... There might still remain a number of irredeemable, idle, and unruly freedmen, particularly among the convicts whom England exported to the colonies. But the numbers were small enough, so that they could be dealt with by the old expedient of drafting them for military expeditions. The way was thus made easier for the remaining freedmen to acquire property, maybe acquire a slave or two of their own, and join with their superiors in the enjoyment of those English liberties that differentiated them from their black laborers (Morgan 1972:27–28).

Jordan points out that slavery did not cause prejudice, nor did prejudice cause slavery. Instead the two "generated each other" (1968:80). But this was not the only result of America's central paradox:

> It was slavery... more than any other single factor, that had made the difference, slavery that enabled Virginia to nourish representative government in a plantation society, slavery that transformed the Virginia of Governor Berkeley to the Virginia of Jefferson, slavery that made the Virginians dare to speak a political language that magnified the rights of freemen, and slavery, therefore, that brought Virginians into the same commonwealth political tradition with New Englanders.... Thus began the American paradox of slavery and freedom, intertwined and interdependent, the rights of Englishmen supported on the wrongs of Africans...
> (Morgan 1972:289).

Scholars have long debated the question of the concomitant rise of freedom and of various forms of repression (racism, slavery, colonial domination), and the suggested explanations are sometimes more thought-provoking than conclusive. Orlando Patterson (1991) has suggested that our Western notion of freedom was generated from the experience of slavery. To extrapolate Patterson's sophisticated and well-documented argument, we might say that freedom and repression are social qualities maintained in internal and/or external balance, that freedom for some members of a society (or an entire society) increases at the expense of other members of the society (or another society).

A second explanation is that freedom is a function or result of the accessibility of resources; for example, the British invasion of other countries was a result of economic imperatives to do with expanding mercantile capitalism, and freedom at home (in England) was a result of greater resource accessibility abroad (in Ireland).

Whatever the accepted explanation, the correlation between increases in both repressions and freedoms is well documented in the scholarly literature and with it, the use of political propaganda to convince people that those "others" (whose rights are being taken away) thoroughly deserve their fate.

Should anyone doubt that political expedience underlies invocations or conceptions of race and racial differences, we can take other examples, from the twentieth century. Richard Milner writes about the Yanomamo of Brazil, studied by Napoleon Chagnon (a case familiar to anthropologists and anthropology students), that in 1989 Chagnon's writings "were being used by the Brazilian government to argue that these tribesmen are murderous, primitive people, incapable of being absorbed into the life of a modern nation. Not so coincidentally, gold has been discovered in their province, and 'sociobiological' arguments about their hereditary fierceness gives a convenient 'scientific' excuse for treating them as less than human" (1990:380).

Another example comes from the words of a well-known twentieth-century leader, who discussed the problems with the idea of nationhood and suggested they might be overcome by substituting the concept of race:

> The conception of the nation has become meaningless... "the nation" is a political expedient of democracy and liberalism. We have to... set in its place the conception of race.... The new order cannot be conceived in terms of the national boundaries of the peoples of the historic past, but in terms of race that transcends those boundaries.... *I know perfectly well... that in a scientific sense there is no such thing as race...* but I as a politician need a conception which enables the order which has hitherto existed on historic bases to be abolished and an entirely new and antihistoric order enforced and given an intellectual basis.... And for this purpose the conception of races serves me well.... With the conception

of race, National Socialism will carry its revolution abroad and recast the world [emphasis added].

These are the words of Adolf Hitler (quoted in Rauschning 1940: 231–232), who tried to do what he promised: to use the idea of race, which he knew to be an unscientific concept, to rebuild Germany, not on historical but on racial grounds.

These examples illustrate another point as well: Scientists are not immune to the prejudices and ideas currently in vogue. If as eminent a scientist as Charles Darwin could endorse the notion of a Celtic race, it is not surprising that Earnest Hooton saw a Keltic physical type. As Anaïs Nin put it, "We don't see things as they are; we see things as we are." ...

## Race, Culture, and Eugenics

I [have] contrasted the ideas of Charles Darwin and Alfred Russel Wallace about human beings and their innate abilities and noted that the answer to Wallace's dilemma was in the concept of culture, the idea of learned abilities available to all humans at whatever level of technology. But this answer was not to be fully accepted in anthropology until the middle of the twentieth century, after race was discarded as a scientific concept. In the meantime, the notion of what constituted a race had undergone some important changes. Before looking at the split between race and culture as anthropological concepts, it is worthwhile to review the phases through which the race concept passed before being discarded by anthropologists. I will summarize its history in anthropology in three phases, which are not mutually exclusive:

1. Race as a *conglomerate descriptive* term, before anthropology came into being (Linnaean, pre-Darwinian, and Darwinian, seventeenth and eighteenth centuries)
2. Race as a *typological device* (Darwinian, largely nineteenth century) in combination with some Darwinian evolutionary' notions
3. Race refined as a category within what is sometimes called the *modern synthetic theory* (the blending of Darwinian theory with genetic theory, twentieth century) and its ultimate replacement by the idea of breeding populations and their adaptation to specific environments (Bleibtreu and Meaney 1973:224).

The question, why are there differences among human groups? is now asked and answered very differently by physical anthropologists. Typologies and inferior/superior rankings no longer enter into the discussions, and very small differences, such as vitamin D absorption or sickling genes, are studied for their adaptive significance within particular environments. And, too, physical anthropologists talk about differences between and within groups, the study of human physical variations. They "believe" not in the existence of races but in populations, usually studied as breeding populations that have a number of physical (not cultural or mental) characteristics in common, such as blood type or eye color.

There are other ways of dividing up these phases. Banton (1987) has described a three-phase view of racial thought in slightly different terms: first, from the sixteenth to the nineteenth century, race as lineage, groups connected by common descent; second, in the early nineteenth century, race as type, as a limited number of permanent forms; and third, after Darwin, in the mid-nineteenth century, race as subspecies (1987:xi).

Nancy Stepan (1982) also divides the phases differently: first, she sees as the "pre-modern" period the time between 1600 and 1800, when involvement in the slave trade and the growth of ethnocentrism contributed to definitions of other races as inferior; second, the modern period between 1800 and 1960 when scientific credence was lent to the notions of racial inferiority and superiority; and third, from 1960 onward, the time when race was discarded by the scientific community as a device for classifying human beings.

Stepan regards the period between 1860 and 1900 as the "heyday of Darwinism" and suggests that the embrace of Darwinism "was compatible with the idea of the fixity, antiquity, and hierarchy of human races"[1] (1982:49). Evolution was used to lend strength to ideas about the superiority of white races, the inferiority of dark races, and eventually, to the cause of the eugenicists. Richard Hofstadter observed that "in some respects the United States during the last three decades of the nineteenth and at the beginning of the twentieth century was *the* Darwinian country. England gave Darwin to the world, but the United States gave to Darwinism an unusually quick and sympathetic reception" (Hofstadter 1955:4–5).

Stocking (1968:115) refers to this period at the end of the nineteenth century as a Darwinian "milieu" in which

> Darwinian evolution, evolutionary ethnology, and polygenist race thus interacted to support a raciocultural hierarchy in terms of which civilized men, the highest product of social evolution, were large-brained white men, and only large-brained white men, the highest products of organic evolution, were civilized. The assumption of white superiority was certainly not original with Victorian evolutionists; yet the interrelation of the theories of cultural and organic evolution, with their implicit hierarchy of race, gave it a new rationale (1968:122).

Banton notes that in response to the question, "'Why are they not like us', the typologists answered, 'Because they have always been different'" (1987:64). Within the typological framework, there was another vexatious question: how long "they" had been different or the general question of the origin of the human species. Those who argued for a single origin were called monogenists, referring to the belief that all humans were descended from one original "Adam and Eve," and those who argued for multiple origins were polygenists, who thought that humans had had separate origins on different continents. Johann F. Blumenbach, Samuel Stanhope Smith (said by Ashley Montagu to be the first American anthropologist), Charles Darwin, Thomas Henry Huxley, and Alfred Russel Wallace were monogenists; Samuel George Morton, Paul Broca, and William Z. Ripley were polygenists.

Franz Boas, a monogenist, and the group of anthropology students he trained took for granted that all human beings learned their ways of behaving, that behavior was not inherent; the eugenics school believed the opposite, that people's behavior was tied to their genetic makeup and could not be changed. The answer Boasian anthropology gave to the question of why there were differences was that differences were primarily a matter of environment and learning, with perhaps some unknown influences of heredity. Here I contrast Boas's ideas about the plasticity of human abilities and physical characteristics with two very different ideas: first, nineteenth-century notions known as "typological" theories, having to do with the fixity of human behavior and, second, the need for improving racial stocks, as formulated in the American school of eugenics in the early decades of the twentieth century.

## Race as a Conglomerate, Descriptive Device

Scientists are uncertain about the origins of the word *race,* but some believe that it might have come originally from an Arabic word, *ras,* which means head or beginning (Boyd 1950). From the Arabic, the word went into Spanish or Italian, and the fourteenth-century Spanish word, *raza,* means kind or sort, a kind or sort of animal, for example (*Webster's New World Dictionary: razza,* Italian; *ratio,* Latin). Before the mid-nineteenth century the word *race* was used in much the same way we might now use the words *strain* or *variety.* Writers spoke in terms of a "race of kings" or a "race of yeomen" (Curtis 1968); John Bunyan in the seventeenth century wrote about a "race of saints" (quoted in Banton and Harwood 1975:13).

The conglomerate descriptive use was "formalized" by Linnaeus, who first published his classifications in 1735 but referred only to *Homo sapiens* (literally, wise man), and did not distinguish the species according to races or varieties in the first edition. In a subsequent (1738) edition of his catalog, Linnaeus added the four "varieties" of *Homo sapiens: americanns; enropaens; asiatiais;* and *aser.* Europeans were "light, lively and inventive," whereas the American Indians (H. *s. americanus)* were "choleric and persevering" (Count 1950:357). The Asiatics (H. *s. asiaticus)* were "yellow, melancholic, inflexible"; and the Africans (H. *s. aser)* were "phlegmatic, indulgent, crafty, lazy and negligent" (Count 1950:357).

These four varieties were essentially geographical classifications; although Linnaeus noted certain temperamental characteristics that went along with the varieties, the divisions were based on the four major geographical divisions of the earth—Europe, Asia, Africa, and the Americas—along with the skin colors found in the human species in each place. As we have seen, early explorers, Herodotus among them, had also noted the differences and speculated that they were due to the environment. Later explorers offered similar speculations and as we have seen, Charles Darwin used facial expressions to judge the cultural characteristics of other groups.

Geography and skin color differences were the main diagnostics—there were yellow people in Asia, white people in Europe, black people in Africa, and red people in America. In the conglomerate descriptive use of race, other characteristics, such as mental or cultural traits, were often mingled with physical attributes; in contemporary terms, this made it a racist scheme because it mixed physical and cultural characteristics. Linnaeus's scientific intent was to classify, not to justify racist social policies, but whatever its difficulties, there were theorists of race who wished for a more scientific set of criteria, one that defined only physical traits. It is a truism of the scientific enterprise that the more closely you look at something, the more complicated it becomes. Broad geographical classifications of race were not useful for scientific purposes; to state that skin color varies from one continent to another is not to explain differences but to state

the obvious. The many descriptions of skin color variations according to geographic region made it clear that skin color varied, even within a group or within broad continental boundaries; at the edges of the continents, skin color was even more varied, and it became apparent to the classifiers that skin color was not a reliable indicator of race.

Later investigators used skin color more systematically and without the personality characteristics the earlier students of human races had ascribed, but the divisions they saw and the concepts they used quickly became unwieldy. However, the conglomerate descriptive use of race continued well into the twentieth century. In 1946, Earnest Hooton (who later studied the physical anthropology of Ireland) offered a different, somewhat dizzying set of categories: there were primary races such as Whites, Negroids, and Mongoloids. Within each primary race there were primary subraces; among whites there were Mediterranean, Ainu, Keltic, Nordic, and Alpine or East Baltic. Further, there were composite races like the Australian, Indo-Dravidian, and Polynesian. There were also composite subraces such as Armenoid and Dinanc, as well as residual mixed types like the Nordic-Alpine and Nordic-Mediterranean. These divisions usually included additional genetically determined traits. ...

## Race as a Typological Device

A key concept of the nineteenth century was "typology," a classificatory system according to which races could be systematically grouped because each had "immutable" or unchanging characteristics. Typological notions were pre-Darwinian, but the school reached its zenith when the typological notions were melded with Darwinian emphasis on evolution's conservative forces. The explanation that was given for racial differences was that variations in constitution and behavior were the expression of differences between types that were relatively permanent, that social categories were aligned with the natural categories, and that individuals belonging to a particular racial group displayed an innate antagonism toward other types (Banton 1987:38).

In this phase, there was an attempt to formalize the race concept even further, based on typologies or the study of ideal types and their variant forms. At the turn of the century, Mendel's findings on inheritance were rediscovered and the search for "racial markers" was ended, as heredity was seen to be an important component of physical makeup, but only one component among many others, including environment and culture.

In the beginning, the investigation of racial differences according to typological notions was a productive enterprise,, in the sense that the investigations yielded a great deal of data. The differences between human groups could be and were quantified; such traits as nose form, blood groups, eye color, head shape, and skin color were carefully counted and recorded. As time went on, more counts were done and then it seemed still more counts were in order, so investigators were kept busy for years with new counts. The refinement of the measuring tools, the endless elaborations of measurements, and of the classifications that grew out of them, would lead finally to the recognition that diversity was as important as the stability the classifiers initially emphasized. But this was not to happen until typological notions had been employed extensively and exhaustively. …

Paul Broca was a French professor of clinical surgery; he founded the Anthropological Society of Paris in 1859, and like Morton, he believed that intelligence could be assessed by brain or skull measurements. Unlike Morton, Broca did not manipulate his measurements; instead he "explained" them. In 1862, Broca published his "demonstration" that the brain size of Europeans had increased in size over the last centuries' progression from medieval to modern times. He obtained samples from three Parisian cemeteries, from the twelfth, eighteenth, and nineteenth centuries. Initially, the average cranial capacities were a disappointment—1,426, 1,409, and 1,462 cc.—but Broca recovered by introducing the factor of social class. The large twelfth-century sample, obtained in a churchyard, had to represent gentry, whereas the (smaller) eighteenth-century skulls

came from a common grave. The nineteenth-century sample came from both individual graves (average 1,484 cc.) and a common grave (1,403 cc.). But the eighteenth-century common grave had a larger average (1,409 cc.) than the nineteenth-century's (1,403 cc.), and Broca explained this by arguing that the eighteenth-century common grave had included a better class of people. In the same way, he resolved another problem, an additional seventeen skulls from the morgue's graveyard, skulls that had a higher value than those from the individual graves of the nineteenth century (1,517 cc. vs. 1,484 cc.). This, Broca said, was because morgues stood on river banks and included a large number of drowned people, many of whom were suicides; many suicides were insane, and many insane people, like criminals, have surprisingly large brains (Gould 1981:96). …

The natural historians used the race concept to arrive at appropriate taxonomic categories or boxes into which to put different groups, but those boxes were difficult and inexact because not all the members of a population necessarily had the traits defined by the boxes. The search began for the "ultimate" trait, a trait that would not vary from one individual or group to the next but would be constant, invariant. When this trait was found, the second or Darwinian phase of racial studies was launched; in this school, the notions of typology were combined with those of eugenics to produce a group that believed absolutely in the fixity of "racial" characteristics, together with the ranking involved (whites on the top, blacks on the bottom) and the additional notion that certain of those fixed characteristics rendered some members of the population "unfit" for civilized social life. The search for the perfect trait produced, at last, what was thought to be an immutable or unvarying characteristic: head form.

Applying their typological notions to head shape, the typologists arrived at the following conclusions:

1. Human heads come in two overall shapes, long and round. Europeans generally have long heads—or at least those who did

the classifying were long-headed—and other peoples, they soon discovered, were round-headed.

2. Long-headedness and round-headedness were then found to account for many differences between groups. Naturally, if "we" were long-headed and superior, it followed that "they" were round-headed and inferior.

According to the typologists, head shape was the perfect indicator of capacity for civilization.

# Holy War Proclaimed

By Thomas Asbridge

● ● ● ● ● ● ● ● ● ● ● ● ● ● ● ● ● ● ● ● ● ● ● ● ● ● ● ● ● ● ● ● ● ● ● ● ● ● ● ● ● ●

## Editor's Introduction
## Asbridge on the First Crusade

The opening paragraphs of this excerpt by Thomas Asbridge reveal the full content of the 1095 papal proclamation that launched the holy war against Islam, today known as the First Crusade (1096). The reader is guided through various issues in medieval Europe, how the First Crusade did not develop "... by some form of pre-existing genetic hatred for Islam[,] and that a desperate clash between these two civilizations was all but inevitable."[1] Another important consideration is that medieval Spain, on the eve of their centuries-long *Reconquista*, "... was once Europe's *most Muslim* and *most Jewish* country."[2]

### Notes

1. Thomas Asbridge. *The First Crusade, A New History: The Roots of Conflict Between Christianity and Islam.* New York: Oxford University Press, 2004, ix.
2. Chris Lowney. *A Vanished World: Muslims, Christians, and Jews in Medieval Europe.* New York: Oxford University Press, 2005, 47.

A race absolutely alien to God has invaded the land of Christians, has reduced the people with sword, rapine and flame. These men have destroyed the altars polluted by their foul practices. They have circumcised the Christians, either spreading the blood from the circumcisions on the altars or pouring it into the baptismal fonts. And they cut open the navels of those whom they choose to torment with loathsome death, tear out their most vital organs and tie them to a stake, drag them around and flog them before killing them as they lie prone on the ground with all their entrails out. What shall I say

of the appalling violation of women, of which it is more evil to speak than to keep silent?

On whom, therefore, does the task lie of avenging this, of redeeming this situation, if not on you, upon whom above all nations God has bestowed outstanding glory in arms, magnitude of heart, litheness of body and strength to humble anyone who resists you.

This horrific imagery and forceful exhortation launched the First-Crusade. On the last Tuesday of November, in the year 1095. Pope Urban II delivered an electrifying speech to a crowd outside the southern French city of Clermont.

Christians living in the East, he alleged, were enduring dreadful oppression and abuse at the hands of their 'savage' Muslim masters, and the epicentre of Christian tradition, the Holy City of Jerusalem, likewise lay in the grasp of Islam. In the face of these intolerable 'injuries', Pope Urban called upon Catholic Europe to take up arms and prosecute a vengeful campaign of reconquest, a holy war that would cleanse its participants of sin. When he proclaimed that those fighting as 'soldiers of Christ' would be purified by the fire of battle, his words set Christendom alight.

In the weeks and months that followed, the pope's impassioned appeal swept across Europe, prompting some 100,000 men and women, from knight to pauper, to take up the call—the largest mobilisation of manpower since the fall of the Roman Empire. One such was the great Norman warrior Bohemond of Taranto. Immersed in the bitter siege of the rebellious southern Italian city of Amalfi, Bohemond apparently underwent a dramatic conversion when news of the gathering crusade arrived. Calling for his most lavishly wrought cloak to be brought forth, he had this treasured garment cut to pieces in front of an astonished assembly. Fashioning the cloth into crosses, he then proudly displayed this badge upon his sleeve as a visible sign of his commitment to the cause and distributed the remainder among the enthralled audience. Together they abandoned the siege to fight a new war, leaving the air afire with their battle cry: 'Gods will! God's will!'

This titanic expedition, known to history as the First Crusade, marked a watershed in relations between Islam and the West. This was not the first war between Christians and Muslims, but it was the conflict that set these two world religions on a course towards deep-seated animosity and enduring enmity. Between 1000 and 1300 CE Catholic Europe and Islam went from being occasional combatants to avowed and entrenched opponents, and the chilling reverberations of this seismic shift still echo in the world today.

The First Crusade stands at the heart of this transformation because it effected change on two intertwined levels: 'reality' and 'myth-history'. In 'reality', the actual progress of the crusade brought Islam and the West into fierce physical conflict, but need not necessarily have prompted an irrevocable divide. Even before the expedition was over, however, its events began passing into 'myth-history', as contemporaries sought to record and explain its remarkable progress, asking why it had happened, who had participated and why, and how the expedition had affected the world. Indeed, from its genesis, the history of the crusade was blurred by distortion. The image of Muslims as brutal oppressors conjured by Pope Urban was pure propaganda—if anything, Islam had proved over the preceding centuries to be more tolerant of other religions than Catholic Christendom. Likewise, the fevered spontaneity of Bohemond's decision to take the cross, dutifully recorded by one of his followers, was almost certainly a facade masking calculated ambition."

## The World of Pope Urban II

The man who unleashed the First Crusade was born to the noble de Lagery family in the northern French town of Chatillon-sur-Marne around the year 1035. Baptised Odo, he is known in the annals of history by another name, for upon ascending the throne of St Peter in Rome in his fifties he followed papal tradition, breaking with his past to become Pope Urban II. But, in spite of this transformation, Urban remained a man of his time, his upbringing and earlier career leaving an unquestionable imprint upon his papacy and serving to shape the momentous call to arms that shook Europe at the end of the eleventh century.

### European Society

Urban's target audience in 1095 was the aristocracy of France, the very group into which lie had been born, a violent warrior class, fighting for survival amid bloodthirsty lawlessness. One thousand years earlier, the region we would think of today as France had been, overrun and absorbed by the relentless expansion of the Roman world For centuries the province enjoyed relative peace and prosperity within the protective fold of this empire, but from the later fourth century C.E. onwards Rome's dominion began to falter, as the force of its law, culture and society receded. The Roman Empire did not implode in one sudden, spectacular moment—rather, it decayed incrementally, and, with the gradual evaporation of its power, the way opened for 'barbarian' peoples to supplant, mimic and finally extinguish Rome's authority. Between the fifth and seventh centuries, groups like the Visigoths, Avars and Lombards redrew the map of Europe, leaving a bewildering patchwork of diverse, warring realms where unity had once prevailed. In north-eastern Gaul one such group, the Franks, came to prominence around 500 CE, carving out a kingdom with which historians now associate their name—Francia, or France—Urban's homeland.

By 800 CE a descendant of the Franks, Charlemagne, had amassed such a collection of dependencies—encompassing regions that would today make up much of France, Italy, Germany and the Low Countries—that he could claim to have restored the glory of the Roman Empire in the West. France and Europe as a whole enjoyed a return to some semblance of centralised authority under Charlemagne and his successors, the Carolingians. But by the year 1000 this had dissolved under the weight of bitter succession disputes and harrowing Viking invasions. Without the controlling hand of centralised rule, disorder spread and effective power devolved into the hands of acquisitive warlords. At the time of Pope Urban II's birth in the eleventh century, only the barest remnant of a Frankish realm survived, and any glimmer of unified French identity endured only in the imagination. The titular kings of France struggled even to control a small territory centred around Paris, while the Frankish realm fractured into numerous dukedoms and counties whose power eclipsed that of the royal house. 'France" was even divided linguistically, with two distinct languages—Languedor and Languedoc—prevailing in the north and south respectively. The people eventually attracted to Urban's crusading ideal in 1095 were certainly not all from France, but contemporaries who wrote about this expedition, especially those looking in

from outside western Europe, tended to categorise all its participants under the single term 'Franks'. Although somewhat misleading, it has therefore become common practice to describe the First Crusaders as the Franks.

Urban II grew up within the Champagne region of north-eastern France, in an intensely localised environment. Here, as in the rest of Europe, even nobles could expect to live their entire lives without travelling more than a hundred kilometres from home. The warrior aristocracy held sway, a class, dominated by the knightly profession, bound by a complex network of lordship, vassalage and obligation—what in the past has been called the 'feudal system"—at the heart of which lay an exchange of military service in return for tenure of a territory or 'fief'. Champagne, and France in general, may not as historians once thought, have been in a state of utter, chaotic savagery, but Urban was still born into an extraordinarily violent society, dominated by bloody feud and vendetta. Even the more peaceable nobles engaged in rapine and plunder as a matter of course, and vicious internecine struggles for power and land were a fact of daily life.

### Medieval Christianity

For all the violence and mayhem of Urban's childhood world, he was, from his earliest clays, surrounded by and immersed in the Christian religion. The medieval society in which he lived was obsessively dedicated to this faith, almost every feature of daily existence being conditioned by its doctrines. Europe's devotion to Christianity can be traced back to the fourth century CE, when the Roman emperor Constantine the Great embraced Christian dogma, injecting this small-scale eastern Mediterranean sect into the lifeblood of Rome. Pumped through the arteries of the empire, Christianity eventually became the state religion, displacing paganism. In a strange quirk of history, the earthly power that had overseen the execution of Christ now catapulted his teachings on to the world stage. Even as Rome's might crumbled, this creed continued to spread to almost every corner of Europe, and by the eleventh century the region could accurately be described as western. Christendom. Following what would today be thought of as Roman Catholicism, its people can most precisely be termed the 'Latins' to distinguish them from adherents of the various other branches of Christianity.

In. Urban's day; this faith dominated and dictated everyday life to an extent that can seem almost inconceivable to a modern observer attuned to the attitudes and preconceptions of an increasingly secularised contemporary society. Urban lived in an authentically spiritual age, one in which there was no need to question the existence of God because his absolute power was plain for all to see, made manifest on earth in the form of 'miracles'—the sudden curing of a 'blind' man after prayer, the 'divine punishment' of a murderer struck by lightning. Events that would today be interpreted as natural phenomena, or put down to the vagaries of chance, sewed to confirm the efficacy of the Christian message to a medieval audience. In eleventh-century Europe, the full pantheon of human experience—birth, love, anger and death—was governed by Christian dogma, and the cornerstone of this system of belief was fear. Medieval minds were plagued by one overwhelming anxiety: the danger of sin. In death, it was believed, every human soul would be judged. Purity would bring everlasting paradise, but an eternity of gruesome torment awaited those polluted by sin. This universal obsession, shared by king and peasant alike, shaped all custom, morality and law.[1] Urban's early life, like that

of his contemporaries, was essentially a struggle to avoid sin and attain heavenly salvation.

The problem was that sin and temptation were everywhere. Natural human impulses—hunger, lust, pride—all carried inherent dangers, and the Bible failed to offer medieval mankind a clear-cut definition of an 'ideal' Christian lifestyle. In Late Antiquity some Christians had gone to extremes to avoid worldly contamination: the celebrated fifth-century hermit St Simeon spent forty-seven years in lonely isolation atop a pillar in northern Syria, striving for purity. By Urban's day, a more attainable path to perfection had become popular in western Europe. Monasticism, in which Christians dedicated their lives to prayer and the service of God within an enclosed environment embracing the principles of poverty, chastity and obedience, was accepted as the pinnacle of spiritual existence. It was this path to 'perfection' that Urban eventually chose to follow. As a young man, he was sent to study at the cathedral school in Rheims and soon joined the (church, attaining the position of archdeacon, an indication that Urban had probably been a younger son and was therefore not bound to a knightly future.

Remaining in Rheims until his mid-thirties, Urban then made a dramatic decision. We might imagine that as a member of the Church, he was already cradled in the bosom of Christian purity, but in reality the eleventh-century clergy were a notoriously dissolute bunch. Priests and bishops often reaped rich profits from land, some might marry, hold two or three ecclesiastical offices at once and perhaps even fight in wars. Around 1068 Urban turned aside from this worldly 'secular" arm of the Church to become a monk, although his decision was probably inspired by a mixture of personal ambition and piety. He was professed into perhaps the most influential and respected monastery of the day, the Burgundian house of Cluny, an institution just reaching the apogee

---

1 In an age before printing, when illiteracy was the norm across all levels of society, the threats posed by sin and damnation were pressed home through dreadful, arresting imagery. Religions art was the mass media of the central Middle Ages, and the frescoes and stone sculptures that decorated churches provided graphic representations of the danger of impurity. Any visitor to the Cathedral of St Lazare in Autun, Burgundy, to the south of Urban's homeland, could not fail to get the message, for the arch above the main entrance contained a stunning sculpted tableau of the Last Judgement. Carved in the first decades of the twelfth century by the master craftsman Giselbert, the weighing of souls—the moment at which a human's worth would he measured—is depicted with agonising clarity, as a grinning devil strives to tip the scales in his favour and then drag condemned souls into

hell. Elsewhere, giant demonic hands reach out to strangle a sinner, with the utter horror of the moment etched on to the victim's lace. Confronted with these ghastly images, and the equally compelling representation of the blessed lifted into eternal paradise by graceful angels, it is little wonder that medieval Christians were fixated upon the battle against sin.

of its power. Cluny epitomised two interlocking concepts: liberty and purity. In an age when even monasteries commonly fell prey to worldly contamination, as lords, princes and bishops sought to meddle in their affairs, Cluny had one massive advantage. From the moment of its birth, in the early tenth century, it had been placed under the direct protection of the pope in Rome, Immune from local interference, Cluny was effectively its own master, free to appoint its own abbots, govern as it saw fit and pursue monastic perfection in true isolation. ... Even within this vast, supranational edifice, Urban's piety and administrative skill did not long go unnoticed. He rose to become grand prior of Cluny, second in command to the abbot, and helped to cement the monastery's reputation as a bastion of uncompromising spiritual purity.

But Urban's career was not to end within the confines of a monastery. As a papal protectorate, Cluny had long enjoyed an intimate, mutually beneficial alliance with Rome. It is no surprise then that Urban's position within the monastery brought him to the notice of the pope. Around 1080, he was recruited to become cardinal-bishop of Ostia, one of the most powerful ecclesiastical offices in Italy. Urban had now entered the inner sanctum of spiritual authority, but he could not have arrived at a more tumultuous moment; for the papacy was in the midst of a ferocious dispute.

## The Medieval Papacy

To understand the arena now confronting Urban, one must first appreciate the differences between the theoretical and actual status of the medieval papacy. In Christian tradition there were five great centres of ecclesiastical power on earth, five patriarchates, of which Rome was just one. But late-eleventh-century popes claimed preeminence among all these on the basis that Christ's chief apostle St Peter had been the first bishop of Rome. Scripture indicated that St Peter had been empowered by Christ to manifest God's will, becoming, in essence, the most potent spiritual figure on earth. The papacy maintained that an unbroken chain of descent ran from St Peter across the centuries, connecting all popes and

thus making them successors to this authority, indeed, it went one step further, arguing that this unique 'apostolic power' was not handed clown from pope to pope and thus subject to dilution, but was instead directly conferred, fresh and unsullied, upon each new incumbent of the office. As far as Rome was concerned, this meant that papal authority was unassailable and infallible. Medieval popes thus regarded themselves as the world's foremost spiritual power and believed they were entitled to exert absolute control over the Latin Church of Europe.

When Urban joined the Roman camp, however, the reality of papal authority was but a pale, almost pathetic, reflection of these lofty aspirations. Far from being recognised as the leader of the Christian faith on earth, the pope struggled to manage the spiritual affairs of central Italy, let alone all western Christendom. The theoretical underpinnings of papal power had for centuries lain, dormant and untapped, as the office of pope remained mired in localised interests and abuse, and any attempts to break free of these confines faltered in the face of massive obstacles. ...

At the same time, any hope of wielding absolute ecclesiastical power in Europe was unrealistic, because the dividing line between the spiritual realm of the Church and the temporal world of kings, lords and knights was at best blurred, at worst non-existent. In the medieval age, these two spheres were so intertwined as to be practically inseparable. Kings, believing themselves to be empowered by divine mandate, felt a responsibility to care for and, if necessary, govern the Church. Meanwhile, virtually all bishops wielded a measure of political authority, being major landholders in possession of their own wealth and military forces. To curb the political independence of these powerful figures, many kings sought to control the selection, appointment and investiture of churchmen based within their realm, even though in theory this was a papal prerogative. At the end of the first millennium of Christian history, the Latin Church was in disarray and the limited efforts to control it were being offered not by the papacy, but by secular rulers.

It was not until the mid-eleventh century that the first significant steps towards redressing this imbalance were taken. Amid a general atmosphere of heightened devotional awareness, inspired in part by the example of monasteries like Cluny, western Christians began to look at their Church and perceive sickness. A clergy rife with abuse and 'governed' by a powerless pope offered little prospect of guiding society towards salvation. Arguing that the Latin Church would have to clean up its act, starting in Rome itself and working outwards, a 'Reform Movement' emerged, advocating a twin agenda of papal empowerment and clerical purification. This campaign enjoyed some early success, establishing a rigorous new process for electing popes and launching public attacks on vices such as clerical marriage and the buying and selling of ecclesiastical office.

The champion and chief architect of the cause was Pope Gregory VII (1073–85), the very man who recognised Urban's talents and brought him to Italy. A profoundly ambitious, wilful and intransigent figure, Gregory fought harder than any pope before him to realise the potential of his office, struggling to unify and cleanse Latin Christendom under the banner of Rome. With audacious single-mindedness, lie identified what he believed to be the root cause of the Church's problems—the polluting influence of the laity—and then sot about attacking it with near-rabid tenacity, in what has been termed the 'Investiture Controversy'. Gregory was not interested in tempered diplomacy or negotiated reform—he went straight for the jugular of the mightiest secular force in Europe, hoping to cow the rest of Christendom into submission by example.

In 1075 Gregory banned the German king Henry IV, a man who could trace the lineage of his office to Charlemagne and beyond, from interfering in the affairs of the Church. When Henry resisted, Gregory mobilised the ultimate weapon in his arsenal. As yet possessing no military might with which to coerce, he chose instead to strike Henry with spiritual censure. In February 1076, he excommunicated the most powerful Latin Christian alive and instructed the king's subjects to renounce him. So dramatic was this act that legend later declared it to have caused the ancient papal throne of St Peter to crack in two. Ejecting Henry from the Church, denying his stains as a Christian, was an immense gamble; should Gregory's edict be ignored, his bluff would be called and his authority shattered, but were this condemnation to be heeded, then the Roman pontiff, who just decades earlier had seemed a marginal nonentity on the European stage, would he confirmed as the arbiter of ultimate justice.

In the final analysis, Gregory's strategy did not succeed, his papacy ending with the glorious ambition of papal empowerment unrealised. Henrys excommunication did initially prompt the king to adopt a more penitent stance, but the pope soon overplayed his hand, enraging his enemies and alienating supporters with his radical and unbending vision of spiritual reform and his intensely personal, autocratic notion of papal authority. Along the way, Gregory experimented with the concept of a papal army, a move that prompted indignation in some quarters but broke crucial ground on the road towards the concept: of crusading.

It was into a world of unrealised papal aspirations and seething diplomatic discord that: Urban was propelled by his appointment as prelate of Ostia c. 1080. In spite of Gregory VII's hard-line fanaticism and failing fortunes, Urban remained among his staunchest allies, … [until] 25 May 1085 [when] Pope Gregory VII died in ignominious exile in southern Italy. In the chaos that followed his death no obvious candidate immediately emerged to champion the Gregorian cause or challenge the authority of the German, anti-pope. The first, short-lived choice of a successor was not consecrated until May 1087, and, after his death in September of that same year, it took a further six months of infighting before Urban II could step forward to assume the office of pope.

Given the extraordinary impact he was to have upon European history, the most striking feature of Urban's early pontificate was the position of extreme weakness and vulnerability from which he began. … A far more skilful diplomat than his predecessor … Urban chose to encourage gradual change through cautious suggestion rather than affect brazen dominance. ... Urban [and he] capitalised upon the network of contacts established during his days at Cluny and worked to rejuvenate the web of aristocratic clients, known as 'the faithful of St Peter. ... Rejecting despotism in favour of consultative government, Urban was the first pope to institute a functioning *curia Romana* or papal court, in which he worked alongside ecclesiastical advisers instead of presenting himself as the sole, perfected mouthpiece of St Peter.

By 1095, Urban's restrained touch had begun to pay off, bringing the doctrine of reform to regions that Gregory's closed fist had failed to penetrate. ... [I]n March [1095] Pope Urban convened a major ecclesiastical comical at the southern Italian city of Piacenza. It was during this meeting that a fateful embassy arrived bearing envoys from Constantinople (modern-day Istanbul), capital of the mighty Greek Christian Empire of Byzantium. Beset by aggressive Islamic neighbours, these Byzantines appealed for military aid from their Christian brethren in the West. The pope's initial reaction was to urge 'many' to promise, by taking an oath, to aid the emperor most faithfully as fur as they were able against the pagans", but this seems to have provoked little or no reaction. The idea of promoting a more vigorous response was, however, beginning to take shape in Urban's mind. Before the year was out, and with the backbone of papal authority barely rebuilt he would issue a call to arms that would drive a multitude of Latins swarming to the gates of Constantinople and beyond.

## The Crusading Ideal

In the autumn of 1095, with the power of Rome taking its first tentative steps towards recovery, Pope Urban II made a grand preaching tour of France. It was during this visit to his old homeland that Urban launched the First Crusade. He called upon the warriors of the Latin West to avenge a range of ghastly 'crimes' committed against Christendom by the followers of Islam, urging them to bring aid to their eastern brethren and to reconquer the most sacred site on earth, the city of Jerusalem. This speech, the moment of genesis for the concept of a crusade, bound the Christian religion to a military cause. To understand how the pope achieved this fusion of faith, and violence and why Europe ultimately responded to his appeal with enthusiasm, we must: begin by asking what prompted Urban to preach the crusade when he did.

## The Threat to Latin Christendom?

The first point to acknowledge is that the call to arms made at Clermont was not directly inspired by any recent calamity or atrocity in the East. Urban's sermon may have been stimulated, at least in part, by the Byzantine appeal for military aid received some eight months earlier at the council of Piacenza, but this request was not itself tied to any recent Greek defeat, resulting instead from decades of mounting Muslim aggression in Asia Minor (modern-day Turkey). And although the Holy City of Jerusalem, the expedition's ultimate goal, was indeed in Muslim hands, it had been so for more than 400 years—hardly a fresh wound. At the start of the eleventh century, the Church of the Holy Sepulchre, thought to enclose the site of Christ's crucifixion and resurrection, had been partially demolished by the volatile Islamic leader known to history as the Mad Caliph Hakim. His subsequent persecution of the local Christian population lasted for more than a decade, ending only when he declared himself a living god and turned on his own Muslim subjects. Tensions also seem to have been running high in 1027, when Muslims reportedly threw stones into the compound of the Holy Sepulchre. More recently, Latin Christians attempting to make devotional pilgrimages to the Levant of whom there continued to be many, may have reported some difficulties in visiting the Holy Places, but the volume and severity of such complaints was far from overwhelming.

The reality was that, when Pope Urban proclaimed the First Crusade at Clermont Islam and Christendom had coexisted for centuries in relative equanimity. 'There may at times have been little love lost" between Christian and Muslim neighbours, but there was, in truth, little to distinguish this enmity from the endemic political and military struggles of the age. When, in the seventh century, Muhammad first revealed the teachings of Allah and Islam exploded out of the Arabian peninsula, the eastern Roman Empire of Byzantium raced a seemingly unstoppable tide of expansion. Arab forces swept through Palestine, Syria and Asia Minor, finally breaking upon the walls of the Creek capital, Constantinople. As the years passed, Islam and Byzantium developed a tense, sometimes quarrelsome respect for one another, but their relationship was no more fraught with conflict than that between the Greeks and their Slavic or Latin neighbours to the west.

At the other end of the Mediterranean, Islamic forces had overwhelmed the Iberian peninsula in 711 CE. So dynamic was their advance that only the might of Charlemagne's grandfather, Charles the Hammer, could turn them back from the borders of France and the heartlands of Latin Christendom, Partially detached from the rest of Europe by the physical barrier of the Pyrenean mountains, these Muslims settled in Spain and Portugal, leaving the indigenous Christians only a thin sliver of territory in the north. Muslim power held fast for generations, allowing culture, learning and trade to flourish, and Islamic Iberia blossomed into one of the greatest centres of civilisation in the known world. When decay and political fracture finally set in during the eleventh century, the surviving Christian realms of the north were quick to capitalise. In the decades leading up to the First Crusade, the nature of Iberian Latin-Muslim contact did alter: animosities hardened; the Christians went into the ascendant; and the frontier dividing these two faiths gradually began to inch southwards. But even in this period the scavenging Latins were far more interested in draining the Muslim south of its fabled wealth than they were in prosecuting any sort of concerted religious warfare. When blood was shed in battle, it was usually the result of Christian in-fighting, fractious squabbling over the spoils.

At the end of the eleventh century, Christendom was in one sense encircled by Islam, with Muslim forces ranged against it to the east along Byzantium's Asian frontier and to the south in the Iberian peninsula. But Europe was a long way from being engaged in an urgent, titanic struggle for survival. No coherent, pan-Mediterranean onslaught threatened, because, although the Moors of Iberia and the Turks of Asia Minor shared a religious heritage, they were never united in one purpose. Where Christians and Muslims did face each other across the centuries, their relationship had been unremarkable, characterised, like that between any potential rivals, by periods of conflict and others of coexistence. There is little or no evidence to suggest that either side harboured any innate, empowering religious or racial hatred of the other.

Most significantly, throughout this period indigenous Christians actually living under Islamic law, be it in Iberia or the Holy Land, were generally treated with remarkable clemency. The Muslim faith acknowledged and respected Judaism and Christianity, creeds with which it enjoyed a common devotional tradition and a mutual reliance upon authoritative scripture. Christian subjects may not have been able to share power with their Muslim masters, but they were given freedom to worship. All around the Mediterranean basin, Christian faith and society survived and even thrived under the watchful but tolerant eye of Islam. Eastern Christendom may have been subject to Islamic rule, but it was not on the brink of annihilation, nor prey to any form of systematic abuse.

It is true that, ten years before the council of Clermont, Iberia entered a period of heightened religious intolerance. In 1086, a fanatical Islamic sect invaded Iberia from north Africa, supplanting surviving, indigenous Muslim power in the peninsula. This new regime set about resisting and then repelling the acquisitive Christian north, scoring a number of notable military victories that reestablished the balance of power in Islam's favour. This did cause a reaction in the Latin West. In 1087 the king of France urged his subjects to offer military support to their Iberian brethren, and a number of French potentates duly led companies across the Pyrenees, among them a number of knights who later joined the

First Crusade. Then in 1089 Pope Urban II took a limited interest in Iberian affairs. He focused his attention upon the ancient Roman port of Tarragona in north-eastern Spain, a city which had for generations lain in ruins, adrift amid the unclaimed wasteland between Christian and Muslim territory. Urban sponsored the rebuilding of Tarragona as a papal protectorate, but, although he created a new archbishopric there and construction was apparently begun, it is not clear whether the port was actually reoccupied. Iberia did serve as something of a testing ground for crusading ideology, because Urban offered a remission of sin to those engaged in the restoration of Tarragona, but his involvement on the peninsula was still extremely limited and there was no direct link between the needs of this theatre of conflict and his eventual decision to launch a campaign to the Levant.

## Pope Urban's Motives in 1095

The problems addressed by the First Crusade—Muslim occupation of Jerusalem and the potential threat of Islamic aggression in the East—had loomed for decades, even centuries, provoking little or no reaction in Rome. Urban II's decision to take up this cause at Clermont was, therefore, primarily proactive rather than reactive, and the crusade was designed, first and foremost, to meet the needs of the papacy. Launched as it was just as Urban began to stabilise his power-base in central Italy, the campaign must be seen as an attempt to consolidate papal empowerment and expand Rome's sphere of influence. It was no accident that Urban chose to unleash the concept of crusading in France, a region in which his roots gave him connections and local knowledge, and over which the papacy had long wished to strengthen its hold. Indeed, the crusade was just one of the weapons used in pursuit of this agenda, Urban's entire grand tour of France in 1095–6 being a transparent attempt to manifest papal authority.

But for Urban the real beauty of the crusade was that it also had the potential to fulfil a range of other papal ambitions. Since the start of his pontificate, Urban had sought to re-establish friendly contact with the Greek Church of Byzantium. ... [And] at the same time; it offered the prospect of expanding Latin influence over the Levantine Church in Asia Minor, Syria and Palestine, a significant step along the road towards papal pre-eminence in all Christendom.

The First Crusade also held more altruistic benefits. It is likely that Urban earnestly desired to help his Byzantine brethren and those eastern Christians living under Islamic rule. Although probably aware that the latter were not suffering desperate abuse, he still sought to liberate all Christendom, thus ending any threat of oppression. And while the Muslim rulers of the Holy Land might have been willing to grant pilgrims access to the sacred sites of Jerusalem, in Urban's mind it was still infinitely preferable for that revered city to be under Christian control. At the same time, he came to realise that the very means by which these goals might be achieved could also serve to purify the Latin West. Having grown up among the Frankish aristocracy, the pope was only too aware of the spiritual dilemma facing this knightly class. Bombarded by a stream of warnings about the dreadful danger of sin, but forced to resort to soul-contaminating violence in order to fulfil their duty and defend their rights in this lawless age, most nobles were trapped in a circle of guilt, obligation and necessity. As Roman pontiff, the father of the Latin Church, Urban was personally responsible for the soul of every single Christian living in the West. It was incumbent upon him to lift as many of his flock as possible towards salvation. The campaign launched at Clermont was therefore, in one sense, designed to answer the prayers of a polluted class in Urban's care, because it offered the nobility a new path to redemption. The message in 1095 was that knights would now be able to prosecute violence in the name of God, participating in a holy war.

### The Long Road to Holy War

Turning bloodshed into a sacred act required the pope to reconcile Christian teaching with the ruthlessness of medieval warfare. With the preaching of the First Crusade the Latin Church went far beyond simply condoning violence; it energetically encouraged military conflict and promoted carnage as an expression of pious devotion. This sanctification of warfare, in which two seemingly immiscible elements—violence and Christianity—were fused, now stands as the defining characteristic of the First Crusade, the feature which has catapulted this expedition into the popular imagination and aroused generations of scholarly attention. The very concept of Christian holy war, of which the crusade was the dominant species, can elicit a sense of dismay and censure in modern observers, who view it as a distortion of Christ's teaching, an abomination that directly contradicts his promotion of pacifism. Many are driven to ask how the medieval papacy could have developed such an extraordinary concept.

In fact, the First Crusade was not utterly abnormal, but an extreme product of concerns common to all ages of human society: the need to contain mankind's innate appetite for violence; and the desire to distinguish between 'good' and 'evil' warfare. Across millennia of recorded history and in every corner of the planet, civilisations have struggled to control and harness human aggression, most often by categorising certain types of bloodshed as acceptable and outlawing or vilifying the remainder. Even modern societies posit a moral distinction between 'private' murder and killing performed in the midst of sanctioned 'public' warfare. Ruling elites also tend to promote their own wars as justifiable and those of their enemies as morally corrupt. The medieval theory of crusading similarly sought to redirect the energies of Europe's feuding warlords, channelling their bloodlust out beyond the borders of the Latin West for the 'good' of all Christendom. In the long term, however, this approach to the management of violence had a bleak and lasting impact upon the relationship with Islam.

This still begs the question of how Christianity, seemingly a pacifistic religion, was so readily militarised. Pope Urban II did not conjure the idea of a crusade from thin air, nor did he consider the concept of holy war to be revolutionary or even novel. In his mind, centuries of Christian, and even pre-Christian, tradition legitimised the principles espoused at Clermont. It was inevitable that his ideas would be influenced by precedent because eleventh-century Latin society was profoundly retrospective. ... Fixated by [a] vision of a golden age in which the apostles supposedly created an ideal Christian order, and governed by an immoveable, authoritative text, the medieval world was obsessed with the past.

But Urban and his contemporaries viewed their Christian history through a cracked and clouded lens. The glorious 'perfection' of a bygone era to which they aspired too often owed more to fiction than to fact. The sheer malleability of history—stretched and distorted by the imprecisions of memory and twisted through wilful manipulation and forgery—meant that the 'past' that informed and enabled Urban's sanctification of violence was actually a shifting, tangled web of reality and imagination. Although the pope earnestly believed that the campaign he preached in 1095 conformed to Christ's teaching, a deep chasm separated the ideals promoted by scripture and those that sustained the concept of crusading. ...

Urban's vision of his religion was, however, coloured by the work of Christian theologians who, in the course of the first millennium CE, decided that scripture might not actually offer such a decisive or universal condemnation of violence and warfare. In part, these theorists were initially sent scurrying to reconsider Christian doctrine by the living reality with which they were confronted. It was always going to prove difficult to maintain an unwavering policy of pacifism in the face of mankind's inherent bellicosity, but, with the conversion of the Roman Empire, it became virtually impossible to sustain the absolute rejection of violence. ...

The most influential patristic writer to grapple with these problems was the north African bishop St Augustine of Hippo (354–430 CE), perhaps the most eminent theologian in all Christian history and author of a long series of works exploring human existence and religious devotion. St Augustine's work on Christian violence laid the foundation upon which Pope Urban II eventually erected the crusading ideal. St Augustine argued that a war could be both legal and justified if fought under strictly controlled conditions. His complex theories were later simplified and consolidated to produce three prerequisites of a Just War: it must be proclaimed by a 'legitimate authority', like a king, prince or bishop; it ought to have a 'just cause', such as the recovery of lost property or defence against enemy attack; and it should be fought with 'right intention', that is without cruelty or excessive bloodshed. These three Augustinian principles were the basic building-blocks of the crusading ideal. But, although Augustine's work shaped the format and nature of Pope Urban II's crusade sermon at Clermont, it did not actually provide the western Church with a working doctrine of holy war. St Augustine broke Latin Christian theology from the shackles of pacifism, and his ideas gradually filtered down into European society, helping to salve general anxieties about the relationship between faith and military service. But there were distinct limitations to his theory as it was applied to the medieval West. It was seen to demonstrate that certain forms of necessary, public warfare might be 'justified'—that is, acceptable and lawful in the eyes of God.

A significant conceptual divide separates this from 'sanctified' violence. This latter form of warfare was not deemed simply to be tolerable to God, a potentially sinful act to which he was prepared to turn a blind eye because its evil would lead to a greater good. Instead, a holy war was one that God actively supported, even demanded, which could be of spiritual benefit to its participants. Pope Urban's crusading ideal was an extension of this second class of sanctified warfare, but it was not until the eleventh century that the Latin Church really developed a working theory of holy war.

Between the age of St Augustine and the council of Clermont, western Christendom gradually became acculturated to the concept of sanctified violence, This was an incremental, organic process, marked by sporadic episodes of theological experimentation, not a driven programme of linear development. Before the year 1000, the papacy occasionally dabbled in the rhetoric of holy war when facing significant threats. In the ninth century, two successive popes sought to rally military support by promising rather vaguely defined spiritual benefits—a 'heavenly reward' or 'eternal life'—to those who fought and died in defence of Rome. But this type of appeal seems to have garnered only a limited response and soon fell into disuse.' ... The prominent role of Carolingian bishops in sponsoring, even directing, brutal campaigns to conquer and convert the pagans of eastern Europe helped stimulate the idea that warfare might have a pious goal. The Christianisation of Germanic 'barbarian' traditions also encouraged reverence for the martial qualities of the warrior class and the adoption of the ritual blessing of the weapons of war by the clergy. It was a relatively small step to imagine that esteemed Christian knights, bearing sanctified arms and armour, might be capable of performing some sort of devotional service to God. ...

It was not until the second half of the eleventh century that Latin Christendom truly began to edge towards the acceptance of sanctified violence and thus became receptive to the idea of crusading. The first step was the accelerated incidence of papally sponsored warfare. With elements of the Reform Movement urging Rome to pursue an energetic policy of empowerment, successive popes began taking a more active interest in the protection of their Italian territories and the extension of their international influence. It soon became apparent that, if Rome wished to stand on the world stage, it would, on occasion, need some form of material military power with which to enforce its spiritual will. ...

### Pope Gregory VII and Sanctified Violence

During the pontificate of Gregory VII the doctrine and application of sacred violence underwent a radical transformation. Gregory's ambitious and uncompromising vision of papal authority prompted him to pursue the sponsorship and sanctification of warfare at an unprecedented pace. His work created the platform upon which Urban stood in 1095. Possessed by an intensely personal notion of his office and believing more wholeheartedly than any pope before him that he was the literal, living embodiment of St Peter, Gregory was utterly convinced that he could wield full apostolic authority on earth. In his mind, there seems to have been no question but that the pope should have total, unchecked control over the spiritual wellbeing of mankind. He was, equally, in no doubt that this power took precedence over that exercised by kings and princes. To realise this audacious ideal, Gregory took a massive step towards the militarisation of the Latin Church. He decided that what Rome really needed was not the martial backing of potentially unreliable secular allies, but a fully fledged papal army owing its allegiance, first and foremost, to St Peter.

In pursuit of this goal, Gregory made a series of sweeping pronouncements that slowly percolated throughout western society, threatening to reshape the Latin world order. He set about reinterpreting Christian tradition in order to establish a precedent for his combative policies. Centuries earlier, patristic theologians had described the internal, spiritual battle waged against sin by devoted Christians as the 'warfare of Christ'. In time, it became popular in learned circles to conceive of monks as the 'soldiers of Christ', ascetics armed with prayer and ritual, engaged in a metaphorical war with temptation. Gregory appropriated this idea and twisted it to suit his purpose. He proclaimed that all lay society had one overriding obligation: to defend the Latin Church as 'soldiers of Christ' through actual, physical warfare.

The laity had, in recent decades, been encouraged to reimagine their spiritual relationship with God and the Latin Church in terms that mirrored the structure of temporal society. With God conceived of as 'lord' and 'ruler' of the 'kingdom' of heaven, Christians were conditioned to believe that they owed him loyalty and service as they would a mortal king. To turn this diffuse theory into reality, Gregory harnessed and adapted a popular fixture of Christianity. Latin Europe was accustomed to the notion that saints—Christians who had lived meritorious lives or been martyred, and thus, in death, attained a special place in heaven—deserved reverence. Throughout the West, men and women championed patron saints, offering them dutiful veneration in return for protection and support Gregory sought to transform this localised patchwork of allegiance by harnessing the universal appeal of St Peter. Rome had, for some time, described its supporters as *fideles beati Petri*, the 'faithful' of St Peter. But Gregory chose to focus on a different aspect of the word *fideles*, emphasising its implication of service and vassalage to suggest that all Latin Christians were, in fact, Vassals of St Peter and so by implication vassals of the pope.

By fusing the vision of Christendom as God's 'kingdom', the practice of venerating saints and the feudal connotations of the term *fideles*, Gregory concocted an elaborate justification for his claim that all lay society owed him a debt of military service. In truth, much of Europe would not have fully understood this intricate web of distorted precedent and warped tradition, and certainly, in the divisive atmosphere of the Investiture Controversy, not all Latins answered Gregory's call to obedience. But he did manage to recruit a powerful network of *fideles* willing to do the bidding of Rome, many of whom would later support Urban's crusade. ...

Early in his pontificate, Gregory laid plans for a grand military enterprise that can be regarded as the prototype for a crusade. In 1074 he tried to launch a holy war in the eastern Mediterranean that would, had it come to fruition, have borne a striking resemblance to the campaign initiated by Urban II in 1095. Gregory sought to recruit lay military support in France and Germany for an expedition to bring aid to the Greek Christians of Byzantium, who were, he claimed, 'daily being butchered like cattle' by the Muslims of Asia Minor. He proposed to lead this bold defence of Christendom in person, declaring that the venture might take him all the way to the Holy Sepulchre of Jerusalem, and expressed the hope that success might bring about the reunification of the eastern and western Churches under the authority of Rome. ...

Gregory's planned expedition did, nonetheless, begin to crystallise the ideal of holy war. His predecessor had already implied that violence in the service of God might be meritorious; Gregory's

1074 scheme explained why. The spiritual benefits of participating in his campaign still seem to have been somewhat vague, described simply as a 'heavenly reward', but the reason why such a prize might be on offer was made much clearer. Gregory argued that his projected war would be fought in defence of the Christian faith and that the very act of bringing aid to Byzantium was an expression of love for one's Christian brethren and thus charitable. This formula of charitable defence made it much easier for contemporaries to believe that fighting in a holy war might truly earn them merit in the eyes of God. ...

For all this, Gregory VII cannot be regarded as the sole architect of the crusading ideal. He certainly never successfully launched a campaign on the scale of the First Crusade, nor was he particularly concerned to direct the energy of sanctified violence against Islam. But he did break crucial ground on the road to the idea of crusading. ...

[Additionally,] Gregory's achievements and those of his predecessors also meant that, by the start of Urban's pontificate in 1088, the concept of holy war had been formulated. The Latin West had been acculturated to the idea that certain classes of violence might be justified, and was slowly waking up to the notion that warfare directed by the papacy might have a penitential character and thus be capable, in some sense, of cleansing the soul of sin. ...

### The Sermon at Clermont

The First Crusade was proclaimed in November 1095 during Urban II's momentous visit to France. His was the first journey made by any pope outside Italy for almost half a century. With the ongoing Investiture Controversy and the recent diminution of papal authority, the journey north of the Alps was designed to affirm Urban's legitimacy and assert Rome's presence in his old homeland. ...

To rally the Latin Church to his cause, Urban called the clergy to a grand ecclesiastical council. Held in late November at Clermont, in the Auvergne region of south-eastern France, this meeting was attended by some twelve archbishops, eighty bishops and ninety abbots—not a massive assembly by medieval standards, but the largest of Urban's pontificate to date. For more than a week, the council considered an array of ecclesiastical business, as Urban sought to disseminate his plans for the continued reform of the Church. Then, on 27 November, with the council drawing to a close, the pope announced that he would deliver a special sermon to an open-air assembly held in a field outside Clermont. Urban probably arranged for this public spectacle in the hope that his preaching would draw a large crowd, and later tradition maintained that the meeting had to be moved outside because of the sheer weight of numbers that gathered to hear him speak, but in reality perhaps only 300 or 400 people braved the chill November air. These select few were to bear witness to a captivating sermon.

### Pope Urban's Message

Unless new evidence comes to light, we will never know exactly what Pope Urban II said in his momentous sermon. Even though this speech initiated a campaign that would change the face of European history, no precise record of Urban's words survives. In the years that followed, a number of men, including three eyewitnesses, did record versions of his address, but all of them wrote after the end of the First Crusade. Their accounts must, therefore, be read with a healthy dose of suspicion in mind, given that their versions of the events at Clermont were composed with the benefit of hindsight. They knew only too well what powerful emotions Urban's words would stir in western Christendom, the tide of humanity that would respond to his call and the dreadful progress of the crusade that followed. ...

We know that Urban urged western Christendom to pursue two interlocking goals: the liberation of the eastern Churches, most notably by bringing military support to the beleaguered Byzantine Empire; and the reconquest of the Holy Land, in particular the city of Jerusalem. From the start, he conceived of the campaign as a war of defence and repossession. The crusade was not launched as an evangelical enterprise to bring about the conversion of Muslims, forced or voluntary, but to protect and recover Christian territory. This was to be a war of religion, but one that focused upon physical power, not ephemeral theology. Rather than emphasise complex questions of dogma and creed, Urban promoted a war that his audience could understand, stressing the theme of Christian brotherhood and highlighting the fact that all Latin knights had a duty to defend Christ's patrimony by participating in an impassioned battle to recover the Holy Land.

His appeal seems to have been loosely structured around the three Augustinian principles of Just War—legitimate authority, just cause and right intention—bolstered by remodelled Gregorian ideals. He took 'just cause' as the key theme for his proposed campaign, launching into a polemical oration, peppered with inflammatory images of Muslim atrocities.

> We want you to know what grievous cause leads us to your territory, what need of yours and all the faithful brings us here. A grave report has come from the lands of Jerusalem and from the city of Constantinople that a people from the kingdom of the Persians, a foreign race, a race absolutely alien to God... has invaded the land of those Christians [and] has reduced the people with sword, rapine and fire.

A central feature of Urban's doctrine was the denigration and dehumanisation of Islam. He set out from the start to launch a holy-war against what he called 'the savagery of the Saracens', a 'barbarian' people capable of incomprehensible levels of cruelty and brutality.

Their supposed crimes were enacted upon two groups. Eastern Christians, in particular the Byzantines, had been 'overrun right up to the Mediterranean Sea'. Urban described how the Muslims, 'occupying more and more of the land on the borders of [Byzantium], were slaughtering and capturing many, destroying churches and laying waste to the kingdom of God. So, if you leave them alone much longer they will further grind under their heels the faithful of God.' The pope also maintained that Christian pilgrims to the Holy Land were being subjected to horrific abuse and exploitation. While the wealthy were regularly beaten and stripped of their fortunes by illegal taxes, the poor endured even more terrible treatment:

> Non-existent money is extracted from them by intolerable tortures, the hard skin on their heels being cut open and peeled back to investigate whether perhaps they have inserted something under it. The cruelty of these impious men goes even to the length that, thinking the wretches have eaten gold or silver, they either put scammony in their drink and force them to vomit or void their vitals, or—and this is unspeakable—they stretch asunder the coverings of all the intestines after ripping open their stomachs with a blade and reveal with horrible mutilation whatever nature keeps secret.

These accusations had little or no basis in fact, but they did serve Urban's purpose. By expounding upon the alleged crimes of Islam, he sought to ignite an explosion of vengeful passion among his Latin audience, while his attempts to degrade Muslims as 'sub-human' opened the floodgates of extreme, brutal reciprocity. This, the pope argued, was to be no shameful war of equals, between God's children, but a 'just' and 'holy' struggle in which an 'alien' people could be punished without remorse and with utter ruthlessness. Urban was activating one of the most potent impulses in human society': the definition of the 'other'. Across countless generations of human history, tribes, cities, nations and peoples have sought to delineate their own identities through comparison to their neighbours or enemies. By conditioning Latin Europe to view Islam as a species apart, the pope stood to gain not only by facilitating his proposed campaign, but also by propelling the West towards unification. ...

[Furthermore,] The pope promoted the crusade as a distinct form of warfare, set apart from the grubby contamination of the inter-Christian struggles afflicting the West. According to one account, he proclaimed:

> Let those who in the past have been accustomed to spread private war so vilely among the faithful advance against the infidels… Let those who were formerly brigands now become soldiers of Christ; those who once waged war against their brothers and blood-relatives fight lawfully against barbarians; those who until now have been mercenaries for a few coins achieve eternal rewards.

This approach was an offshoot of the Augustinian principle of 'right intention', requiring a Just War to be fought with restraint and control. Urban suggested that 'normal' violence was both illegal and corrupting, that only a war fought under regulated conditions could be considered licit or sanctified. But he proclaimed that in this campaign the regulating factor would be not the degree of brutality, but rather the 'alien' status of its target. … Pope Urban twisted and extended this idea, declaring that the crusade would be a distinct class of warfare, prosecuted under a particular set of controlled conditions. In this instance, however, the 'controlling' feature that established a 'right intention' had nothing to do with degrees of violence or the tempered prosecution of warfare. Instead, it was entirely dependent upon the 'alien' nature of the enemy to be confronted. The expedition would be 'just' because it was directed against 'inhuman' Muslims, not because it was executed with moderation. This may, to some extent, help to explain why the First Crusaders proved capable of such extreme brutality.

### A New Form of Holy War

Perhaps the most significant feature of Pope Urban's sermon at Clermont was the formula of sanctified violence he associated with the proposed campaign. His predecessors, like Gregory VII, had experimented with the concept of holy war, seeking to promote the idea that military service in the name of God might bring participants a spiritual reward. But, more often than not, their calls to arms had attracted only a limited response. In one sense, Urban followed their lead: he promised that Latins who fought to protect their eastern brethren and recapture Jerusalem would enjoy a remission of sin, that is a cleansing of the soul. But he took a crucial further step, refining the ideological framework of sanctified violence to produce a new model of sacred warfare that, for the first time, truly resonated with the needs and expectations of medieval Europe. It was this new recipe for salvation that produced such an electric reaction among his audience.

Urban performed a relatively simple feat. He repackaged the concept of sanctified violence in a devotional format that was more comprehensible and palatable to lay society. Earlier popes may have argued that holy war could purify the soul, but Latin arms-bearers seem to have harboured nagging doubts about the efficacy of this notion. Urban sold the idea in terms that were familiar, convincing and attractive.

Western Christians were programmed to think of themselves as being critically contaminated by sin and conditioned to pursue a desperate struggle for purification through the outlets of confession and penance. Among the most recognised and fashionable of penitential activities in the eleventh century was the practice of pilgrimage. These devotional journeys to sites of religious significance were specifically designed to be gruelling, potentially dangerous affairs and thus capable of purging the soul. Urban's sermon at Clermont interwove the theme of holy war with that of pilgrimage to produce a distinct, new class of sanctified violence: a crusade. In this sacred expedition, the purificational properties of fighting for Christ were married to the penitential rigours of the pilgrim's journey, creating ideal conditions for the cleansing of sin. In this First Crusade, Urban's target audience, the Frankish knights of western Europe, would be able simultaneously to pursue two of their favourite pastimes—warfare and pilgrimage—in a devotional activity that seemed to them a natural extension of current Christian practice. This crusade promised to engender an unquestionably purgative atmosphere within which the intense burden of transgression and guilt might be relieved. The allure of this armed pilgrimage was all the more intense because its ultimate target was the premier devotional destination in Christian cosmology, the most revered physical space on earth: the Holy City of Jerusalem.

Jerusalem has a singular devotional resonance for three of the world's great religions, being the third city of Islam and the centre of the Christian and Judaic faiths. By the end of the eleventh century, it was popular in the Latin West to conceive of the city and its surroundings as a physical relic of Christ's life. Pope Urban was fully conscious of the almost irresistible appeal of the Holy City and he took pains to underline its significance during his sermon. ...

The spiritual rewards offered by Urban for making this armed pilgrimage to Jerusalem were immensely attractive, but not theologically audacious. Later, unsanctioned preachers did extend and simplify Urban's message, but the pope himself never suggested that joining the crusade would 'magically' guarantee all participants a place in heaven. To a modern observer, the very idea of fighting to purify ones soul might seem absurd and irrational, but Urban's vision of the crusade indulgence was firmly grounded in medieval reality. He conceived of the purificational properties of the crusade in terms that mirrored current devotional practice, incorporating existing language and ritual to produce a system that, in eleventh-century terms, offered a clear and rational pathway towards salvation. ...

For the first time, fighting in the name of God and the pope brought with it a spiritual reward that was at once readily conceivable and deeply compelling: a real chance to walk through the fires of battle and emerge unsullied by sin.

# The Devastation of the Indies

## A Brief Account

By Bartolomé de Las Casas

•••••••••••••••••••••••••••••••••••••••••••

## Editor's Introduction

Like Christopher Columbus, whose writings he edited, few figures in the early history of the Spanish Conquest have inspired as much praise or fallen into as much disrepute. Bartolomé de Las Casas, the polemic figure blamed by Spain for almost single-handedly creating the Black Legend of Spanish cruelty, was published widely and translated into many languages. This latter aspect provided the English with the rationale and justification to invade Spanish territories in the Caribbean. Falling into obscurity after this publication, Las Casas was resurrected in the middle nineteenth century in a favorable light as part of the White Legend created by revisionist historians in Spain and her remaining colonies: Cuba, Puerto Rico, and the Philippines.

The White Legend reinstated both Las Casas and Columbus as proof of Spain's humanity and bridged the gap between Old and New Worlds. After all, Las Casas, while bishop of Chiapas, was bestowed the title "Protector of the Indians" by the Crown. His legacy, however, does not always include his early advocacy of escalating African slavery to replace the exploited indigenous labor on Spanish *encomiendas* (land grants with obligatory labor laws). His role in the slave trade was recanted on his deathbed.

Throughout this excerpt, Las Casas's views of the native peoples, although sympathetic and passionate, cannot refrain from Eurocentric interpretations and exudes paternalism. Las Casas, like many during this time and after, felt that Indians were like children and inferior, but if they accepted the white man's religion, they could enjoy reasonable amounts of help and protection.

### References

Las Casa, Bartolomé. *A Short Account of the Destruction of the Indies.* Translated by Nigel Griffin. New York: Penguin, 1999.

Restall, Matthew. *Seven Myths of the Spanish Conquest.* New York: Oxford, 2003.

Schmidt-Nowara, Christopher. *The Conquest of History: Spanish Colonialism and the National Histories in the Nineteenth Century.* Pittsburgh: University of Pittsburgh Press, 2006.

The Indies[1] were discovered in the year one thousand four hundred and ninety-two. In the following year a great many Spaniards went there with the intention of settling the land. Thus, forty-nine years have passed since the first settlers penetrated the land, the first so-claimed being the large and most happy isle called Hispaniola,[2] which is six hundred leagues in circumference. Around it in all directions are many other islands, some very big, others very small, and all of them were, as we saw with our own eyes, densely populated with native peoples called Indians. This large island was perhaps the most densely populated place in the world. There must be close to two hundred leagues of land on this island, and the seacoast has been explored for more than ten thousand leagues, and each day more of it is being explored. And all the land so far discovered is a beehive of people; it is as though God had crowded into these lands the great majority of mankind.

And of all the infinite universe of humanity, these people are the most guileless, the most devoid of wickedness and duplicity, the most obedient and faithful to their native masters and to the Spanish Christians whom they serve. They are by nature the most humble, patient, and peaceable, holding no grudges, free from embroilments, neither excitable nor quarrelsome. These people are the most devoid of rancors, hatreds, or desire for vengeance of any people in the world. And because they are so weak and complaisant, they are less able to endure heavy labor and soon die of no matter what malady. The sons of nobles among us, brought up in the enjoyments of life's refinements, are no more delicate than are these Indians, even those among them who are of the lowest rank of laborers. They are also poor people, for they not only possess little but have no desire to possess worldly goods. For this reason they are not arrogant, embittered, or greedy. Their repasts are such that the food of the holy fathers in the desert can scarcely be more parsimonious, scanty, and poor. As to their dress, they are generally naked, with only their pudenda covered somewhat. And when they cover their shoulders it is with a square cloth no more than two varas in size[3]. They have no beds, but sleep on a kind of matting or else in a kind of suspended net called *hamacas*. They are very clean in their persons, with alert, intelligent minds, docile and open to doctrine, very apt to receive our holy Catholic faith, to be endowed with virtuous customs, and to behave in a godly fashion. And once they begin to hear the tidings of the Faith, they are so insistent on knowing more and on taking the sacraments of the Church and on observing the divine cult that, truly, the missionaries who are here need to be endowed by God with great patience in order to cope with such eagerness. Some of the secular Spaniards who have been here for many years say that the goodness of the Indians is undeniable and that if this gifted people could be brought to know the one true God they would be the most fortunate people in the world.

Yet into this sheepfold, into this land of meek outcasts there came some Spaniards who immediately behaved like ravening wild beasts, wolves, tigers, or lions that had been starved for many days. And Spaniards have behaved in no other way during the past forty years, down to the present time, for they are still acting like ravening beasts, killing, terrorizing, afflicting, torturing, and destroying the native peoples, doing all this with the strangest and most varied new methods of cruelty, never seen or heard of before, and to such a degree that this Island of Hispaniola, once so populous (having a population that I estimated to be more than three millions), has now a population of barely two hundred persons.

The island of Cuba is nearly as long as the distance between Valladolid and Rome; it is now almost completely depopulated. San Juan[4] and Jamaica are two of the largest, most productive and attractive islands; both are now deserted and devastated. On the northern side of Cuba and Hispaniola lie the neighboring Lucayos[5] comprising more than sixty islands including those called

---

1 Caribbean Islands
2 Present-day Dominican Republic and Haiti

3 A *vara* is an old Spanish unit of length.
4 Puerto Rico
5 Bahamas

*Gigantes,* beside numerous other islands, some small some large. The least felicitous of them were more fertile and beautiful than the gardens of the King of Seville. They have the healthiest lands in the world, where lived more than five hundred thousand souls; they are now deserted, inhabited by not a single living creature. All the people were slain or died after being taken into captivity and brought to the Island of Hispaniola to be sold as slaves. When the Spaniards saw that some of these had escaped, they sent a ship to find them, and it voyaged for three years among the islands searching for those who had escaped being slaughtered, for a good Christian had helped them escape, taking pity on them and had won them over to Christ,[6] of these there were eleven persons and these I saw.

More than thirty other islands in the vicinity of San Juan are for the most part and for the same reason depopulated, and the land laid waste. On these islands I estimate there are 2,100 leagues of land that have been ruined and depopulated, empty of peopled.[7]

As for the vast mainland, which is ten times larger than all Spain, even including Aragon and Portugal, containing more land than the distance between Seville and Jerusalem, or more than two thousand leagues, we are sure that our Spaniards, with their cruel and abominable acts, have devastated the land and exterminated the rational people who fully inhabited it. We can estimate very surely and truthfully that in the forty years that have passed, with the infernal actions of the Christians, there have been unjustly slain more than twelve million men, women, and children. In truth, I believe without trying to deceive myself that the number of the slain is more like fifteen million.

The common ways mainly employed by the Spaniards who call themselves Christian and who have gone there to extirpate those pitiful nations and wipe them off the earth is by unjustly waging cruel and bloody wars. Then, when they have slain all those who fought for their lives or to escape the tortures they would have to endure, that is to say, when they have slain all the native rulers and young men (since the Spaniards usually spare only the women and children, who are subjected to the hardest and bitterest servitude ever suffered by man or beast), they enslave any survivors. With these infernal methods of tyranny they debase and weaken countless numbers of those pitiful Indian nations.

Their reason for killing and destroying such an infinite number of souls is that the Christians have an ultimate aim, which is to acquire gold, and to swell themselves with riches in a very brief time and thus rise to a high estate disproportionate to their merits. It should be kept in mind that their insatiable greed and ambition, the greatest ever seen in the world, is the cause of their villainies. And also, those lands are so rich and felicitous, the native peoples so meek and patient, so easy to subject, that our Spaniards have no more consideration for them than beasts. And I say this from my own knowledge of the acts I witnessed. But I should not say "than beasts" for, thanks be to God, they have treated beasts with some respect; I should say instead like excrement on the public squares. And thus they have deprived the Indians of their lives and souls, for the millions I mentioned have died without the Faith and without the benefit of the sacraments. This is a well-known and proven fact which even the tyrant Governors, themselves killers, know and admit. And never have the Indians in all the Indies committed any act against the Spanish Christians, until those Christians have first and many times committed countless cruel aggressions against them or against neighboring nations. For in the beginning the Indians regarded the Spaniards as angels from Heaven.[8] Only after the Spaniards had used violence against them, killing, robbing, torturing, did the Indians ever rise up against them.

---

6 blank [*sic*]

7 His numbers are spurious, but depopulation was rampant.

8 Part of a cultural myth begun by Columbus in his writings.

On the Island Hispaniola was where the Spaniards first landed, as I have said. Here those Christians perpetrated their first ravages and oppressions against the native peoples. This was the first land in the New World to be destroyed and depopulated by the Christians, and here they began their subjection of the women and children, taking them away from the Indians to use them and ill use them, eating the food they provided with their sweat and toil. The Spaniards did not content themselves with what the Indians gave them of their own free will, according to their ability, which was always too little to satisfy enormous appetites, for a Christian eats and consumes in one day an amount of food that would suffice to feed three houses inhabited by ten Indians for one month. And they committed other acts of force and violence and oppression which made the Indians realize that these men had not come from Heaven. And some of the Indians concealed their foods while others concealed their wives and children and still others fled to the mountains to avoid the terrible transactions of the Christians.

And the Christians attacked them with buffets and beatings, until finally they laid hands on the nobles of the villages. Then they behaved with such temerity and shamelessness that the most powerful ruler of the islands had to see his own wife raped by a Christian officer.

From that time onward the Indians began to seek ways to throw the Christians out of their lands. They took up arms, but their weapons were very weak and of little service in offense and still less in defense. (Because of this, the wars of the Indians against each other are little more than games played by children.) And the Christians, with their horses and swords and pikes began to carry out massacres and strange cruelties against them. They attacked the towns and spared neither the children nor the aged nor pregnant women nor women in childbed, not only stabbing them and dismembering them but cutting them to pieces as if dealing with sheep in the slaughter house. They laid bets as to who, with one stroke of the sword, could split a man in two or could cut off his head or spill out his entrails with a single stroke of the pike. They took infants from their mothers' breasts, snatching them by the legs and pitching them headfirst against the crags or snatched them by the arms and threw them into the rivers, roaring with laughter and saying as the babies fell into the water, "Boil there, you offspring of the devil!" Other infants they put to the sword along with their mothers and anyone else who happened to be nearby. They made some low wide gallows on which the hanged victim's feet almost touched the ground, stringing up their victims in lots of thirteen, in memory of Our Redeemer and His twelve Apostles, then set burning wood at their feet and thus burned them alive. To others they attached straw or wrapped their whole bodies in straw and set them afire. With still others, all those they wanted to capture alive, they cut off their hands and hung them round the victim's neck, saying, "Go now, carry the message," meaning, Take the news to the Indians who have fled to the mountains. They usually dealt with the chieftains and nobles in the following way: they made a grid of rods which they placed on forked sticks, then lashed the victims to the grid and lighted a smoldering fire underneath, so that little by little, as those captives screamed in despair and torment, their souls would leave them.

I once saw this, when there were four or five nobles lashed on grids and burning; I seem even to recall that there were two or three pairs of grids where others were burning, and because they uttered such loud screams that they disturbed the captain's sleep, he ordered them to be strangled. And the constable, who was worse than an executioner, did not want to obey that order (and I know the name of that constable and know his relatives in Seville), but instead put a stick over the victims' tongues, so they could not make a sound, and he stirred up the fire, but not too much, so that they roasted slowly, as he liked. I saw all these things I have described, and countless others.

And because all the people who could do so fled to the mountains to escape these inhuman, ruthless, and ferocious acts, the Spanish captains, enemies of the human race, pursued them with the fierce dogs[9] they kept which attacked the Indians, tearing them to pieces and devouring them. And because on few and far between occasions, the Indians justifiably killed some Christians, the Spaniards made a rule among themselves that for every Christian slain by the Indians, they would slay a hundred Indians.

## The Kingdoms That Once Existed on the Island Hispaniola

On the island Hispaniola there were five very large principalities ruled by five very powerful Kings to whom almost all the other rulers paid tribute, since there were other princes in distant provinces who recognized no one as their superior. There was a kingdom called Magua, the last syllable accented, which name means "The Realm of the Fertile Lowlands." This land is among the most notable and admirable places in the world, for it stretches across the island from the southern sea to the northern sea, a distance of eighty leagues. It averages five leagues in width but at times is eight to ten and is of very high altitude from one part to another and is drained by more than thirty thousand rivers and creeks, twelve of the rivers being as large as the Ebro and Duero and Guadalquivir combined. All the rivers flow from the western highland, which means that twenty or twenty-five thousand of them are rich in gold. For in those highlands lies the province of Cibao, where are the famous Cibao mines harboring a fine and remarkable pure gold.

The King who ruled this realm was called Guarionex. Great lords were his vassals, one of them having assembled an army of sixteen thousand men to serve Guarionex, and I know or knew some of them. That virtuous King Guarionex was by nature very pacific and was devotedly obedient to the Kings of Castile and in certain years gave them, through the nobles under his command, a generous amount of gold dust. Each man who had a house was given for this purpose a spherical

bell, or rather, a spherical grain measure resembling a bell. This was stuffed full with gold dust (brought down by the rivers) for the people of this realm did not have the skill to work the mines. When there was not enough, some years, to fill the measure, then it was cut in half and one half was filled. This King Guarionex proclaimed himself ready to serve the King of Castile with a labor force that would be brought to Santo Domingo from the city of Isabella, the first Christian settlement, fifty leagues distant, and said, with reason, that they should not have to pay in gold because his vassals did not know how to procure it. That labor force, he said, would work the mines with great heartiness and their labor would be worth to the King of Spain, each year, more than three million castellanos.[10] And had that labor force been so employed, there would be, today, more than fifty cities the size of Seville, on this island.

The recompense they gave this great and good Indian ruler was to dishonor him through his wife, who was raped by a Christian officer. And King Guarionex, who, in time, could have assembled his people to avenge him, chose instead to go alone into hiding and die exiled from his kingdom, deprived of his rank and possessions, placing himself under the protection of the chieftain of the province called Ciguayos, one of his vassals.

When his hiding place was discovered, the Christians waged war on Ciguayos, massacring a great number of people until they finally took the exiled King and, in chains, put him on a vessel that was to take him to Castile. But the vessel was lost at sea and with it were drowned many Christians along with the captive King, and in this shipwreck was lost a quantity of gold dust and gold nuggets weighing the equivalent of 3,600 castellanos. Such was God's vengeance for so many terrible injustices.

Another kingdom on the island was called Marien and is now called Puerto Real. It is situated at the end of the fertile lowlands toward the north and is larger than Portugal, although much more suitable for development and settlement.

---

9 Bull Mastifs were commonly employed in this capacity.

10 A unit of measure based on refined ore (gold).

Many mountain chains exist here, which are rich in copper and gold. The King of this province was called Guacanagari, many of whose vassals were known to me. It was this King who welcomed the Admiral[11] when he first landed in the New World and set foot on the island of Hispaniola.

The welcome extended by this King to the Admiral and all those accompanying him could not have been more cordial and generous, even had it been the voyagers' native land and their own King greeting them with food and provisions of every kind, everything that was needed, which was a great deal, for the vessel on which Columbus had voyaged was lost here.

I know all this from conversations with the Admiral.

Well, that same King, while fleeing to the mountains to escape the cruel persecutions meted out to him and his people by the Christians, died, having been stripped of his rank and possessions by those same Christians, and all his vassals perished in the tyrannical persecutions and enslavements which I shall later on describe.

The third kingdom on the island of Hispaniola was Maguana, where the best sugar in that island is now made. The King of that realm was called Caonabo and in condition and importance he surpassed all the others. The Spaniards captured this unhappy King by using great and wicked subtlety, laying hands on him while he was in his house. Afterward, they put him on a ship outward bound for Castile. But while still in port with six other outward-bound vessels, God desired to manifest Himself against this great iniquity and sent a violent storm that sank all the vessels and drowned all the Christians on board, along with the shackled King of Maguana.

This native ruler had three or four brothers, who, like him, were strong and fearless. When their brother and lord was taken captive and his subjects killed or enslaved, these brothers, upon seeing the slaughter being carried out by the Christians, took up arms in revenge. The Christians met their attack with cavalry (horses being the most pernicious weapon against the Indians) and in the battles that followed half the land was laid waste and depopulated.

The fourth kingdom was that of Xaragua and it was like the marrow and medulla of the island, its sovereign court. Its King surpassed all the other princes in eloquence, refinement, and education and good breeding. Likewise, his government was the best ordered and the most circumspect. At his court there was a multitude of nobles whose beauty and elegance excelled all others.

Behechio, the King of Xaragua, had a sister, by name Anacaona. Together, the brother and sister rendered great services to the Kings of Castile and afforded great benefactions to the Christians, helping them to avoid countless mortal dangers. After the death of her brother the King, Anacaona continued to rule the land.

Then, one day the Christian Governor[12] of the island arrived with a cavalry force of sixty horses and three hundred foot soldiers. The cavalry alone could lay waste the land. Having been promised safe conduct there soon arrived three hundred Indian nobles. These, or most of them, were tricked into entering a very big Indian house of straw where they were shut in and burned alive when the house was set on fire. Those who did not perish in the conflagration were put to the sword or the pike, along with a countless number of the common people. As a special honor, the lady Anacaona was hanged.

And it happened that those Christians, either out of piety or cupidity, took some boys to shield them from the slaughter and placed them on the croup of their horses. But other Spaniards came up from behind and ran the boys through with their pikes. When the victims fell from the horses the Spaniards cut off their legs with a sword.

Some of the nobles who managed to flee from this inhuman cruelty took refuge on a small island nearby, about eight leagues out to sea. And the said Christian Governor condemned all those who had gone there to be sold as slaves because they had fled the butchery.

The fifth kingdom was called Higuey and its ruler was an aged queen who was called

11 blank [*sic*]

12 blank [*sic*]

Higuanama. They hanged her. And there were countless people that I saw burned alive or cut to pieces or tortured in many new ways of killing and inflicting pain. They also made slaves of many Indians.

Because the particulars that enter into these outrages are so numerous they could not be contained in the scope of much writing, for in truth I believe that in the great deal I have set down here I have not revealed the thousandth part of the sufferings endured by the Indians, I now want only to add that, in the matter of these unprovoked and destructive wars, and God is my witness, all these acts of wickedness I have described, as well as those I have omitted, were perpetrated against the Indians without cause, without any more cause than could give a community of good monks living together in a monastery. And still more strongly I affirm that until the multitude of people on this island of Hispaniola were killed and their lands devastated, they committed no sin against the Christians that would be punishable by man's laws, and as to those sins punishable by God's law, such as vengeful feelings against such powerful enemies as the Christians have been, those sins would be committed by the very few Indians who are hardhearted and impetuous. And I can say this from my great experience with them: their hardness and impetuosity would be that of children, of boys ten or twelve years old. I know by certain infallible signs that the wars waged by the Indians against the Christians have been justifiable wars and that all the wars waged by the Christians against the Indians have been unjust wars, more diabolical than any wars ever waged anywhere in the world. This I declare to be so of all the many wars they have waged against the peoples throughout the Indies.

After the wars and the killings had ended, when usually there survived only some boys, some women, and children, these survivors were distributed among the Christians to be slaves. The repartimiento or distribution was made according to the rank and importance of the Christian to whom the Indians were allocated, one of them being given thirty, another forty, still another, one or two hundred, and besides the rank of the Christian there was also to be considered in what favor he stood with the tyrant they called Governor. The pretext was that these allocated Indians were to be instructed in the articles of the Christian Faith. As if those Christians who were as a rule foolish and cruel and greedy and vicious could be caretakers of souls! And the care they took was to send the men to the mines to dig for gold, which is intolerable labor, and to send the women into the fields of the big ranches to hoe and till the land, work suitable for strong men. Nor to either the men or the women did they give any food except herbs and legumes, things of little substance. The milk in the breasts of the women with infants dried up and thus in a short while the infants perished.

And since men and women were separated, there could be no marital relations. And the men died in the mines and the women died on the ranches from the same causes, exhaustion and hunger. And thus was depopulated that island which had been densely populated.

I will speak only briefly of the heavy loads the Indians were made to carry, loads weighing three to four arrobas,[13] Christian tyrants and captains had themselves carried in hammocks borne by two Indians. This shows that they treated the Indians as beasts of burden. But were I to describe all this and the buffetings and beatings and birchings endured by the Indians at their labors, no amount of time and paper could encompass this task.

And be it noted that the worst depredations on these islands in the New World began when tidings came of the death of Her most Serene Highness, Queen Isabel, which occurred in the year one thousand five hundred and four. Because, up to that time, only a few provinces on the island of Hispaniola had been destroyed in unjust wars, but not the entire island, since, for the most part, the island was under the royal protection of the Queen and she, may God rest her, took admirable and zealous care of these people, their salvation and prosperity, as we saw with our own eyes and touched with our hands.

---

13 A unit of measure, approximately 26 pounds.

Another rule should be noted: in all parts of the Indies, wherever they have landed or passed through, the Christians have always committed atrocities against the Indians, have perpetrated the slaughters and tyrannies and abominable oppressions against innocent people that we have described, and have added worse and more cruel acts, ever since God allowed them most suddenly to fall into dishonor and opprobrium. ...

## The Island of Cuba

In the year one thousand five hundred and eleven, the Spaniards passed over to the island of Cuba, which as I have said is at the same distance from Hispaniola as the distance between Valladolid and Rome, and which was a well-populated province. They began and ended in Cuba as they had done elsewhere, but with much greater acts of cruelty.

Among the noteworthy outrages they committed was the one they perpetrated against a cacique, a very important noble, by name Hatuey, who had come to Cuba from Hispaniola with many of his people, to flee the calamities and inhuman acts of the Christians. When he was told by certain Indians that the Christians were now coming to Cuba, he assembled as many of his followers as he could and said this to them: "Now you must know that they are saying the Christians are coming here, and you know by experience how they have put So and So and So and So, and other nobles to an end. And now they are coming from Haiti (which is Hispaniola) to do the same here. Do you know why they do this?" The Indians replied: "We do not know. But it may be that they are by nature wicked and cruel." And he told them: "No, they do not act only because of that, but because they have a God they greatly worship and they want us to worship that God, and that is why they struggle with us and subject us and kill us."

He had a basket full of gold and jewels and he said: "You see their God here, the God of the Christians. If you agree to it, let us dance for this God, who knows, it may please the God of the Christians and then they will do us no harm." And his followers said, all together, "Yes, that is good,

that is good!" And they danced round the basket of gold until they fell down exhausted. Then their chief, the cacique Hatuey, said to them: "See here, if we keep this basket of gold they will take it from us and will end up by killing us. So let us cast away the basket into the river." They all agreed to do this, and they flung the basket of gold into the river that was nearby.

This cacique, Hatuey, was constantly fleeing before the Christians from the time they arrived on the island of Cuba, since he knew them and of what they were capable. Now and then they encountered him and he defended himself, but they finally killed him. And they did this for the sole reason that he had fled from those cruel and wicked Christians and had defended himself against them. And when they had captured him and as many of his followers as they could, they burned them all at the stake.

When tied to the stake, the cacique Hatuey was told by a Franciscan friar who was present, an artless rascal, something about the God of the Christians and of the articles of the Faith. And he was told what he could do in the brief time that remained to him, in order to be saved and go to Heaven. The cacique, who had never heard any of this before, and was told he would go to Inferno where, if he did not adopt the Christian Faith, he would suffer eternal torment, asked the Franciscan friar if Christians all went to Heaven. When told that they did he said he would prefer to go to Hell. Such is the fame and honor that God and our Faith have earned through the Christians who have gone out to the Indies.

On one occasion when we went to claim ten leagues of a big settlement, along with food and maintenance, we were welcomed with a bounteous quantity of fish and bread and cooked victuals. The Indians generously gave us all they could. Then suddenly, without cause and without warning, and in my presence, the devil inhabited the Christians and spurred them to attack the Indians, men, women, and children, who were sitting there before us. In the massacre that followed, the Spaniards put to the sword more than three thousand souls. I saw such terrible cruelties done there as I had never seen before nor thought to see.

A few days later, knowing that news of this massacre had spread through the land, I sent messengers ahead to the chiefs of the province of Havana, knowing they had heard good things about me, telling them we were about to visit the town and telling them they should not hide but should come out to meet us, assuring them that no harm would be done to them. I did this with the full knowledge of the captain. And when we arrived in the province, there came out to welcome us twenty-one chiefs and caciques, and our captain, breaking his pledge to me and the pledge I had made to them, took all these chieftains captive, intending to burn them at the stake, telling me this would be a good thing because those chiefs had in the past done him some harm. I had great difficulty in saving those Indians from the fire, but finally succeeded.

Afterward, when all the Indians of this island were subjected to servitude and the same ruin had befallen there as on the island Hispaniola, the survivors began to flee to the mountains or in despair to hang themselves, and there were husbands and wives who hanged themselves together with their children, because the cruelties perpetrated by one very great Spaniard (whom I knew) were so horrifying. More than two hundred Indians hanged themselves.

And thus perished a countless number of people on the island of Cuba.

That tyrant Spaniard, representative of the King of Spain, demanded, in the *repartimiento*, that he be given three hundred Indians. At the end of three months all but thirty of them had died of the hard labor in the mines, which is to say only a tenth of them had survived. He demanded another allocation of Indians, and they also perished in the same way. He demanded still another large allocation, and those Indians also perished. Then he died, and the devil bore him away.

In three or four months, when I was there, more than seventy thousand children, whose fathers and mothers had been sent to the mines, died of hunger.

And I saw other frightful things. The Spaniards finally decided to track down the Indians who had taken refuge in the mountains. There they created amazing havoc and thus finished ravaging the island. Where had been a flourishing population, it is now a shame and pity to see the island laid waste and turned into a desert.

## Study Terms

Black Legend
White Legend
Paternalism
Eurocentrism
Ethnocentrism
Repartimiento
Encomienda

# Introduction

*from Genealogical Fictions: Limpieza de Sangre, Religion, and Gender in Colonial Mexico*

By María Elena Martínez

● ● ● ● ● ● ● ● ● ● ● ● ● ● ● ● ● ● ● ● ● ● ● ● ● ● ● ● ● ● ● ● ● ● ● ● ● ●

## Editor's Introduction

In this selection by María Elena Martínez, the Spanish concept *limpieza de sangre* (purity of blood) is examined, and also how it evolved during the *Reconquista*, played a role in the Spanish Inquisition, and ultimately, continued in the Americas well into the eighteenth century. What is clear is that near-pathological obsession with purity of blood led to families keeping meticulous genealogical histories. What makes this more fascinating is that the practice was mandated "by the state, church, Inquisition, and other institutions in colonial Mexico..."[1]

What can be learned here is how folk taxonomy, discussed in Eugenia Shanklin's reading, was instilled on a grand scale, and its legacy can still be traced today, even if the sistema de castas (system of caste) disappeared after Mexico's independence from Spain in the nineteenth-century.

### Notes

María Elena Martínez. *Genealogical Fictions: Limpieza de Sangre, Religion, and Gender in Colonial Mexico.* Stanford: Stanford University Press, 2008, quoted from the back cover.

## Problem and Objectives

This book charts the rise of categories of *limpieza de sangre* ("purity of blood") in Spain and their journey from the Iberian Peninsula to the Americas, where they eventually took on a life of their own. Having originated in late medieval Castile, the concept of purity of blood and its underlying assumptions about inheritable characteristics had by the late seventeenth century produced a hierarchical system of classification in Spanish America that was ostensibly based on proportions of Spanish, indigenous, and African ancestry, the *sistema de castas* or "race/caste system." This use of the concept would probably have surprised the Spaniards who first deployed it against Jewish converts to Christianity, the *conversos,* or "New Christians." They defined blood purity as the absence of Jewish and heretical antecedents and, as of the middle of the fifteenth century, they increasingly wielded the notion to deprive the conversos of access to certain institutions and public and ecclesiastical offices. The concept acquired greater force during the next one hundred years, as limpieza de sangre statutes—requirements of unsullied "Old Christian" ancestry—were adopted by numerous religious and secular establishments in Castile and Aragon, the Spanish Inquisition was founded to identify "secret Jews" and root out heresy, and the category of impurity was extended to the descendants of Muslims. By the middle of the sixteenth century, the ideology of purity of blood had produced a Spanish society obsessed with genealogy and in particular with the idea that having only Christian ancestors, and thus a "pure lineage," was the critical sign of a person's loyalty to the faith. Descent and religion—"blood" and faith—were the two foundations of that ideology, and the same would be true in Spanish America.

The transfer of the Castilian discourse of limpieza de sangre to Spanish America did not mean, however, that it remained the same in the new context. As much as Spaniards tried to recreate their society in "New Spain" (colonial Mexico), they had to face circumstances, peoples, and historical developments that inevitably altered their transplanted institutions, practices, and cultural-religious principles. The survival of native communities and part of the pre-Hispanic nobility, the importance of the conversion project to Spanish colonialism and to Castile's titles to the Americas, the introduction of significant numbers of African slaves into the region, the rapid rise of a population of mixed ancestry, the influx of poor Spaniards seeking to better their lot if not ennoble themselves, and the establishment of a transatlantic economy based largely on racialized labor forces—these and other factors ensured that the Iberian concept of limpieza de sangre would be reformulated and have different implications than in Spain. In Castile, for example, it did not produce an elaborate system of classification based on blood proportions as it did in the colonies, though signs that such categories might develop appeared in the sixteenth century, particularly

in the Inquisition's genealogical investigations. Furthermore, in Spanish America, the notion of purity gradually came to be equated with Spanish ancestry, with "Spanishness," an idea that had little significance in the metropolitan context. The language of blood and lineage also underwent modifications. Nonetheless, at the end of the colonial period, the concept of limpieza de sangre was still partly defined in religious terms. What were the implications of this religious dimension for colonial categories of identity, racial discourses, and communal ideologies? Answering this question is one of the central aims of this book.

More to the point, the book seeks to expose the connection between the concept of limpieza de sangre and the sistema de castas. Although a number of scholars of colonial Mexico have referred to this connection, they have not fully explained it. They have not clarified how a concept that had strong religious connotations came to construct or promote classifications that presumably were based on modern notions of race. Exactly when, how, and why was the notion of purity of blood extended and adapted to the colonial context? This critical question has received little attention in the literature because, until recently, most historical studies of the sistema de castas have focused on the eighteenth century (when notions of race were starting to become secularized) and in particular on the problem of the saliency of "race" versus "class" as mercantile capitalism expanded. The privileging of the late colonial period in the historiography has meant that both the origins of the system and its relation to the concept of limpieza remain unclear. Works that do refer to the system in the early colonial period generally link the concept of purity of blood to race without elaborating on what exactly either of these terms meant at that time. Furthermore, they normally describe its rise as a function of the displacement of main peninsular status categories (noble, commoner, and slave) onto the three primary colonial groups (respectively, Spaniards, Indians, and blacks) and explain the disruption of this tripartite order by the growth of populations of mixed ancestry. This rendition of the emergence of the sistema de castas is seductive because of its simplicity; but it is also deceptive because it deprives the process of its contingency, does not explain why more than one category of mixture was created, and obscures the religious dimension of limpieza de sangre and therefore also its implications.

This book provides an analysis, first, of the linkages between the concept of limpieza de sangre and the sistema de castas with special consideration to the role of religion in the production of notions of purity and impurity, the historical specificity of Castilian categories such as *raza* (race) and *casta* (caste), the intertwined nature of peninsular and colonial discourses of purity, and the fluidity and ambiguities that characterized the system of classification throughout the colonial period. It is informed by critical race theory and in particular by scholarship that posits that race is not merely a consequence of material interests (an "effect" of class) but rather is linked in complex ways to economic, political, and ideological structures; social conditions; and systems of signification. Philosopher Cornel West has termed this approach "genealogical materialist." He has stressed the importance of investigating the origins and trajectory of racial ideas within specific cultural and historical traditions and their dynamic interaction with both micro- and macrolevel processes, including those related to political economy (local and global), the reproduction and disruption of power (say, through particular languages, idioms, or representations), and the construction of notions of self. West chose Nietzsche's concept of genealogy because he wanted to underscore the importance of undertaking deep and careful excavations of the meanings of race within the particular cultural-historical context in which it develops and of explaining its connections to different levels of existence.

In this study, the concept of genealogy is central both because it alludes to the process of historicizing race and because in the early modern Hispanic world it was ubiquitous and consequential, the foundation of a multitude of practices and identities that helped mold historical memory at both the individual and collective levels. It does not presuppose the automatic deployment of the concept of limpieza de sangre against colonial populations and simple displacement of peninsular status categories onto them. Nor does it assume that the meanings of early modern notions of purity and race are self-evident, a mistake that can lead to the tautological argument that the system of classifying "blood mixture" arose because "race mixture" occurred, an argument that reproduces the idea of races as biological givens rather than challenging it by interrogating why categories arise, become reified, and get contested. Instead, this book prioritizes analyzing the discursive tradition that the concepts of limpieza and raza were part of and which, together with certain practices, those two notions helped to constitute. It begins by addressing the following questions. What exactly did the concepts of limpieza de sangre and raza mean in Spain, when and why did they first start to be deployed in Mexico, and how were they adapted to the colonial context? Was their growing usage related to events in the metropole, Spanish America, or both? Which institutions adopted purity-of-blood requirements and when did they begin to target people of mixed ancestry? Did definitions of limpieza de sangre change over time, and if so, how? And what practices and identities did the ideology of purity of blood promote? These are the questions that constitute the first of three main lines of inquiry in the book.

A second line of investigation pertains to the connections of the concept of limpieza de sangre to gender and sexuality. The book argues that these connections were strong not just because of the centrality of biological reproduction (and by extension, female sexuality) to the perpetuation of community boundaries and the hierarchical social order in general. They were also powerful because Spanish notions regarding sexual and reproductive relations between the three main populations reflected and interacted with other discourses of colonial power. Recurring ideas regarding blood purity and mixture, for example, construed native people—the transmission of their traits—as weak, thereby echoing paternalistic religious and government policies that depicted relations among Spaniards, indigenous people, and blacks in gendered forms. Political, religious, and genealogical discourses in fact mirrored, complemented, and reinforced each other through the use of notions of strength and weakness that by coding different colonial groups as male or female naturalized socially created hierarchies.

Only in the eighteenth century, however, would invocations of nature as the basis of difference between men and women as well as between human groups begin to emerge as a prominent discourse. A growing interest, particularly among natural philosophers, in questions about the origins of different populations and function of men and women in the generation of life influenced how the sistema de castas was represented. As scientific explanations to sexual and racial difference gained ground over religious ones, colonial Mexico's population became subject, like the animals and plants in natural histories, to increasingly elaborate and visual taxonomic exercises that made the gendering of race and racing of gender as well as social hierarchies seem to be ordained by nature. This penchant for classification and naturalization was manifested in "casta paintings," a genre that illustrated and labeled the unions of different "castes" as well as their offspring and that betrayed both how some of Mexico's artists conceived of the appropriate relationship of gender, race, and class and the lingering importance of the discourse of limpieza de sangre.

A third main line of inquiry tracks the importance of the state-sponsored organization of colonial society into two separate commonwealths or "republics"—one Spanish, the other indigenous—to discourses of blood and lineage. Although strict segregation between the two populations was never achieved and some Spanish jurists and legislation allowed for the day when the native people would be fully incorporated into Hispanic colonial society, the dual model of social organization nevertheless had profound repercussions. At least in central Mexico, the *republica de indios* ("Indian

Republic") was not just an ideological device, and it continued to have practical significance well into the eighteenth century. It promoted the survival of *pueblos de indios* (native communities) with their own political hierarchies and citizenship regime, the creation of special legal and religious institutions for the indigenous people, and the official recognition of Indian purity. This recognition, which mainly pivoted on the argument that the original inhabitants of the Americas were unsullied by Judaism and Islam and had willingly accepted Christianity, made it possible for some of the descendants of pre-Hispanic dynasties to successfully claim the status of limpieza de sangre, in the long run altering some of their conceptions of blood and history. Their genealogical claims became more frequent in the last third of the seventeenth century, amid increasing efforts to preserve communal lands and histories.

But native nobles and rulers were not the only group to be influenced by the Spanish state's promotion of two polities and corresponding dual citizenship and purity regimes. All colonial identities, after all, were the results of complex colonial processes. Maintaining a system of "proving" purity in the "Spanish republic" necessitated the creation of birth records, classifications, and genealogies and obliged those who wanted access to the institutions or offices with limpieza requirements to submit lineages, produce witnesses, and keep records of their ancestors. Among creoles (Spaniards born and/or raised in the Americas), these administrative and archival practices helped foster a historical consciousness that encouraged their identification with a broader Spanish community of blood even as they developed a strong attachment to the land. By the eighteenth century, they established their purity not so much by stressing their lack of Jewish and Muslim ancestors as by providing evidence of their Spanish descent. Yet this formulation of limpieza de sangre as Spanishness did not entirely undermine the idea that the indigenous people were pure and redeemable because of their acceptance of Christianity. Instead, it produced paradoxical attitudes toward reproduction or *mestizaje* ("mixture") with Amerindians among Creole elites, particularly as their patriotism intensified and they began to imagine the merger of the two republics in reproductive and biological terms.

The book, then, centers on three main issues: the relationship between the Spanish notion of limpieza de sangre and Mexico's sistema de castas; the intersection of notions of purity, gender, and sexuality; and the linkages of religion, race, and patriotic discourses. Framing the exploration of these subjects is an emphasis on the role of the state, church, and archives in promoting a preoccupation with lineage in central Mexico, particularly among Creole and native elites. In other words, one of the book's thematic threads is how the routinization of genealogical requirements in the secular and religious hierarchies helped shape social practices, notions of self, and concepts of communal belonging. Which is not to say that the Spanish colonial state was powerful and that its laws were always or even frequently obeyed, only that it set guidelines for government and religious institutions and through them shaped the nature of social relations. The term *archival practices* thus generally refers to the record-keeping activities of the state, church, and Inquisition that produced and reproduced categories of identity based on ancestry linked to particular legal statuses (to certain responsibilities, rights, or privileges). These archival practices promoted genealogical ones, including official and unofficial investigations into a person's ancestors—involving examinations of birth records, interrogations of town elders, inspections of tributary lists, and so forth—and the construction of family histories through, among other things, the maintenance, purchase, or falsification of written genealogies, certifications of purity of blood, and copies of baptismal and marriage records.

Another recurring theme in the book is the interaction of metropolitan and colonial notions of purity and, more broadly, discourses about the New Christians—which drew on anti-Semitic tropes—and the converted populations of the Americas. Special attention is drawn to the similarities and differences in Spanish attitudes toward the conversion potential of Jews and native people and especially to how stereotypes that were used to describe one group tended to be mapped onto the other. Finally, the book underscores the instability of the sistema de castas. It stresses that, like all hegemonic projects, it was a process, powerful and pervasive because it was promoted by the state and the church but fluctuated and was subject to contestation. The relative fluidity of the sistema de castas was partly due to inconsistencies in the discourse of limpieza de sangre, which, for example, characterized native people *as* pure and impure, as both perfect material for Christianization and incorrigible idolaters. Hegemonic discourses tend to derive power from their construction of subjects in a doubled way.

The sistema's fluidity was also a by-product of the Spanish imperial structure, which incorporated Spanish America into the Crown of Castile but failed to clearly outline what that meant in terms of the rights and privileges of different populations. For example, despite the various compilations of laws for the "Indies" *(derecho indiano)* that Spain produced in the seventeenth century, it did not issue a legal code specifically for the castas and did not entirely clarify the status of Creoles as "natives" of a particular jurisdiction. The political vagueness of imperial space and piecemeal nature of colonial legislation prompted individuals and groups to attempt to challenge or redefine statuses, policies, and classifications. These features also resulted in unexpected political imaginaries, ones that a rigid distinction between a metropolitan core and colonial periphery cannot begin to capture.

## Limpieza De Sangre, Race, and Colonialism in the Early Modern Period

Scholars of early modern Spain have not paid much attention to the relationship between the concept of limpieza de sangre and Spanish American racial ideology. Their disinterest in the problem can be blamed on the lamentably persistent tendency within the profession to treat the histories of the Iberian Peninsula and colonial Latin America *as* separate analytical fields. But it is also indicative of a broader Spanish denial about certain aspects of Spain's colonial past. I first encountered this denial when I arrived at the Archivo General de Indias (AGI) in Seville to conduct research for this book. After I explained the purpose of my visit, the director of the archive informed me that I would not find any sources on limpieza de sangre there. The response took me aback because I had a list of references for documents related to my topic that other historians had found at that archive. But after being in Spain for a few months, I realized that it was part of a general reluctance among contemporary Spaniards to recognize the importance that the concept of purity of blood had in the Americas, namely because of what it implies for their national history, which has tended to minimize (if not deny) the role of processes of racialization in Castile's overseas territories. This reluctance cannot simply be attributed to ignorance, for even some Spanish historians of colonial Latin America tried to convince me, when at the onset of my research I presented at a reputable research institution in Seville, that the problem of purity of blood was one that never spilled out of the borders of the Iberian Peninsula and that the concept was used exclusively against converted Jews and Muslims. It soon became clear that the organization of archives—the way that many limpieza de sangre documents were classified or not classified, subsumed under other records, or mislabeled—was intimately connected to this national historical narrative.

That the same historians who tried to convince me of the irrelevance of the concept of limpieza de sangre outside of Spain were well acquainted with purity documents produced in Spanish America only added a surreal quality to the discussion that followed my presentation in Seville. But the strangeness of the experience did not end there. To bolster his case, a specialist in Andean history offered the observation that many Spanish colonists had reproduced with native women and, in cases where acquiring land was at stake, even married them! A people concerned with blood purity would not be willing to "mix" with the Amerindians was his point, one that clearly echoed the arguments made by some scholars in the first half of the twentieth century regarding Iberians' relatively benign attitudes toward native people and Africans. This current of thought, which had among its many flaws the propensity to see early colonial sexual relations not as acts of power but as signs of a more gentle or open approach to colonization (sometimes attributed to the history of Spanish and Portuguese "commingling" with Jews and Muslims) is part of the white Legend of Spanish history, an apologetic view of Spain's actions in the Americas. The view to some extent surfaced in reaction to the body of propagandistic literature that began to be produced by Spain's European rivals (especially the British and Dutch) in the late sixteenth century and which gave rise to the Black Legend. Seeking to discredit Castile's claims to the Americas, this legend focused attention on the conquerors' cruelty toward indigenous peoples, their unbridled greed, and their hypocritical use of religion as justification for their deeds.

The Black Legend survived into the twentieth century and colored Anglophone scholarship on both Spain and Spanish America. Its influence is evident, for example, in the modernization studies of the 1950s that compared Latin America's apparent continuity in political, social, and economic forms—its history of authoritarianism, sharp inequalities, and financial dependency—with the more democratic and capitalist trajectory of the United States. These studies tended to blame the "feudal" and "absolutist" foundations of Spanish colonial societies for the region's troubled path to modernity. Many framed the problems associated with the latifundia (the absence of a yeomanry), the Inquisition (the suppression of freedom of political and religious thought), and the church's collusion with the state (the clergy's ongoing support of absolutism) as medieval holdovers that Castilians took to the Americas, where they obstructed economic entrepreneurship, individualism, and democratic ideals, among other things. The causes of Spain's inability to modernize à la other parts of Western Europe and the United States also explained Latin America's "backwardness."

In the past few decades, the Black Legend has taken on a new twist. Some of the scholarship on the history of race and racism has been casting early modern Iberia as the site of a precocious elaboration of racial concepts and practices. A recent historical overview of the problem, for example, begins by discussing developments in Spain, "the first great colonizing nation and a seedbed for Western attitudes toward race." Iberia's pioneering role in the development of racial ideologies is sometimes linked to its participation in the early stages of the transatlantic African slave trade and in the colonization of the Americas. But it is more often associated with the Spanish statutes of limpieza de sangre. Indeed, particularly in the literature that seeks to excavate the "origins" of race, it has become almost commonplace to postulate that the Castilian concept of blood purity was the first racial discourse produced by the West or at least an important precursor to modern notions of difference. Anti-Semitism was endemic in late medieval Europe, and in the two centuries preceding Spain's 1492 expulsion of its Jews France and England had on repeated occasions tried to do the same with their Jewish populations, but it apparently makes for a much more satisfying narrative when race and racism can be given a single starting point and a linear trajectory. Thanks to its contribution to racism via the purity statutes and Inquisition, early modern Spain can finally make a claim to modernity. It was ahead of its time in something.

Whether the intention of its proponents or not, the argument that credits Spain with establishing the first modern system of discrimination fits neatly into the package of the Black Legend, which might help to explain why Spanish historians would be less than enthusiastic about studying the extension of the concept of limpieza de sangre to the other side of the Atlantic. To acknowledge that a discourse of purity of blood surfaced in the Americas would

be to risk adding yet another dark chapter to a history that includes the expulsion of the Jews, the establishment of the Inquisition, the forced exile of Muslims *and* moriscos (Muslim converts to Christianity), and the conquest and colonization of native peoples. Given that the concept of purity of blood was relevant in all of these developments, how does one approach the subject in ways that avoid presenting historical actors in terms of simplistic dichotomies and, more generally, the politicization of history? Perhaps, as the historian Steve Stern has stressed, the conquest and colonization of the Americas can never be disentangled from politics—from the politics of the past and the present, the history and historiography—but the point here is not to vilify Spaniards or suggest that they were worse, as the Black Legend would have it, than other colonial powers, or for that matter better, as the White Legend camp claimed. No expansionist European country could claim the moral high ground with respect to their attitudes toward and treatment of the peoples they colonized and/ or enslaved, only some differences in timing, methods, and guiding principles. This book does not intend, therefore, to provide material for the perpetuation of the Black Legend (whether it is used as such is another matter) or to reinforce the tendency in recent studies on the origins of race and racism to single out early modern Iberia, as if those phenomena were unknown in other parts of Europe or somehow spread from the peninsula to the rest of the continent. Its main concern is not with the history of Spain but with that of New Spain, although the two are clearly interrelated, and that in itself is a point that the study tries to reiterate as it charts the transatlantic paths of the problem of limpieza de sangre.

If Spanish historians can be criticized for their failure to recognize the importance of limpieza de sangre in the colonial context, U.S. scholars of Spanish America can be accused of not having paid adequate attention to the complexity of the uses and meanings of the concept in Iberia, which has tended to result in oversimplified and at times anachronistic renditions of the ways in which it shaped racial discourses in the American context. For their part, Mexican and other Latin American academics can be taken to task for their general aversion to treating race as a legitimate subject of inquiry for understanding their region's history. It is fair to say that they tend to regard it as an issue that mainly has had relevance in the United States and other former slave societies (as opposed to "societies with slaves"), whereas they see class as much more salient for understanding the Iberian American past (even when it comes to regions in which slavery was extremely important, such as Brazil and Cuba). Thus, although some Mexican specialists of the colonial period might agree that the notion of limpieza de sangre was of some significance (it is hard to miss references to it in the archives), they commonly dismiss the problem of race by stressing that social organization was based on an estate model. If different groups had distinct rights, privileges, and obligations, it was because of the hierarchical nature of Spanish society, which at the time of the conquest continued to consist of three main estates and numerous corporations with specific functions within the social body, not because of modern notions of biological difference.

The argument that using the notion of race to study the period prior to the nineteenth century is anachronistic has of course not been made exclusively by Latin Americans. Indeed, the standard chronology (and teleology) of the concept is that it had not yet crystallized—assumed its full essentializing potential—in the early modern period because attitudes regarding phenotype usually combined or competed with ideas of cultural or religious difference. According to this account, race did not appear until the nineteenth century, when pseudoscience anchored it in biology, or rather, when biology anchored it in the body much more effectively than natural philosophy and natural history ever did. It is true that the concept of race generally became more biologistic in that period, and it is of course important not to project its modern connotations to previous eras. But arguing that racial discourses took a particular form in the nineteenth century

is one thing; contending that they did not operate in the early modern period, quite another. In the past three decades, a number of scholars have demonstrated that the meanings and uses of the concept of race have varied across time, space, and cultures and that even in modern times, it has not relied exclusively on biological notions of difference but rather has often been intertwined with culture and/or class. To elevate "race as biology" to an ideal type is to set up a false dichotomy—to ignore that racial discourses have proven to be remarkably flexible, invoking nature or biology more at one point, culture more at another. The shifting meanings and uses of race simultaneously underscore its social constructedness and suggest that there is no single, transhistorical racism but rather different types of *racisms,* each produced by specific social and historical conditions. The historian's task is precisely to excavate its valences within particular cultural and temporal contexts, study the processes that enable its reproduction, and analyze how it rearticulates or is "reconstructed as social regimes change and histories unfold.

Several historians of colonial Latin America have argued that it is necessary to keep limpieza de sangre and race analytically distinct for the sake of historical specificity and in particular to attempt to be faithful to the ways in which people of that time and place understood their social identities. Some scholars fear that equating notions of lineage, blood, and descent with race would mean characterizing all pre modern societies, and those studied by anthropologists, as racially structured. The argument is compelling, and it is certainly difficult to dispute the point that there is a significant difference between the racial discourses that European colonialism unleashed and indigenous kinship systems. But attempting to draw a rigid analytical line between purity of blood and race is tricky, first, because the two concepts gained currency at about the same time and appear side by side in virtually all *probanzas* (certificates) of limpieza de sangre, and second, because the former influenced the latter in no small ways. Indeed, there was no neat transition from early modern notions of lineage to race. In the Hispanic Atlantic world, Iberian notions of genealogy and purity of blood—both of which involved a complex of ideas regarding descent and inheritance (biological and otherwise)—gave way to particular understandings of racial differences.

There is nothing original about asserting that there was a link between European genealogical notions and racial discourses. As the anthropologist Ann Laura Stoler has observed, both Michel Foucault and Benedict Anderson alluded to this link, albeit in different ways. Foucault, who viewed the problem of race mainly as part of Europe's "internal and permanent war with itself" and therefore did not consider colonialism's relevance to it, implied that a discourse of class had emerged from the "racism" of the European aristocracy. For his part, Anderson suggested that race had its origins in ideologies of "class" sprung from the landed nobility. Thus, for one scholar, the aristocracy's racism informed class; for the other, its elitism shaped race. To some extent, these two different formulations stem from confusion over how to characterize the nobility's obsession with "blood," which more often than not was accompanied by concerns with biological inheritance, anxieties about reproduction outside the group, and a series of insidious assumptions about the inferiority and impurity of members of the commoner estate. Medieval representations of peasants, for example, rendered them as a lower order of humanity and associated them with animals, dirt, and excrement. The beastialization of the peasantry could reach such extremes that a historian of slavery has suggested that it was an important precursor to the early modern racialization of Jews and blacks.

Whether medieval and early modern concerns with blood and lineage—in Europe and elsewhere—can be classified as racism will most likely continue to be debated, especially by those who favor using a loose definition of race that makes it applicable to most naturalizing or essentializing discourses and those who opt for a narrow one that basically limits its use to the nineteenth century and beyond. The debate is important but frankly less pressing than analyzing the historical significance of those concerns—the social tensions that produced them, the terms people used to express them, and the ways in which they were reproduced or rearticulated over time and across geocultural contexts. This book therefore uses the word *race* in relation to the discourse of limpieza de sangre but does so with caution, stressing that both concepts were strongly connected to lineage and intersected with religion. Through much of the early modern period, they remained part of a grid of knowledge constituted not by scientific (biologistic) discourses but by religious ones and operated through an "episteme of resemblance" in which similitude dominated the organization of symbols and interpretations and representations of the universe. The book also emphasizes that concepts of blood purity and race were neither contained in Europe nor simply a consequence of the continent's "internal war with itself." They operated in a transatlantic context, and their continued salience and fluctuating meanings over the centuries were partly, if not greatly, determined by colonialism.

In sum, by underscoring the interrelated nature of discourses of purity of blood in Iberia and the Americas, this study undermines the view (especially prominent among Spanish historians) that the problem of limpieza de sangre was primarily an Iberian phenomenon as well as the contention (made by some scholars of Spanish America) that it can be separated from that of race. Furthermore, it problematizes the conceptual division that the literature on race sometimes makes between colonial racism and anti-Semitism. Some studies have argued that the two types of discriminatory regimes are manifestly different: that whereas the former has been characterized by the construction and maintenance of (colonial) hierarchies, the latter has typically promoted exclusion or outright extermination (as in the case of Nazi Germany). But as Etienne Balibar has stressed, a stark distinction between an "inclusive" colonial racism and an "exclusive" (usually anti-Semitic) one is untenable because historically, the two forms have not only exhibited similar characteristics but have depended on each other; rather than having separate genealogies, they have a "joint descent." Few historical phenomena demonstrate this close relationship between anti-Semitic and colonial discourses of difference better than the ideology of purity of blood, which spread while Spain was forging its overseas empire. Like the ships, people, and merchandise moving to and from Europe, Africa, and the Americas, the ideas and practices associated with the notion of limpieza de sangre circulated within, and helped forge, the Hispanic Atlantic world.

If the area to which this book most directly contributes is the study of race in Spanish America, it also has implications for a number of other topics, including ones related to periodization, nationalism, and comparative colonialisms. For one, the centrality of the seventeenth century to the development of the sistema de castas places the focus on a period that historians of colonial Latin America have tended to understudy. Perhaps unduly influenced by anthropologist George Foster's characterization of colonial Latin American culture as having "crystallized" or acquired its basic social institutions by 1580, the historiography has generally regarded the years between that decade and 1750 as largely uneventful. Neglect of this "long seventeenth century" or middle phase of Spanish colonialism might also be explained by its shortage of events as dramatic as those of the conquest and its aftermath. How can the period compete, for example, with the years that witnessed the early evangelizing campaigns and their inspiration in biblical, messianic, and eschatological interpretations of history; the Spanish "debates" about the humanity of the Amerindians; and the civil war that erupted among some of Peru's conquerors? It may also be that the seventeenth-century's difficult paleography and less extensive secondary literature have made studying other eras more appealing.

Whatever the case, the period was anything but static. Seventeenth-century Spanish America not only had strong connections with Spain but underwent crucial social and cultural transformations. Included among these changes was the rise of Creole patriotism, a topic that has been explored by David Brading, Bernard Lavalle, and others and which is analyzed in the present study in relation to the ideology of limpieza de sangre. By interrogating the complex relationship of patriotic, religious, and blood discourses, the book makes an intervention in discussions of nationalism in Latin America. Nationalism, however, is not an explicit subject of inquiry, in part because it did not appear until the end of the colonial period, if then. The region's independence movements were primarily triggered by Napoleon's invasion of Spain in 1808 and imposition of his brother Joseph as the new king, which on both sides of the Atlantic led to political assemblies and discussions that quickly became much more than about the restitution of Ferdinand VII to the throne. Thus, Latin American nationalism seems to have been the result, not the cause, of the independence movements, and to speak of eighteenth-century "creole nationalism" is to walk on shaky argumentative ground. Furthermore, as a number of historians who responded to Benedict Anderson's thesis about its rise in Spanish America have pointed out, not only was creole patriotism compatible with continued loyalty to the Spanish Crown, but the early modern notion of "nation" *(nation)* was exceedingly ambiguous with regard to territory and bloodlines.

That a strong identification with the local community existed prior to independence does not mean that there was a causal connection between the two or between *criollismo* (creolism) and nationalism. Assuming such a connection amounts to "doing history backwards," that is, projecting modern categories onto a world in which those forms of thinking had not yet come about. It also forecloses the possibility of studying Creole patriotism on its own terms—its meanings, motivations, and political effects at different points in time. But if patriotism and nationalism should not be conflated, examinations of colonial political ideology, social developments, and cultural movements are necessary to understand the form that Mexican nationalism took after independence. By exploring the relationship between the religiously inflected concept of limpieza de sangre and notions of citizenship *(vecindad)* in New Spain, this study seeks to provide a basis for further discussions about how the particularities of colonialism in Mexico shaped its postindependence political projects, gendered and racialized imaginings of the nation, and legal formulations of the citizen.

It also aims to highlight some of the specificities of Spanish colonialism. Although there are continuities and similarities between different colonial projects, colonialism cannot be reduced to a single model; it has multiple historicities. The Spanish colonial project, the earliest in the Americas, was driven by historically and culturally specific forces, and its course was determined by early modern dynamics on both sides of the Atlantic. It differed most from modern imperial projects. For example, unlike Britain and France when they launched the second major phase of European colonialism starting in the second half of the eighteenth century, when Spain invaded the Americas, it was not an industrial power seeking raw materials and markets for its manufactured goods. Its expansion west was initially propelled by the search for gold (increasingly important as a medium of exchange in international commerce), and its economic project came to be based primarily on the exploitation of mineral wealth and on state-controlled systems of extracting labor and tribute from native populations that had few parallels.

Furthermore, Spanish colonialism began long before the emergence of the politics of nationhood, liberalism, and Enlightenment-inspired universalist concepts of freedom, equality, rights, progress, and citizenship. Together with the expansion of capitalist relations, these modern developments generated new ideological frameworks for justifying colonial rule as well as a deep tension between the particularism of colonialism (predicated on the creation and perpetuation of colonial hierarchies) and the universalism of western European political theory. Spanish colonialism in the Americas, based more on the concept of status than on the notion of rights,

did not have to contend with this tension, at least not at first. During its first two centuries, its main ideological contradiction stemmed from, on one hand, universalist Christian doctrines that touted the redemptive powers of baptism and the equality of all members of the church and, on the other, the construction of different categories of Christians. The extent to which religion played a role in justifying expansion and colonial rule was another aspect of the early modern Spanish colonial project that distinguished it from modern ones.

Readily distinguishable in certain respects from nineteenth- and twentieth-century imperialism, Spanish colonialism becomes less distinctive when it is compared to other formative or early colonial projects in the Americas. Contrary to what the Black Legend would have us believe, during the initial phase of European expansion, Spaniards did not have a monopoly on the unbridled use of violence against native peoples. The British and Dutch amply demonstrated their capacity for barbarity. Furthermore, Spanish, Portuguese, English, and French colonial projects shared a number of features, including expansion through settlement; efforts to recreate European ways of life; and religious Utopias, Catholic and Protestant alike. But similarities among these "settler-type" colonialisms can be overstated, among other reasons because each power had its own economic, political, and religious agendas, even if at certain historical moments some of these overlapped. The Spanish state's control over some systems of labor, its transformation of large indigenous populations into tributaries, and its collective incorporation of native people as Christian vassals of the Crown of Castile were exceptional, especially when compared to British policies in Anglo North America. And although efforts to convert native people to Christianity were by no means exclusive to Spaniards, no other European colonial power, not even the other Catholic ones of Portugal and France, relied on the church to spread the faith, support the government, and structure colonial society as much as Castile. The historical moment and cultural context were both crucial. That religion was integral to Spanish colonialism was due in large measure to its importance in sixteenth-century Spain itself, where Catholicism was the only religion allowed, where the church and state had developed an extraordinarily strong relationship, and where the twin notions of "Old Christian blood" and genealogical purity had emerged as powerful cultural principles and exclusionary weapons. Religion, lineage, and blood would in turn be used to organize the Spanish colonial world.

In conclusion, Spanish colonialism was shaped by particular economic, political, and religious goals; by historical circumstances in early modern Spain and Spanish America; and by distinctive principles of social organization. As a result, its categories of discourse, mechanisms of inclusion and exclusion, and forms of establishing the boundaries of the Spanish community were unique or, at the very least, substantially different from modern colonial projects in Africa and Asia.

## Study Terms

Critical Race Theory
Black Legend
White Legend
Limpieza de Sangre
Sistema de Castas
derecho indiano
mestizaje
pueblo de indios
Archival Practices
probanzas
conversos
Genealogy

# Scientific Racism
# and Nationalism

# Race and IQ

By Alexander Alland, Jr.

● ● ● ● ● ● ● ● ● ● ● ● ● ● ● ● ● ● ● ● ● ● ● ● ● ● ● ● ● ● ● ● ● ● ● ● ● ● ● ●

## Editor's Introduction to Race and IQ

One of the longest-standing tenets of racism is the assumption or perception that non-whites are biologically inferior, and, by extension, less intelligent than whites. This essay on Race and IQ closely examines and refutes the findings of a study conducted in 1969 by Arthur Jensen. One controversial finding was "an average genetic deficit in IQ among people of black ancestry when compared to whites."[1] Jensen's report was immediately utilized as "proof" that remedial educational programs should cease because if IQ was hereditary, then time and money was being wasted.

In the 1990s, a polarizing book, *The Bell Curve*, claimed that its empirical studies agreed with the Jensen Report, and had expanded upon it. However, the book's claimed empirical studies were thoroughly picked apart by the late Stephen Jay Gould and other scholars.[2] Nonetheless, the "Jensen Report" resurfaces from time to time as an argument to cut federal spending, often camouflaged as an "austerity" measure, or reduction in the size of government.

### Notes

1. Alexander Alland, Jr. *Race in Mind: Race, IQ, and other Racisms.* New York: Palgrave, 2002, 79.
2. Stephen Jay Gould. *The Mismeasure of Man.* New York: W.W. Norton, 1996.

This chapter deals primarily with race and IQ in the work of Arthur Jensen, the author of a 1969 report on race and IQ that was essentially an attack on the governmental program known as Project Head Start. The program's goal was to help children from poor neighborhoods prepare for their entry into the regular school system through attendance at free government-supported preschools. The assumption behind Head Start was that the children of the poor suffered a learning deficit in their early formative years due to an impoverished intellectual environment. For those who believed that IQ and, therefore, performance was hereditary, Head Start was seen as a waste of federal monies.

Jensen is an educational psychologist specializing in psychological statistics who, after many years as a professor at Teachers College, Columbia University, moved to the University of California at Berkeley. His highly controversial article "How Much Can We Boost IQ and Scholastic Achievement?" published in the *Harvard Educational Review* in 1969, made a case for the preponderance of heredity in the production of intelligence as measured by IQ tests, and an average genetic deficit in IQ among people of black ancestry when compared to whites. Although the argument had been made before, Jensen's article drew a vast amount of positive attention from the press and among some educators and strong criticisms from many, but by no means all, professional psychologists and anthropologists. It is important to note that the "Jensen Report" came shortly after the Supreme Court decision banning segregation in public schools and the successes of the civil rights movement to desegregate schools in the South. Therefore, it should come at no surprise that Jensen's conclusions were seized upon immediately by those who opposed remedial educational programs, such as Project Head Start, for young poor children and, in particular, poor black children. In a nutshell their argument was: If, as Jensen has proved, IQ is largely hereditary, it is a waste of money and time to develop and pursue programs for children in order to enhance their intelligence. Because even today this article stands as a model for those who continue to believe the IQ argument concerning race, this chapter will focus on its major shortcomings. Later work concerning group differences and IQ will be taken up in chapter eight, which is devoted to Herrnstein and Murray's *The Bell Curve*.

In discussions concerning hereditary group differences in IQ, race has not always been the crucial variable. In Great Britain, for example, the focus has been on class rather than race. The man most associated with modern work on class and IQ in Britain, and who had a significant impact on Jensen's methods of research, was Cyril Burt. Burt attempted to prove that heredity played a major role in intelligence by studying identical twins reared apart. Because such twins are genetically identical, any differences in IQ found among them must be due to environment. However, because no one has ever argued that genetics plays the *only* role in the determination of IQ, such studies are putatively used to determine the proportional contributions of genetics and environment to a trait that varies among populations with different genetic profiles and brought up under different environmental conditions. Since at the time that Cyril Burt did his work class and not race was a major concern in Britain, he set out to prove that IQ was the *major* variable in *class* differences in intelligence.

This idea was not new with Burt. It was first proposed in the middle of the nineteenth century by Darwin's brilliant cousin, one of the founders of mathematical statistics, Francis Galton. Galton warned that class differentials in fertility, with the lower class having more children than the upper classes, would inevitably produce a gradual decrease in the average IQ of the entire British population. Burt represented a modern version of Galton's hypothesis and provided what he claimed was solid evidence of the phenomenon that would bring about the decline in IQ predicted by his predecessor.

Before I criticize Jensen's and Burt's work in detail let me turn to the concept of race and its purported relation to behavioral traits including—but not exclusive to—IQ. As we have already seen, the concept of race is often confused with ethnic, cultural, or religious identity. People speak of the French race, the Irish race, or the Jewish race. In societies where racism is current, individuals of mixed ancestry are usually assimilated into whichever part of their ancestry is downgraded by society. Thus, in the United States even individuals who are phenotypically white may be classed as black if it is known that they have even a small degree of black ancestry. It is fair to say, therefore, that even if race is a false concept in biology it is *real* from a sociological perspective. When members of a society classify an individual by race then that person *is by definition* a member of that race!

Racial identity is by no means a neutral concept. Wherever used it implies superiority or inferiority. Which "racial" groups are esteemed or denigrated is determined by subjective factors linked to historical and sociological factors. During the middle of the nineteenth century the Protestant establishment in New England tended to characterize the Irish as a distinct race. At that time the Irish were said to display a range of primarily negative biological characteristics. Later, as the Irish gained in population and political power, this attitude changed.

One of the favorite and eternal arguments of dominant groups is that they *merit* their place in the social hierarchy (see also chapter eight). In times of absolutist royal power kings and nobles ruled through the doctrine of hereditary power. Ever since the enlightenment and the rise of industrial capitalism in the West, large segments of the middle class have rested their claim to social and political dominance on "social selection," a process said to be akin to natural selection. People might rise to the top from humble social origins, but if they did so it was on the basis of *merit* According to this theory, merit was linked directly to heredity. Since the beginning of the twentieth century merit has come to be objectified as intelligence *plus* socially acceptable hard work.

Meanwhile, the somewhat vague concept of intelligence was converted into a supposedly measurable entity through the statistical concept of IQ. It is common for people to believe not only that IQ is hereditary but also that whole "racial" groups differ in average IQ. This has led to what is known as the "IQ argument." As noted above, the IQ argument was originally associated with class relations, particularly in Europe, and with race in the United States. In discussing the assumed link between race and IQ it must be made clear that we are about to deal with two nebulous concepts. We have already seen that race has no firm reality in biology. Now we need to examine the pitfalls in the concept of IQ as well as the notion that whole groups have different *hereditary* averages for intelligence.

What is intelligence? It should be obvious that tests designed to measure it are structured in relation to some theory, but I wish to delay discussion of this problem for the moment. Let us begin with test results and work backward to their origin and the concepts they reflect. Suffice it to say here that intelligence is a comparative phenomenon. Tests are standardized on the basis of a mean average in a population of test takers. Once this has been established individuals can be ranked above, at, or below the mean. It is also possible to give IQ tests to different groups of people, compare average scores, and rank one group against another. When such rankings are made in this country the data show that some sociological categories consistently score lower than the standard white American rage. These groups include American Indians, African Americans, and other ethnic groups, such as Latinos of various origin. Class breakdown of scores shows that middle- and upper-class whites score better than lower-class whites and that people in the North score higher than those in the South. Much has been made of the fact that African Americans from the *North* scored better on one type of test (the army alpha given around the time of World War I), than *Southern* whites. When compared to *Northern* whites, however, they scored below the mean. The lower scores for African Americans in the North when compared to northern whites have been attributed to differences in social environment and education. It is important to note, however, that these results were couched in terms of differences among biological groups. But data actually concern four distinct *sociological* categories. These are: Southern *sociologically* defined whites, Southern *sociologically* defined African Americans, Northern *sociologically* defined whites, and Northern *sociologically* defined African Americans. In no case do any of these groups represent a distinct biological population, although it *is* fair to say that the gene pools of each group differs from the others to some unquantifiable degree.

It must be stressed as well that IQ data is subject to variation in two ways. First, they depend on particular test protocols (many different kinds of IQ tests exist), and second, tests are given under varying conditions. It has been shown that *different* IQ tests produce *different* results and the *same* tests can produce *different* results when the testing conditions are varied.

Let us return to the concept of intelligence for a moment. What is it? The French psychologist Alfred Binet and his colleague, Theodore Simon, developed a set of tests between 1905 and 1911 that were meant to predict success in French middle-class elementary schools. They suggested that in intelligence there is a fundamental mental facility, the alteration or the lack of which is of utmost importance for practical life. That facility is judgment, or good sense, initiative, the faculty of adapting ones self to circumstances, judging well, comprehending well, and reasoning well. The concept of intelligence became a major preoccupation of American educational psychologists in the first half of the twentieth century. This led to various modifications of the definition. For example, Spearman (1904) reduced it to the ability to deduce relations and correlations. Thorndike (1927) regarded it as the power to make good responses from the standpoint of truth and fact. Terman (1937) defined it as the ability to think in abstract terms. All three definitions imply that intelligence can be measured as the rapidity of accommodation or adaptation to unique environmental situations through learning and conceptualization.

As the attention of psychologists turned to the concept of intelligence and how to test it, a debate began to emerge over the degree to which it is genetically determined. None of the definitions imply directly that IQ is genetic nor does anyone concerned with it claim that it is 100 percent hereditary. Rather, as I have already noted, arguments center over the relative contributions of heredity and environment to individual and group intelligence and how to measure objectively the contribution of each. Not so curiously, given the history of discrimination in the United States, most scholars who take a strong hereditarian position on IQ also assume that group differences in measured IQ are hereditary and that whites are genetically superior in intelligence to blacks. These arguments comfort the "racial" situation in the United States and have strong backing from many politicians and, unfortunately, psychologists

(see epilogue), who have a strong academic stake in testing. The "new" field of evolutionary psychology (another name for sociobiology) reinforces the simplistic notion that most of human behavior is genetic in origin and that differences among cultural groups are biological in nature (see Wilson 1975).

Here it should be clear that we are concerned with two different problems. It is *not* the same thing to say that (1) genetics are responsible for individual differences in IQ within populations and (2) that population differences in IQ are due to genetics. The human species is highly *polymorphic*. Thus all human populations display wide internal variation in genetic traits, not to mention cultural variation. I have already noted that genetic differences *within* populations are wider than genetic differences among different populations. It is also true that, in the case of the human species, it is difficult, if not impossible, to separate genetic from environmental factors in the expression of phenotypic behavioral traits. Experiments designed to do this are impossible for both ethical and cultural reasons. We cannot breed humans in the laboratory the way we can breed rats. As we shall see in this chapter as well as the chapter on *The Bell Curve,* so far all attempts to empirically separate environmental from genetic factors in behavioral testing have been seriously flawed.

There are other problems as well. The selection and maintenance of a definite goal and the ability to criticize one's own behavior contain elements that are surely subject to environmental modification. No two children ever grow up under the same conditions. In addition, individual psychological differences other than intelligence may affect the way an individual responds to new situations. A hesitant, demurring child might do less well on tests than a more confident one even though both might have the same potential capacities. And, of course, when we deal with test results the testing situation must be considered, for these conditions are bound to be influenced by an individuals cultural and psychological background. Although intelligence tests are supposed to be self-contained units, that is, units that contain all the information necessary to make judgments within the context of the test, the intellectual background, interests, and experience of the individuals tested appear to have significant effects on the responses of test takers. In addition different cultures have a tendency to treat "truth" or "fact" in very different ways. In American society Aristotelian logic is imposed early on children, while in the East not only is a paradoxical type of logic taught in some areas, but some intellectuals there strive to change their basic thought patterns so that they can come to accept a kind of inversion of what Westerners would call truth: The obvious is always false; truth often lies in opposites.

IQ tests themselves are subject to artifactual errors that render interpretation difficult. Among these are such cultural factors as attitudes toward testing in general, the amount of test sophistication an individual brings to a particular experiment, and the structure of the tests themselves. Thus the tests may or may not actually measure what the experimenter assumes they do. For example, such tests are poor measures of biologically based *group* differences. The *independent* variable (the group being tested) is most frequently more *social* than biological. There are major problems with the *dependent* variable (what is being tested) as well. In addition to whatever that is, such items as motivation to take the test, intellectual background based on prior learning, and many other psychological factors affect test results.

Let me summarize those factors that go into an intelligent (successful) response to environmental stimuli. First, the nature of the stimulus must be considered. While there is evidence that the ability to respond to specific cues is partially inherent (humans in general have good vision and hearing and a relatively poor sense of smell), there is also evidence that a good deal of learning goes into the process. Perceptions are always selective (even when the process of selection is unconscious). The response to a cue involves such psychological factors as perceptual acuity, ability to discriminate among stimuli (which is partly hereditary and partly learned), and the ability to generalize, that is, to form classes of data from a range of sense perceptions. The latter is also clearly a process involving both learning and

heredity. Accurate responses involve memory and the ability to retrieve necessary bits of information to be employed in problem solving. Interest and span of attention, both of which are highly dependent upon social and psychological factors, speed of response, and effectiveness of feedback from behavior are all important variables. No single gene, of course, could underlie all of these (and other) psychological processes. In addition each variable, dependent as it may be on a hereditary base, would be subject to environmental modification in different ways. Divergent behavioral phenotypes could emerge from the same basic genotype. This would arise through environmental shaping in the same way that similar phenotypes are derived from different genotypes.

Let us return to those "bright" and "dull" rat strains developed by Tryon. Later experimentation demonstrated that the rats were reacting to specific tests. Environmental factors had a strong effect on the performance of these inbred (and thus genetically pure) strains. More specifically, in three out of five maze measures "dulls" were either equal in performance or better than the "brights." The "brights" were more food-driven, low in motivation to escape water, timid in open field situations, more purposive, and less destructive. "Dulls" were not highly food-driven, were better on average in motivation to escape water, and were fearful of mechanical apparatus features. Note how important these additional facts are to a full understanding of Tryon's results.

Intelligence tests are designed to measure a series of abilities: for example, spatial relations, reasoning, verbal fluency, and facility with numbers. But these are no more culture-free than the concepts behind them. For although it is possible to define intelligence *operationally* as the ability to achieve high scores on IQ tests, we must never forget that certain socially significant concepts lie behind the operational definition. The major concept relates IQ to academic performance under existing forms of education. Our system of education, however, is geared to middle-class success, not necessarily innate ability. Arthur Jensen (1969a) has pointed out that many of the psychological properties that contribute to response potential intercorrelate, even though specific tasks such as spatial relationships, verbal analogies, and numerical problem solving might bear no resemblance to one another. In this he follows Spearman, who separated out a factor ("g") that he believed accounted for "general intelligence." This conclusion led Spearman to define intelligence as the ability to deduce relations and correlates. Nonetheless, Jensen, himself unsatisfied with a unidimensional concept of intelligence, delineated two *genotypically* (genetically based) distinct basic processes that he called level one (associational ability) and level two (conceptual ability). Jensen related level one to the formation of associations between related stimuli, red with danger, for example, and level two to concept learning and problem solving, for him by far the most important factor in intelligence.

Another author, Rosalind Cohen (1969), identified two conceptual styles that she called "relational" and "analytic":

> The analytic cognitive style is characterized by a formal or analytic mode of abstracting salient information from a stimulus or situation and by a stimulus-centered orientation to reality and is parts-specific (i.e., parts or attributes of a given stimulus have meaning in themselves). The relational cognitive style, on the other hand, requires a descriptive mode of abstraction and is self-centered in its orientation to reality; only the global characteristics of a stimulus have meaning to its users, and these only in reference to some total context. (Cohen 1969, 829–30)

For what I hope are obvious reasons, the analytic style is clearly correlated with success in the academic context. While they are perhaps not identical, the analytic style is certainly close to what Jensen (1969a, 114) refers to as level two learning, or conceptual ability. Cohen, however, rejects a genetic hypothesis and substitutes one in which socialization and group structure constitute the independent variables in the formation of cognitive style. I would claim that Cohen's arguments are more convincing than Jensen's.

> Observation indicated that relational and analytic cognitive styles were intimately associated with shared-function and formal styles of group organization.… When individuals shifted from one kind of group structure to the other, their modes of group participation, their language styles, and their cognitive styles could be seen to shift appropriately to the extent that their expertise in using other approaches made flexibility possible. It appeared that certain kinds of cognitive styles may have developed by day-today participation in related kinds of social groups in which the appropriate language structure and methods of thinking about self, things, and ideas are necessary components of their related styles of group participation and that these approaches themselves may act to facilitate or impede their "carriers" ability to become involved in alternate kinds of groups. (Ibid., 831)

As long ago as the 1930s C. C. Brigham, who had been convinced that IQ differences between immigrant groups could be objectively tested, offered this strong renunciation of his own past theoretical bias. "This review has summarized some of the most recent test findings, which show that comparative studies of national and racial groups may not be made with existing tests, and which show, in particular, that one of the most pretentious of these comparative racial studies—the writer's own—was without foundation" (Brigham 1930,165).

Such candor is rare even in science. Once Brigham had reversed himself on culture-free testing he was able offer the following analysis for differential responses to tests. Note how his discussion parallels the analysis of behavioral responses of animals to test situations.

The assumption is made that people taking the alpha test [a U.S. Army test used during World War I] adopted two different attitudes or sets, viz., a "directions attitude"—an attitude of careful attention to the examiner's instructions without looking at the test questions while the directions were read; and "reading attitude"—partially or completely ignoring the examiners instructions while studying the test questions during the time in which the examiner was reading. The adoption of the first attitude would tend to give the individual higher scores in test 1 (entirely oral directions), test 6 (an unusual form of mathematical test), and 7 (a novel type of verbal test). On the other hand a person adopting the second attitude might quickly find out what was required in tests 3,4,5, and 8, and his score would be better if he ignored what the examiner was reading and studied the test questions during the period of instruction. (Brigham 1930, 162–63)

To my knowledge this analysis was the first published indication that the problem of constructing a "culture-free" test is not the only one in testing. The procedures themselves appear to have strong and differential effects on the responses of individuals taking the tests.

As I have noted above, in the United States, for what are clearly social and historical reasons, the argument over IQ and heredity has centered around black-white differences. By 1966 Audrey Shuey could publish a heavy tome with the title *The Testing of Negro Intelligence*. Her summary of this issue ended with the conclusion not only that African Americans scored lower on most tests but also that the studies reviewed confirmed the hypothesis that differences between whites and blacks were largely due to heredity.

A search of the literature shows that this issue has been with us almost since IQ testing was invented. It was of course of great concern during the integration battles of the 1960s. Those who fought to maintain the status quo in the South argued that ending segregation would lower standards in the public schools through an influx of genetically inferior students. Those in favor of integration claimed that the poor showing of African Americans in the school system was an effect of segregation. This, they believed, was true in the North as well as in the South. Under then-president Lyndon Johnson in the middle 1960s, segregation as law was abolished officially in the entire country but continued de facto through residential patterns and educational inequality.

In an attempt to improve educational opportunity and to prepare young children for school, Project Head Start was begun in poor neighborhoods in the middle of the 1960s. Head Start nursery schools were designed to provide cultural stimulus for children before they entered kindergarten. While this project was welcomed by many in the country, there were those who felt that it was a waste of federal monies. Then, in 1969 a media bombshell struck. It was an article by Arthur Jensen, "How Much Can We Boost IQ and Scholastic Achievement?" published in what the press referred to as the "prestigious" *Harvard Educational Review,* By this time a new administration had taken over the White House. The country was in the midst of the Vietnam War, begun under Johnson, and priorities had shifted from domestic programs to foreign relations. Jensen's article, soon to be known as the "Jensen Report," argued that Head Start and programs like it were bound to fail. IQ was, he claimed, primarily hereditary, and African Americans were genetically inferior in IQ to whites. The Jensen article was reported in *Time* magazine to have shown up on the President's desk only a week after its publication. It was certainly taken seriously among those holding political power in the country.

I shall attempt to show below that in my opinion Jensen's paper fails the test of scientific validity. First, however, I should like to call attention to a point that has been overlooked by many on both sides of the IQ argument. Suppose, for a moment, that Jensen was completely right. He claimed that the total deficit between whites and blacks translated into 15 IQ points of difference and that of these, seven or seven and one-half points could be attributed to a genetic deficit among blacks. Now what could this seven to seven and one-half points mean in terms of educability? It should be clear that the answer must be: "Not much and probably nothing!"

Now to the failures of the report itself: Technically Jensen committed a major error when he claimed that his data concerning the degree to which IQ was hereditary, drawn as it was from white populations, could be used to speak about black populations. The genetic factor in IQ, estimated at 80 percent, was taken largely from studies by a well-known British psychologist, Cyril Burt. Burt based his conclusions on data from identical twins reared apart. Such twins are rare and important finds. They *are* identical genetically. Because they are raised in different environments, what measurable differences in behavioral traits occur between each individual in a set of twins can be attributed to the effects of the environment. If the difference between twins is 20 percent on a behavioral measure, for example, then one can say that the maximum effect of the environment is 20 and that the trait is, therefore, 80 percent genetically determined. The problem is that Burt's studies, even if they were correct (see below), were based exclusively on white twins. Additionally, one cannot say that the environments of identical twins reared apart are different enough to reveal genetic similarities as opposed to environmental ones. It is the general practice of adoption agencies to place children in homes that are similar in many respects to the homes of birth parents, except in cases where the birth parents maintained dysfunctional homes. It is even more likely that adoption agencies would go out of their way to place twins to be reared apart in similar homes regardless of the home situation of the birth parents.

The major statistic used in the Jensen Report is known technically as the *heritability* of a trait. The term can be very misleading. In fact, in biology it is employed in two contradictory ways. First, it is sometimes used loosely to indicate that a trait is genetic in origin. In this usage, when a trait is said to be "heritable" it simply means that it is in some way genetic. In the second, more correct and technical usage, heritability is *exclusively* a measure of *variance.* This means that it applies only when *variation* of some kind is present in a population. For example, the condition is satisfied when a population is made up of both blue-eyed and brown-eyed individuals. One can then ask the question: "What percentage of the variance (between blue and brown eyes) is due to heredity and what percentage is due to the environment?" The answer in this case is that the observed variation is 100 percent hereditary. Now if we are faced with a situation in which *everyone* is blue eyed, *then* there is *no* variance in the population (every individual is the same in reference to the trait in question, all have blue eyes). Because in this second case the trait does *not vary* among individuals the heritability is *zero* even though the trait is *100* percent genetic! This is a crucial point since laypeople are often confused by the term "heritability," and it is also misused even by some professional psychologists.

Because the concept of heritability deals with two variables, genetic *and* environmental, as a *statistic* it is subject to a very important restriction. No two populations ever live in exactly the same environment. If a trait with a genetic component is subject to environmental effects, as most are, these effects may differ in value from one environment to another. In other words the *penetrance* of the gene can be different in different environments. The genetic factor in height in humans is certainly based in large measure on heredity. But average height between two different populations might differ for such an environmental reason as nutrition (the degree to which proteins are found in the average diet of each population, for example). For this reason a measure of heritability in one population, let us say .80, is no guarantee that the heritability will be the same (for the same trait) in another population in another environment. It is always possible that the environment has acted differently on the same genetic potential. Thus the problem is that all the heritability figures available to Jensen came from white populations.

What this means is that he had no right (from an experimental point of view) to extrapolate this figure for African Americans. Even in the most integrated parts of American society it is not possible to say that the environment for African Americans is identical to that of whites. IN FACT it is most likely that there are significant environmental differences for the two groups. Therefore, we have no idea what the heritability of IQ might be among African Americans. As the population geneticist James Crow put it in a response to Jensen published in 1969:

> It can be argued that being white and being black in our society changes one or more aspects of the environment so importantly as to account for the difference [in IQ]. For example, the argument that the American Indians score higher than Negroes on IQ Tests—despite being lower on certain socioeconomic scales—can and will be dismissed on the same grounds: some environmental variable associated with being black is not included in the environmental ratio. (Crow 1969, 308)

Did Jensen know any of this when he wrote his report? Yes, he did. In an article published one year before his report he said the following:

> The inventors and developers of intelligence tests—such men as Galton, Binet, Spearman, Burt, Thorndike and Terman—clearly intended that their tests assess as clearly as possible the individuals innate brightness or mental capacity. If this is what a test attempts to do, then clearly the appropriate criterion for judging the test's "fairness" is the *heritability* of the test scores in the population in which the test is used. The quite high value of *H* for tests such as the Stanford-Binet attests to the success of the test-makers aim to measure innate ability.... However, I would be hesitant to generalize this statement

beyond the Caucasian population of the United States and Great Britain, since nearly all the major heritability studies have been performed in these populations. At present there are no really adequate data on the heritability of intelligence tests in the American Negro population. (Jensen 1968, 94)

The problem does not end here. Jensen's major heritability estimates were drawn from data provided by Cyril Burt (born 1883, died 1971). In 1972 and 1973 a Princeton University professor, Leon Kamin, began to speak out concerning what he saw as problems in Burt's data. Scientific models and the experimental data to support them rarely, if ever, show absolute statistical uniformity. Kamin became suspicious of Burt's material on heritability and IQ because it was just too good to be true. Burt published several studies of twins both reared apart and reared together. The correlation between IQ scores of the twins reared *apart* was given as 0.771. In addition Burt used a single statistic, 0.94, for twins reared *together*, again in every study. Kamin's criticisms were aired verbally in 1972. While Kamin had accused Burt of fraud, in a 1978 article published in *American Psychologist* Jensen attempted to excuse Burt by saying that the peculiarities in Burt's data were probably due to carelessness. Jensen also claimed that whatever the reasons for Burt's data, they were no longer necessary to support his own arguments.

Kamin is not the only one to believe that Burt intentionally skewed the data to support his hypothesis. L. S. Hearnshaw (1979), an avowed fan of Burt's who gave the memorial address at the University of Liverpool on the occasion of Burt's death and who was chosen by the Burt family to write Burt's definitive biography, admits in that book that the evidence points to fraud, at least in the case of IQ: "The verdict must be, therefore, that at any rate in three instances, beyond reasonable doubt, Burt was guilty of deception. He falsified the early history of factor analysis....; he produced spurious data on MZ twins; and he fabricated figures on declining levels of scholastic achievement. Moreover, other material on kinship correlations is distinctly suspect" (Hearnshaw 1979, 259).

A stronger argument, published in the *British Journal of Psychology* in 1983, was made against Burt by James Hartley and Donald Rooum. In a survey of Burt's work in the field of typographical research (one less likely to be controversial than heredity and IQ) they concluded:

> Sir Cyril Burt contributed to five main areas of typographical research: spacing words and text; the use of serifs; the effects of typefaces, type sizes and line-lengths on reading comprehension; and aesthetic preferences. Hearnshaw (1979) assessed this contribution as worthy of "well merited acclaim." In this article we examine what Burt had to say on each of these issues, and how far what is said is applicable to typographic practice today. It appears, despite the wisdom of some of the sentiments expressed, that many of them were opinions that were not supported by the data that Burt presented. Indeed there is possible evidence of deceit. We conclude, therefore (and Hearnshaw accepts) that Burt's contribution to typographic practice was marred by the same defects that one can find in his other work (Hartley and Rooum 1983, 203)

Michael McAskie also disagrees with Jensen in reference to Burt. In a May 1978 article published in *American Psychologist* he argued that Burt's data "points more to invention than to genuine derivation." McAskie concluded by saying:

> It is a great pity that Jensen chose to write so ill-prepared a reply to the fraud allegations concerning Burt. Jensen does not even appear to have applied some of the tools of his trade in trying to distinguish between fraud and carelessness. He had no right to suppose that

people suggesting fraud were merely speculating, nor was he particularly informed about the background of the *Sunday Times* article by Oliver Gillie or the political persuasions of those involved, "Sheer surmise and conjecture, and perhaps wishful thinking" are words that Jensen was not in a strong position to throw accusingly at others on this issue. (McAskie 1978, 498)

Perhaps one of the problems here is that Jensen was a post-doctoral student of Hans Eysenck (see chapter nine) who himself was a student of Burt's. What we have here is a (nongenetic) family connection. Beyond the fact that Jensen's work was based on Burt's statistics, Jensen's defense may, at least in part, be due to family loyalty.

It is apparent that Jensen accepts race as a valid biological division. Yet when Jensen talks about African Americans, the genes he is talking about (or better, a good percentage of them) come from a huge and varied continent. Thus, some analysis of ethnic and genetic diversity in Africa must be germane to the discussion.

Irving Gottesman (1968) in a book edited by Jensen (!) and others, discussed the geographic range of populations in Africa from which slaves were imported to Charleston during the period 1733 to 1807. His figures, taken from a study by William Pollitzer, show the following percentages: Senegambia 20 percent, Winward Coast 23 percent, Gold Coast 13 percent, Whydah-Bennin-Calibar 4 percent, and Angola 23 percent. Such a distribution covers more than a thousand miles of coastline and a territory extending for six hundred miles inland. The range of genetic and ethnic groups tapped was extensive.

In the United States itself, it is a vast simplification to speak of a single black or white genetic population. According to Gottesman: "The variation observed in the studies reviewed… are probably valid and reflect the genetic heterogeneity of Negro Americans living in different geographical and social distances away from their white neighbors. Such heterogeneity prevents us from speaking validly of an average Negro American with x percentage of white genes" (Gottesman 1968, 20).

In sum, genetic studies of black versus white intelligence (whatever that is) based upon undifferentiated U.S. samples are naive in the extreme because they do not consider distributions of genetic variation in either Africa or the United States.

The problem does not end here. As we have seen, Jensen found an overall intelligence deficit of 15 percentage points among African Americans. He was willing to attribute about half of this difference to environmental influences. The other 7.5 points were then assumed in the report to be due to genetic factors. Yet on page 100 of his 1969a article Jensen states:

> In addition to these factors, something else operates to boost scores five to ten points from first to second test, provided the first test is really the first. When I worked in a psychological clinic, I had to give individual intelligence tests to a variety of children, a good many of whom came from an impoverished background. Usually I felt these children were really brighter than their IQ would indicate. They often appeared inhibited in their responsiveness in the testing situation on their first visit to my office, and when this was the case I usually had them come in on two to four different days for half-hour sessions with me in a "play therapy" room, in which we did nothing more than get acquainted by playing ball, using finger paints, drawing on the blackboard, making things out of clay, and so forth. As soon as the child seemed to be completely at home in this setting, I would retest him on a parallel form of the Stanford-Binet, a boost in IQ of 8 to 10 points or so was the rule; it rarely failed, but neither was the gain very often much above this.

Was Jensen unaware that these are the conditions that are not met by the majority of studies he cites in his report, particularly those drawn together by Shuey (1966)? If the deficit he notes is consistent in disadvantaged children, then all the IQ differences noted between whites and blacks in the United States may be subsumed under a combination of testing errors and environmental effects.

The Jensen Report contains other distortions and misinformation concerning cited data. The following material was extracted by Dr. Carol Vance and myself from a close reading of the Jensen Report and a comparison of his citations with what was actually said in the original sources.

On page 23 of the report, Jensen refers to an article by Cyril Burt (1963). He says that in the general Negro population there is an excess of IQs in the 70–90 range (see Jensens illustration on page 25 of the Report). This excess is explained as the combined effects of severe environmental disadvantage and emotional disturbance, both of which act to depress test scores. On page 27 Jensen says that Burt corrected for this bulge by eliminating scores of those having depressing factors. However, according to the original Burt article there is a lack rather than an excess in 70–90 range (see figure 1 in Burt 1963, 180).

On page 40–41, Jensen cites Cooper and Zubek (1958). He stresses the effects of rearing bright rats in normal and enriched environments and says, "While the strains differ greatly when reared under 'normal' conditions… they do not differ in the least when reared in a restricted' environment and only slightly in a 'stimulating environment.'"

Our reading of the same article puts things the other way around. Cooper and Zubek stress the benefits of stimulation to dull animals. "A period of early enriched experiences produces little or no improvement in the learning of the bright animals, whereas dull animals are so benefited by it that they become *equal* to bright animals. On the other hand dull animals raised in a restricted environment suffer no deleterious effects, while bright animals *are* retarded to the level of the dulls in learning ability" (Cooper and Zubek 1958, 162). This result extrapolated to humans supports the hypothesis that deprived environments such as those known to exist for the poor and particularly black Americans should have an effect on IQ scores.

If one compares Jensen's figure 6 on page 50 of the Report with figure 1 of Erlenmeyer-Kimling and Jarvik's (1963) article, from which some of Jensen's data is drawn, we find that Jensen shows only the midpoints for correlations between relatives reared together and reared apart. This emphasis stresses the discreteness and difference among the correlational scores while the original diagram, which shows the range and the median, demonstrates the overlap of correlational range and hence an overlap in the strength of genetic inheritance.

On page 63 Jensen cites a study by Wheeler (1942) of IQ among Tennessee mountain children and notes that environmental improvements do not counteract a decline in IQ of "certain below average groups." Jensen neglects to mention Wheeler's discovery that the decline in IQ is due to the large percentage of held-back children. This factor raised the age level in every grade and therefore depresses IQ scores because these are always correlated with age. When Wheeler separated out the scores of older children in each grade he found that the other children performed normally. Comparing chronologically "true" members of each grade over time (with those overage weeded out) he found that in most years there was no decline. Wheeler says that the chronological IQ drop of 20 points is accounted for by children being repeatedly held back, which means more older children will be found as the grades get higher. Their presence depresses IQ scores most in the higher grades. If Wheeler's logic is followed the decline that Jensen presents as ranging from 103 to 80 points of IQ is reduced to the range 102.76 to 101.00 points!

On page 74 Jensen says that on the average first-born children are superior mentally and *physically* to their siblings. His citation here is Altus (1966). Altus, however, presents no evidence about physical superiority. Altus does cite a study by Huntington showing differences in birth order and achievement that suggests that the differences are caused by superior physical strength of the first born. Altus has the following to say about Huntington's hypothesis: "While his finding is typical of all those reported thus far, his explanation of the linkage is *not* typical: He argued that the first born probably tend to be physically stronger and healthier. ... *One may safely accept his data on the birth order of the eminent without accepting his explanation* (Altus 1966, 45; italics mine).

On page 76 Jensen cites Burt's (1961) contention that the inheritance of intelligence conforms to a Mendelian, polygenic model. Yet, he fails to note the wide variety of intelligence within a social class and the fact that children's scores are not as narrow as those of their parents. In fact, if there were no social mobility at all and class were totally static, the result of breeding over five generations would be a disappearance of class means. "After about five generations the differences between the class-means would virtually vanish, and the proportional range within each class would spread out almost as widely as the proportional range of the population as a whole" (Burt 1961,15).

Other British studies show that IQ scores within social classes have been remarkably stable over the past hundred years. This is because bright lower-class children have moved up the social scale while less bright upper-class children have moved down. Burt's study appears to bear this out for England. Needless to say the notions of bright and less bright used here do not necessarily imply genetic differences, although they might.

Now if the same model is applied to African Americans, intelligence would have remained constant by class if social mobility operated as it is supposed to operate in England. But even in the lowest class, there would be children of above-average intelligence who would rise so that the range of child intelligence would be much wider than adult intelligence. This is the process known to statisticians as "regression to the mean." In any case, Jensen does not mention this aspect of African American performance, that is, unexpected *over* performance.

In any case the model cannot be applied in the United States, because when Jensen published his report little real social mobility existed for African Americans. Even today, in spite of some increased social mobility, African Americans do not experience the same degree of social mobility as whites. Additionally, it is necessary to stress yet again that from the point of view of genetics, blacks in America do not constitute a homogeneous population.

On page 83 Jensen cites research by Heber and Dever on education and habitation of the mentally retarded. While we did not have access to Jensen's original source for this citation (a paper read at the Conference on Sociocultural Aspects of Mental Retardation), we did read a paper by the same authors entitled "Research on Education and Habilitation of the Mentally Retarded." It appeared in *Social-Cultural Aspects of Mental Retardation,* edited by H. C. Haywood (1968).

Jensen says that Heber has estimated that IQs below 75 have a much higher incidence among African American children than among white children at every level of socioeconomic status (Jensen 1969a, 83). We found no statement by the cited authors that African Americans have a higher frequency of IQs under 75 than whites. Furthermore, Heber's study was not a study of race and intelligence but rather a study of a special group of mentally retarded children from a specific neighborhood in Milwaukee that was:

> Characterized by having the city's highest known prevalence of mental retardation among school age children. The nine census tracts which compose this area, known as the "inner core," also have the city's highest rate of dilapidated housing, the greatest population density per living unit, the lowest median income level, and the greatest rate of unemployment. Though comprising no more than five percent of Milwaukee's population it yields about one-third of the mentally retarded known to the schools. (Heber, et al. 1968, 35)

While it is a good bet that this population is composed primarily of African Americans given its socioeconomic profile, the point of Heber's study was to show that much of what passes for mental retardation is caused by *cultural* rather than genetic factors. One might also wish to take into account the degree to which slum dwellers in urban America are exposed to a high percentage of lead poisoning due to the ingestion of lead dust in old, poorly cared for housing. It is a well-known fact that lead poisoning has a strong effect on mental capacity, particularly in children.

On page 86 Jensen cites a study by Geber (1958) that discusses precocity of African American infants. Jensen mentions motor precocity but neglects to mention intellectual development as well. Geber says, "The result of tests showed an all round advance of development over European standards which was greater the younger the child. The precocity was not only in motor development; *it was found in intellectual development also"* (Geber 1958, 186).

The main thrust of Jensen's paper, which has been somewhat buried by popular accounts, is that there is a wide diversity of mental abilities in humans and that educational programs should be tailored to meet the needs of all children. It is difficult to disagree. It is most unfortunate, however, that Jensen pleads this case in the context of a report centered on a flawed discussion of genetics and IQ. In his report Jensen took a fairly safe, if as yet unproved hypotheses—that intelligence is heritable (that it varies among individuals by genetics and environment)—and forced it to carry the burden of a second argument for which there is no acceptable evidence at all.

In 1977, Jensen published an article in *Developmental Psychology* ("Cumulative Deficit in IQ of Blacks in the Rural South"). Here evidence *is* offered in support of an environmental explanation for IQ deficit! In this study Jensen finds substantial decrements in IQ as a linear function of age and relates it to educational differences. This study did not lead Jensen to change his mind, however. Instead he compares his new data with a previous study of children in Berkeley, California. (In the Berkeley study Jensen found no significant decrements in IQ in either his white or black sample.) This led him to conclude:

However, the present results on Georgia blacks, when viewed in connection with the contrasting results for California blacks, would seem to favor an environmental interpretation of the progressive IQ decrement [in Georgia]. If the progressive IQ decrement were a genetic racial effect per se, it should have shown up in the California blacks as well as in the Georgia blacks, even if one granted that the California blacks have a somewhat larger admixture of Caucasian ancestry than do blacks in Georgia.... But the California blacks showed a slight, though significant decrement only in verbal IQ, which one might expect to be more susceptible to environmental or cultural effects than nonverbal IQ The blacks of rural Georgia, whose environmental disadvantages are markedly greater than in the California sample, show considerable decrements in both verbal and nonverbal IQ, (Jensen 1977, 190)

Apparently Jensen refuses to consider the possibility that even in Berkeley, California, the social and educational environments for whites and blacks might be different and have an effect upon IQ test scores. It might be useful, therefore, before closing this chapter to look at some of the sociological situations that affect the performance of children on IQ tests in American society.

Two studies dating from the 1960s (Cohen's work cited above is also relevant) have amplified the role of culture and social group in both test results and academic performance. Katz (1968) varied test conditions for samples of African American students in relation to "subjective probability of success"—that is, how the individual taking the test feels about how he or she will score. Differences in this attitude were then measured against different types of testing situations in which the race of the tester was varied as well as the kinds of attitude expressed during the testing situation. The theoretical basis for this

study comes from the psychological concept of "need achievement" in which "the strength of the impulse to strive for success on a given task is regarded as a joint function of the persons motives to achieve, the subjective problems of success, and the incentive value of success. According to the model, on a test that has evaluative significance (e.g., a classroom test) motivation is maximal when the probability of success is at the .50 level."

Katz notes that in a number of experiments with black college students, individuals tend to underperform on intellectual tasks in the presence of whites. Katz speculates:

...that for Negroes who find themselves in predominantly white academic achievement situations, the incentive value of success is high but the expectance of success is low because white standards of achievement are perceived as higher than own-race standards. By the same token, the perceived value of favorable evaluation by a white adult authority is high, but the expectancy of receiving it is low. Therefore, by experimentally controlling Negro subjects' expectancy of success on cognitive tasks it should be possible to produce the same, if not higher, levels of performance in white situations as in all-Negro situations. (Katz 1968, 134)

A group of freshmen were given a test that was described to them as part of a scholastic aptitude test. They were told that their scores would be evaluated in comparison to scores achieved in predominantly white colleges. The students were given a pretest and then told what their chances of success on the actual test would be. One-third were led to believe that they had little chance of meeting the standards for their group, one-third were told that they had an even chance, and one-third were told that they had a good chance. Each of these three groups was then divided into subunits, one given a white tester, the other a black tester. "The results showed that in the low and intermediate probability conditions, performance... was better with a Negro tester, but when the stated probability of achieving the white norm was high, the performance gap between the two tester groups closed" (Katz 1968, 134).

Another test, in which a college with no admission standards other than high school graduation was compared to a college with high relative standards, demonstrated that the effects of varying the race of the tester were the same as in the controlled experiment described above. On the other hand, the scores achieved by students at the selective college were higher when the testers were white, no matter what the probability of success. Katz explained these differences:

> In summary, it appears that Negro students who had been average achievers in high school (the non selective college sample) were discouraged at the prospect of being evaluated by a white person, except when they were made to believe that their chances of success were good. But Negro students with a history of high academic standards (the selective college sample) seemed to be stimulated by the challenge of white evaluation, regardless of the objective probability of success. (Katz 1968, 138)

Katz generalized his results in terms of differences in socialization between lower- and middle-class children. "The present assumption is that lower class children... because they have received less parental approval for early intellectual efforts remain more dependent than middle class children on social reinforcement when performing academic tasks" (Katz 1968, 138).

While Katz's experiments do not relate directly to intelligence testing they do go a long way toward explaining why certain sociological groups respond as they do to education. The problem is complicated since it involves the motivation of the individual, which is partly a product of home experience but also of the students' conception of the expectations of teachers defined partially in terms of race. The common educational experience of lower-class African Americans with white

*and* black teachers is often discouraging. This problem is amplified by the environmental setting in which the probability of success is lowered by the experience of daily life. All these factors would act to lower success in any testing situation.

The process of learning in children is even more subtle than Katz's findings would indicate. A study of performance of children in the San Francisco schools supports the hypothesis that a teacher's attitude toward the success of a child will have a profound effect on the outcome of the educational process.

The experimenters established the expectation in teachers that certain children in the school chosen at *random* would show *superior* performance in the coming school year. This expectation was established by testing the children on an intelligence test and informing teachers of the results. The use of this test in the pre-experimental situation had the added advantage of providing a true measure since the children could be reexamined with the same test later in the experiment. A casual method of informing the teachers about the presence of "potential spurters" was used. "The subject was brought up at the end of the first staff meeting with the remark 'By the way, in case you're interested in who did what in those tests they were done for Harvard'" (Rosenthal and Jacobson 1968, 22).

All the children were retested four months after school started, at the end of the school year, and finally in May of the following year. As the children matured, they were given tests appropriate to their level. These were designed to evaluate both verbal skills and reasoning. The results showed that children who were expected to do well by teachers showed the greatest intellectual gains. An unanticipated finding of the study was that when teachers were asked to evaluate the undesignated children, many of whom had gained in IQ during the year, they tended to evaluate them negatively. The more they gained the less favorably they were seen!

Since writing his report Arthur Jensen has continued his work in the field of IQ and race. It seems to me that in these works Jensen ignores all the recent evidence for the nonexistence of racial categories. Among his recent works are Jensen 1974, 1977, 1978a, 1978b, 1980, 1984a, 1984b, 1985, 1986, 1987a, 1987b, 1989, 1990, 1992, 1993a, 1993b. In 1999 he wrote a laudatory comment in the pretext pages of J. Philippe Rushton's book on race, IQ and brain size (criticized in chapter nine of this book). In none of his works that I have seen does Jensen take account of the evidence against the existence of race as a valid category in the classification of humans. Nor does he seriously discuss the many studies that support the flexibility of IQ in the context of environmental differences. Instead he continues to argue as he has always done, relating race to IQ with the persistent claim that the average black is inferior in intelligence to the average white. To my knowledge he has never cleared up the contradiction between his understanding of the concept of heritability, which, as noted above, he admits does not allow for intergroup comparisons, and his consistent use of heritability statistics for samples of whites applied to blacks.

In the next chapter I will discuss the IQ argument from the perspective of Konrad Lorenz and Robert Ardrey. Lorenz was a Nobel Prize winner and internationally acclaimed biologist, and, although his research concerned fish and birds, he ventured well beyond his competence to speculate, in a series of popular books and articles, about human behavior. Robert Ardrey authored three bestsellers, popularizing Lorenz's ideas concerning our species. Although Lorenz's and Ardrey wrote before the official founding of sociobiology by E. O. Wilson, their extreme form of biological determinism, based primarily on extrapolations from nonhuman animal behavior to humans, stands between the vulgar biological determinism, of the nineteenth century and the explosion of a somewhat more scientific form in the last quarter of the twentieth. Both Lorenz and Ardrey preached the doctrine of racial purity and both argued for the inferiority of certain races.

# Nation and Race

## from *Mein Kampf*

### By Adolf Hitler

● ● ● ● ● ● ● ● ● ● ● ● ● ● ● ● ● ● ● ● ● ● ● ● ● ● ● ● ● ● ● ● ● ● ● ● ● ● ● ● ● ● ● ● ● ● ● ● ● ●

### Editor's Introduction
### Adolf Hitler on Nation and Race

Although his views on race and the biological are a pastiche of nineteenth- and early twentieth-century views, Adolf Hitler quickly devised a way to unify a depressed Germany as he rose to power. His National Socialist Party (Nazi) seized power in 1933, and while rebuilding the nation, he plotted a war against the Jews and other peoples he considered inferior, or *untermensch* (subhuman). What is clear, however, as detailed in the Shanklin reading, is that Hitler fully understood there is no scientific basis for different races. Instead, his political treatise and manifesto, *Mein Kampf* (my struggles or my battle), places the concept of nation ahead of all else, and envisioned a world led by the superior Aryan race (racially pure Germans) at the expense of Germany's enemies, real or imagined.

### References

Bullock, Alan. *Hitler: A Study in Tyranny*. New York: Bantam Books, 1961.
Hitler, Adolf. *Mein Kampf*. Translated by Ralph Manheim. New York: Houghton Mifflin, 1943.
Shanklin, Eugenia. *Anthropology and Race*. Belmont, CA: Wadsworth, 1994.
Waite, Roger G.L. *The Psychopathic God: Adolf Hitler*. New York: Da Capo Press, 1993.

There are statements of truth which are so obvious that just for this reason the common world does not see, or at least does not recognize, them. At times the world passes these well-known truisms blindly and it is most astonished if now suddenly somebody discovers what everybody ought to know. The Columbus eggs' are lying about by the hundreds of thousands, only the Columbuses are rarely seen.

Thus, without exception, people wander about in Nature's garden; they think they know almost everything, and yet, with few exceptions, they walk blindly by one of the most outstanding principles of Nature's working: the inner seclusion of the species of all living beings on earth.

Even the most superficial observation shows, as an almost brazen basic principle of all the countless forms of expression of Nature's will to live, her limited form of propagation and increase, limited in itself. Every animal mates only with a representative of the same species. The titmouse seeks the titmouse, the finch the finch, the stork the stork, the field mouse the field mouse, the common mouse the common mouse, the wolf the wolf, etc.

Only exceptional circumstances can change this; first of all the compulsion of captivity, as well as any other impossibility of mating within the same species. But then Nature begins to resist this with the help of all visible means, and her most visible protest consists either of denying the bastards further procreative faculty, or she limits the fertility of the coming offspring; but in most cases she takes away the capacity of resistance against disease or inimical attacks.

This is then only too natural.

Any crossing between two beings of not quite the same high standard produces a medium between the standards of the parents. That means: the young one will probably be on a higher level than the racially lower parent, but not as high as the higher one. Consequently, it will succumb later on in the fight against the higher level. But such a mating contradicts Nature's will to breed life as a whole towards a higher level. The presumption for this does not lie in blending the superior with the inferior, but rather in a complete victory of the former. The stronger has to rule and he is not to amalgamate with the weaker one, that he may not sacrifice his own greatness. Only the born weakling can consider this as cruel, but at that he is only a weak and limited human being; for, if this law were not dominating, all conceivable development towards a higher level, on the part of all organically living beings, would be unthinkable for man.

The consequence of this purity of the race, generally valid in Nature, is not only the sharp limitation of the races outwardly, but also their uniform character in themselves. The fox is always a fox, the goose a goose, the tiger a tiger, etc., and the difference can lie, at the most, in the different measure of strength, force, cleverness, skill, perseverance, etc., of the various specimens. But there will never be found a fox which, according to its inner nature, would perhaps have humane tendencies as regards the geese, nor will there be a cat with a friendly disposition towards mice.

Therefore also, here the fight amongst one another originates less from reasons of inner aversion than from hunger and love. In both cases, Nature looks calm and even satisfied. The fight for daily bread makes all those succumb who are weak, sickly, and less determined, while the males' fight for the female gives the right of propagation, or the possibility of it, only to the most healthy. But the fight is always a means for the promotion of the species' health and force of resistance, and thus a cause for its development towards a higher level.

If it were different, every further development towards higher levels would stop, and rather the contrary would happen. For, since according to numbers, the inferior element always outweighs the superior element, under the same preservation of life and under the same propagating possibilities, the inferior element would increase so much more rapidly that finally the best element would be forced to step into the background, if no correction of this condition were carried out. But just this is done by Nature, by subjecting the weaker part to such difficult living conditions that even by this the number Is restricted, and finally by preventing the remainder, without choice, from increasing, but by making here a new and ruthless choice, according to strength and health.

---

This appeal to the sacred norm of the 'survival of the fittest'—customary in Pan-German literature—had been resorted to as well by critics of Socialism. The 'tearful sentimentality' of the humanitarians, forever attempting to salvage what had better be left to die, is denounced by Spengler and many others. But the application of 'fitness' to mating is something else entirely, deriving from Plato through a number of intermediaries some of whom can be sought out in modern anti-Semitic literature. There are considerable differences. Thus, Ludwig Schemann thinks that Nature does not mean the same thing by 'fitness' that man does, and that therefore any vigorous recourse to eugenics—except in so far as purely negative matters (health, etc.) are concerned—would prove impossible and impractical. Others have gone the whole way and advocated rigid public regulation of procreation.

Just as little as Nature desires a mating between weaker individuals and stronger ones, far less she desires the mixing of a higher race with a lower one, as in this case her entire work of higher breeding, which has perhaps taken hundreds of thousands of years, would tumble at one blow.

Historical experience offers countless proofs of this. It shows with terrible clarity that with any mixing of the blood of the Aryan with lower races the result was the end of the culture-bearer. North America, the population of which consists for the greatest part of Germanic elements—which mix only very little with the lower, colored races—displays a humanity and a culture different from those of Central and South America, where chiefly the Romanic immigrants have sometimes mixed with the aborigines on a large scale. By this example alone one may clearly and distinctly recognize the influence of the race mixture. The Germanic of the North American continent, who has remained pure and less intermixed, has become the master of that continent, he will remain so until he, too, falls victim to the shame of blood-mixing.

The result of any crossing, in brief, is always the following:

1. Lowering of the standard of the higher race,
2. Physical and mental regression, and, with it, the beginning of a slowly but steadily progressive lingering illness.

To bring about such a development means nothing less than sinning against the will of the Eternal Creator.

This action, then, is also rewarded as a sin.

Man, by trying to resist this iron logic of Nature, becomes entangled in a fight against the principles to which alone he, too, owes his existence as a human being. Thus his attack is bound to lead to his own doom.

Of course, now comes the typically Jewish, impudent, but just as stupid, objection by the modern pacifist: Man conquers Nature!'

Millions mechanically and thoughtlessly repeat this Jewish nonsense, and in the end *they* imagine that they themselves represent a kind of conqueror of Nature; whereas they have no other weapon at their disposal but an 'idea,' and such a wretched one at that, so that according to it no world would be conceivable.

But quite apart from the fact that so far man has never conquered Nature in any affair, but that at the most he gets hold of and tries to lift a flap of her enormous, gigantic veil of eternal riddles and secrets, that in reality he does not 'invent' anything but only discovers everything, that he does not dominate Nature, but that, based on the knowledge of a few laws and secrets of Nature, he has risen to the position of master of those other living beings lacking this knowledge; but quite apart from this, an idea cannot *conquer* the presumptions for the origin and the existence of mankind, as the idea itself depends only on man. Without men there is no human 'idea' in this world; thus the idea is always caused by the presence of men, and, with it, of all those laws which created the presumptions for this existence.

---

The argument has been put another way by Professor Carl Schmitt (cited by Kolnai): 'A universal organization in which there is no place for warlike preservation and destruction of human life would be neither a State nor an Empire: it would lose all political character.' Yet this is not Jewish but Christian teaching that is under criticism. Cardinal Faulhaber, meeting the objection that the Old Testament is filled with 'hymns of hate,' responded that Christianity had indeed changed those hymns into canticles of love, and added: There is no alternative: either we are disciples of Christ, or we lapse into the Judaism of antiquity with its hymns of hate.' The letter which the evangelical churches addressed to Hitler in June, 1936, contained these words: 'When blood, race, creed, nationality and honor are thus raised to the rank of qualities that guarantee eternity, the Evangelical Christian is bound, by the first commandment, to reject the assumption.'

---

And not only that! Certain ideas are even tied to certain men. This can be said most of all of just such thoughts the content of which has its origin, not in an exact scientific truth, but rather in the world of feeling, or, as one usually expresses oneself so nicely and 'clearly' today, which reflects an 'inner experience.' All these ideas, which have nothing to do with clear logic in itself, but which represent mere expressions of feelings, ethical conceptions, etc., are tied to the existence of those men to whose spiritual force of imagination and creation they owe their own existence. But precisely in this case the preservation of these certain races and men is the presumption for the existence of these 'ideas'. For example, he who actually desires, with all his heart, the victory of the pacifistic idea in this world would have to stand up, with all available means, for the conquest of the world by the Germans; for if it should come about the Other way round, then, with the last German, the last pacifist would die off, as the other part of the world has hardly ever been taken in so deeply by this nonsense, adverse to nature and to reason, as unfortunately our own people. Therefore, whether one wanted to or not, if one had the serious will, one would have to decide to wage war in order to arrive at pacifism. This and nothing else was what the American world-redeemer [President Woodrow] Wilson wanted to have done, at least our German visionaries believed in this. With this, then, the purpose was fulfilled.

Indeed, the pacifist-humane idea is perhaps quite good whenever the man of the highest standard has previously conquered and subjected the world to a degree that makes him the only master of this globe. Thus the idea is more and more deprived of the possibility of a harmful effect in the measure in which its practical application becomes rare and finally impossible. Therefore, first fight, and then one may see what can be done. In the other case, mankind has passed the climax of its development, and the end is not the rule of some ethical 'idea,' but barbarism, and, in consequence, chaos. Naturally, here the one or the other may laugh, but this planet has driven on its course through the ether for millions of years without men, and the day may come when it will do so again, if people forget that they owe their higher existence, not to the ideas of some crazy ideologists, but to the knowledge and the ruthless application of Nature's brazen laws.

---

The foregoing passages are derived in the main from Houston Stewart Chamberlain, but with *nuances* that suggest the influence of Rosenberg, or at least of the Free Corps which imported so much militaristic anti-Semitism into Germany after the War. For Chamberlain the moral superiority of the disappointed when 1918 seemed to mean perpetual moral degradation for the human race. In his famous letter to Hitler, following their meeting in 1923, he wrote, therefore: 'At one blow you have transformed the state my soul was in. Germany's vitality is proved if in this hour of its deepest need it can produce a Hitler.' Perhaps the basis of this attitude as a whole must be sought in those fears of an eventual 'war between races' which were aired as early as the eighteenth century, but reached a kind of apogee during the nineteenth. Then the inferiority of the ' colored races' was taken for granted, though the interest taken in a newly discovered Indian literature, ascribed in theory to an 'Indo-Germanic invasion' of Asia, tended to make many place the Brahmins on a somewhat higher level. Later on the 'negroid characteristics' of the Mediterranean races were stressed by Pan-German writers. The Latin, the Catholic, was of highly questionable value. The Germanic Aryan had a right to dominate, and eventually he surely would. After the War the stress was shifted to the Jew, partly because French 'inferiority' had not been satisfactorily demonstrated, after all, and partly because the Free Corps encouraged the view that Jewry was responsible for Germany's acquiescence in Allied demands.

---

Everything that today we admire on this earth—science and art, technique and inventions—is only the creative product of a few peoples and perhaps originally of one race. On them now depends also the existence of this entire culture. If they perish, then the beauty of this earth sinks into the grave with them.

No matter how much the soil, for instance, is able to influence the people, the result will always be a different one, according to the races under consideration. The scanty fertility of a living space may instigate one race towards the highest achievements, while with another race this may only become the cause for the most dire poverty and ultimate malnutrition with all its consequences. The inner disposition of the peoples is always decisive for the way in which outward influences work themselves out. What leads one people to starvation, trains the other for hard work.

All great cultures of the past perished only because the originally creative race died off through blood-poisoning.

The ultimate cause of such a decline was always the forgetting that all culture depends on men and not the reverse; that means, that in order to save a certain culture the man who created it has to be saved. But the preservation is bound to the brazen law of necessity and of the right of the victory of the best and the strongest in this world.

He who wants to live should fight, therefore, and he who does not want to battle in this world of eternal struggle does not deserve to be alive.

Even if this were hard, this is the way things are. But it is certain that by far the hardest fate is the fate which meets that man who believes he can 'conquer' Nature, and yet, in truth, only seems to mock her. Misery, distress, and diseases are then her answer!

The man who misjudges and disdains the laws of race actually forfeits the happiness that seems destined to be his. He prevents the victorious march of the best race and with it also the presumption for all human progress, and in consequence he will remain in the domain of the animal's helpless misery, burdened with the sensibility of man.

It is a futile enterprise to argue which race or races were the original bearers of human culture and, with it, the actual founders of what we sum up with the word 'mankind.' It is simpler to put this question to oneself with regard to the present, and here the answer follows easily and distinctly. What we see before us of human culture today, the results of art, science, and techniques, is almost exclusively the creative product of the Aryan. But just this fact admits of the not unfounded conclusion that he alone was the founder of higher humanity as a whole, thus the prototype of what we understand by the word 'man'. He is the Prometheus of mankind, out of whose bright forehead springs the divine spark of genius at all times, forever rekindling that fire which in the form of knowledge lightened up the night of silent secrets and thus made man climb the path towards the position of master of the other beings on this earth. Exclude him—and deep darkness will again fall upon the earth, perhaps even, after a few thousand years, human culture would perish and the world would turn into a deserts.

This idyl of 'Aryan' pre-history is interesting because: of the definition of 'culture' that is involved. For 'culture' in this sense is once again become the principal concern of Europe. The 'Aryan' succeeds in pushing his way onward and upward by conquering lesser peoples and using them as 'helping forces' (slaves). Then, however, master and slave intermarry, and the 'culture' decays. Perhaps this is only an analogy borrowed from some pictorial history of European colonizing effort: perhaps it is more philosophical. Spengler had taught—in the *Decline of the West*—that cultures arise and fall cyclically; and Hitler here provides a convenient illustration of why they fall. Therewith the riddle proposed by Spengler is solved; the 'culture-making' folk is that which, obeying the law that only the fittest survive, embarks on conquest and exploitation; and the 'culture-destroying folk' is the slave breed which tempts the aristocratic group into intermarriage. This is Nietzsche materialized.

If one were to divide mankind into three groups: culture-founders, culture-bearers, and culture-destroyers, then, as representative of the first kind, only the Aryan would come in question. It is from him that the foundation and the walls of all human creations originate, and only the external form and color depend on the characteristics of the various peoples involved. He furnishes the gigantic building-stones and also the plans for all human progress, and only the execution corresponds to the character of the people and races in the various instances. In a few decades, for instance, the entire east of Asia will call a culture its own, the ultimate bases of which will be Hellenic spirit and Germanic technique, just as is the case with us. Only the *external* form will (at least partly) bear the features of Asiatic character. It is not the case, as some people claim, that Japan adds European techniques to her culture, but European science and techniques are trimmed with Japanese characteristics.

But the basis of actual life is no longer the special Japanese culture, although it determines the color of life (because outwardly, in consequence of its inner difference, it is more visible to European eyes), but it is the enormous scientific and technical work of Europe and America, that is, of Aryan peoples. Based on these achievements alone the East is also able to follow general human progress. This creates the basis for the fight for daily bread, it furnishes weapons and tools for it, and only the external makeup **is** gradually adapted to Japanese life.

But if, starting today, all further Aryan influence upon Japan should stop, and supposing that Europe and America were to perish, then a further development of Japan's present rise in science and technology could take place for a little while longer; but in the time of a few years the source would dry out, Japanese life would gain, but its culture would stiffen and fall back into the sleep out of which it was startled seven decades ago by the Aryan wave of culture. Therefore, exactly as the present Japanese development owes its life to Aryan origin, thus also in the dim past foreign influence and foreign spirit were the awakener of the Japanese culture. The best proof of this is the fact that the latter stiffened and became completely paralyzed later on. This can only happen to a people when the originally creative race nucleus was lost, or when the external influence, which gave the impetus and the material for the first development in the cultural field, was lacking

later on. But if it is ascertained that a people receives, takes in, and works over the essential basic elements of its culture from other races, and if then, when a further external influence is lacking, it stiffens again and again, then one can perhaps call such a race a '*culture-bearing*' one but never a '*culture-creating*' one.

An examination of the various peoples from this viewpoint evidences the fact that in nearly all cases one has to deal, not with originally *culture-creating*, but rather always with *culture-supporting* peoples.

It is always about the following picture of their development that presents itself:

Aryan tribes (often in a really ridiculously small number of their own people) subjugate foreign peoples, and now, stimulated by the special living conditions of the new territory (fertility, climatic conditions, etc.) and favored by the mass of the helping means in the form of people of inferior kind now at their disposal, they develop the mental and organizatory abilities, slumbering in them. Often, in the course of a few millenniums or even centuries, they create cultures which originally completely bear the inner features of their character, adapted to the already mentioned special qualities of the soil as well as of the subjected people. Finally, however, the conquerors deviate from the purity of their blood which they maintained originally, they begin to mix with the subjected inhabitants and thus they end their own existence; for the fall of man in Paradise has always been followed by expulsion from it.

Often, after a thousand and more years, the last visible trace of the one-time overlords is shown in the fairer complexion which their blood has left, in the form of the color, to the subjected race, and in a petrified culture which they had founded as the original creators. For, just as the actual and spiritual conqueror lost himself in the blood of the subjected, thus also the fuel for the torch of human culture progress was lost! As through the blood the color of the former masters keeps a faint glimmer as a memory of them, thus also the night of the cultural life is faintly brightened by the creations that remained of the erstwhile bearers of light. These now shone through all the barbarism that has returned, and in the thoughtless observer of the moment they awaken only too frequently the opinion that he sees the picture of the present people, whereas it is only the mirror of the past at which he is looking.

Then it may happen that such a people for a second time, nay, even more often in the life of its history, comes into touch with the race of its one-time suppliers of culture, without a memory of former meetings necessarily being present. The remainder of the blood of the one-time masters will unconsciously turn to the new apparition, and what first was only possible by compulsion will now succeed with the help of their own will. Then a new culture wave makes its entrance and lasts until its bearers have once more been submerged in the blood of foreign peoples.

It will be the task of a future culture and world history to make researches in this sense and not to suffocate by reflecting external facts, as this is unfortunately only too often the case with our present science of history.

Merely from this sketch of the development of 'culture-bearing' nations results also the picture of the origin, the work, and—the decline of the true culture-creators of this globe, the Aryans themselves.

Just as in daily life the so-called genius requires a special cause, often even a real impetus in order to be made conspicuous, the same is also the case with the ingenious race in the life of the peoples. In the monotony of everyday life even important people often seem unimportant and they hardly stand out over the average of their surroundings; but as soon as they are faced by a situation in which others would despair or go wrong, out of the plain average child the ingenious nature grows visibly, not infrequently to the astonishment of all those who hitherto had an opportunity to observe him, who had meanwhile grown up in the smallness of *bourgeois* life, and therefore, in consequence of this process, the prophet has rarely any honor in his own country. Never is there a better opportunity to observe this than during war. In the hours of distress, when others despair, out of apparently harmless children, there shoot suddenly heroes of death-defying determination and icy coolness

of reflection. If this hour of trial had never come, then hardly anyone would ever have been able to guess that a young hero is hidden in the beardless boy. Nearly always such an impetus is needed in order to call genius into action.

---

No definition of the word 'Aryan' is acceptable. German lexicographers were hard pressed to hit upon an accurate description. The term itself is probably of Sanskrit origin, and seems to have meant 'friends.' It was next assumed that these 'friends' were Indo-Germans, who (it was further assumed) had invaded India and subjugated the 'lesser breeds.' Finally 'Aryan' became just a synonym for 'Indo-German.' The 1931 edition of the *encyclopedia Der grosse Herder* said: 'Recently some have used (ethnologically, in an incorrect way) 'Aryan;' to indicate Indo-Germans in general. In this case, the term is used as in the nature of a slogan in the struggle over the self-determination and preservation of our race against Jewry, which is of a different order.' For this and similar definitions (surely discreet enough), the earlier volumes of this encyclopedia were ordered withdrawn from circulation. In practice the word is officially used today as a racial term excluding Jews and negroes. The second are frowned upon because (i.a.) they are admitted into the French army; and because, it is hoped, sympathy for the Nazi cause may be thus awakened among Southerners in the United States. Delegations of 'Brahmins' have, however, been cordially welcomed to the New Germany.

---

Parallels to this can be found in the writings of Pan-Germans like Heinrich Class and Count Reventlow. In an address delivered during 1932, Hitler declared; 'Let them call us inhuman! If we save Germany, we shall have done the greatest deed in the world. Let them call us unjust! If we save Germany, we shall have repaired the greatest injustice in the world. Let them say that we are without morality! If our people is saved, we shall have paved the way for morality!'

---

Fate's hammer stroke, which then throws the one to the ground, suddenly strikes steel in another, and while now the shell of everyday life is broken, the erstwhile nucleus lies open to the eyes of the astonished world. The latter now resists and does not want to believe that the apparently 'identical' kind is now suddenly supposed to be a 'different' being; a process which repeats itself with every eminent human being.

Although an inventor, for instance, establishes his fame only on the day of his invention, one must not think that perhaps his genius in itself had entered the man only just at this hour, but the spark of genius will be present in the forehead of the truly creatively gifted man from the hour of his birth, although for many years in a slumbering condition and therefore invisible to the rest of the world. But some day, through an external cause or impetus of some kind, the spark becomes fire, something that only then begins to stir the attention of other people. The most stupid of them believe now in all sincerity that the person in question has just become 'clever' whereas in reality they themselves now begin at last to recognize his greatness; for true genius is always inborn and never acquired by education or, still less, by learning.

This, however, may be said, as already stressed, not only for the individual man, but also for the race. Creatively active peoples are creatively gifted from the very bottom and forever, although this may not be recognizable to the eyes of the superficial observer. Here, too, external recognition is always only possible as a consequence of accomplished facts, as the rest of the world is not able to recognize genius in itself, but sees only its visible expressions in the form of inventions, discoveries, buildings, pictures, etc.; but even here it often takes a long time till it is able to struggle through to this knowledge. Exactly as in the life of the individual important man his genius or extraordinary ability strives towards its practical realization only when urged on by special occasions, thus also in the life of the peoples the real use of creative forces and abilities that are present can take place only when certain presumptions invite to this.

We see this most clearly in that race that cannot help having been, and being, the supporter of the development of human culture—the Aryans.

As soon as Fate leads them towards special conditions, their latent abilities begin to develop in a more and more rapid course and to mold themselves into tangible forms. The cultures which they found in such cases are nearly always decisively determined by the available soil, the climate, and—by the subjected people. The latter, however, is the most decisive of all factors. The more primitive the technical presumptions for a cultural activity are, the more necessary is the presence of human auxiliary forces which then, collected and applied with the object of organization, have to replace the force of the machine. Without this possibility of utilizing inferior men, the Aryan would never have been able to take the first steps towards his later culture; exactly as, without the help of various suitable animals which he knew how to tame, he would never have arrived at a technology which now allows him to do without these very animals. The words 'Der Mohr hat seine Schuldigkeit getan, er kann gehen' [The Moor has done his duty, he may go] has unfortunately too deep a meaning. For thousands of years the horse had to serve man and to help in laying the foundations of a development which now, through the motor-car, makes the horse itself superfluous. In a few years it will have ceased its activity, but without its former co-operation man would hardly have arrived at where he stands today.

Therefore, for the formation of higher cultures, the existence of inferior men was one of the most essential presumptions, because they alone were able to replace the lack of technical means without which a higher development is unthinkable. The first culture of mankind certainly depended less on the tamed animal, but rather on the use of inferior people.

Only after the enslavement of subjected races, the same fate began to meet the animals, and not vice versa, as many would like to believe. For first the conquered walked behind [in later editions read: before] the plow—and after him, the horse. Only pacifist fools can again look upon this as a sign of human baseness, without making clear to themselves that this development had to take place in order to arrive finally at that place from where today these apostles are able to sputter forth their drivel into the world.

The progress of mankind resembles the ascent on an endless ladder; one cannot arrive at the top without first having taken the lower steps. Thus the Aryan had to go the way which reality showed him and not that of which the imagination of a modern pacifist dreams. The way of reality, however, is hard and difficult, but it finally ends where the other wishes to bring mankind by dreaming, but unfortunately removes it from, rather than brings it nearer to, it.

Therefore, it is no accident that the first cultures originated in those places where the Aryan, by meeting lower peoples, subdued them and made them subject to his will. They, then, were the first technical instrument in the service of a growing culture.

With this the way that the Aryan had to go was clearly lined out. As a conqueror he subjected the lower peoples and then he regulated their practical ability according to his command and his will and for his aims. But while he thus led them towards a useful, though hard activity, he not only spared the lives of the subjected, but perhaps he even gave them a fate which was better than that of their former so-called 'freedom.' As long as he kept up ruthlessly the master's standpoint, he not only really remained 'master' but also the preserver and propagator of the culture. For the latter was based exclusively on his abilities, and, with it, on his preservation in purity. But as soon as the subjected peoples themselves began to rise (probably) and approached the

conqueror linguistically, the sharp separating wall between master and slave fell. The Aryan gave up the purity of his blood and therefore he also lost his place in the Paradise which he had created for himself. He became submerged in the race-mixture, he gradually lost his cultural ability more and more, till at last not only mentally but also physically he began to resemble more the subjected and aborigines than his ancestors. For some time he may still live on the existing cultural goods, but then petrifaction sets in, and finally oblivion.

In this way cultures and realms collapse in order to make room for new formations.

The blood-mixing, however, with the lowering of the racial level caused by it, is the sole cause of the dying-off of old cultures; for the people do not perish by lost wars, but by the loss of that force of resistance which is contained only in the pure blood.

All that is not race in this world is trash.

All world historical events, however, are only the expression of the races' instinct of self-preservation in its good or in its evil meaning.

---

That is, security is better than freedom. And security, carried to its ultimate in the 'total mobilization' of the nation, is very well analyzed by Rauschning. The masses still cling to the residue of personal liberty, of self-determination, which has been left to them. Yet all such things must disappear completely before the absolute 'security' which is the inherent objective of the Hitlerite revolution has been reached.

---

# Colonialism and
# Post-Colonialism

# Discourse on Colonialism

By Aimé Césaire

●●●●●●●●●●●●●●●●●●●●●●●●●●●●●●●●●●●●●●●●●●●●●●●●

## Editor's introduction

Described as "… a declaration of war … [and] a 'third world manifesto …',"[1] Aimé Césaire, raised in the French Caribbean colony Martinique, lashed out against colonialism, the colonizer, and the "deciviliz[ing]"[2] methods employed to subjugate the populace. A central message throughout this reading is that "the colonizer's sense of superiority, their sense of mission as the world's civilizers, depends on turning the Other into a barbarian."[3] Students will find many similarities of thought in the Frantz Fanon passage contained in this anthology.

### Notes

1. Aimé Césaire. *Discourse on Colonialism*. Trans. Joan Pinkham. New York: Monthly Review Press, 2000.
2. Ibid., 89.
3. Ibid., 9.

A civilization that proves incapable of solving the problems it creates is a decadent civilization.

A civilization that chooses to close its eyes to its most crucial problems is a stricken civilization.

A civilization that uses its principles for trickery and deceit is a dying civilization.

The fact is that the so-called European civilization—"Western" civilization—as it has been shaped by two centuries of bourgeois rule, is incapable of solving the two major problems to which its existence has given rise: the problem of the proletariat and the colonial problem; that Europe is unable to justify itself either before the bar of "reason" or before the bar of "conscience"; and that, increasingly, it takes refuge in a hypocrisy which is all the more odious because it is less and less likely to deceive.

### Europe Is Indefensible.

Apparently that is what the American strategists are whispering to each other.

That in itself is not serious.

What is serious is that "Europe" is morally, spiritually indefensible.

And today the indictment is brought against it not by the European masses alone, but on a world scale, by tens and tens of millions of men who, from the depths of slavery, set themselves up as judges.

The colonialists may kill in Indochina, torture in Madagascar, imprison in Black Africa, crack down in the West Indies. Henceforth the colonized know that they have an advantage over them. They know that their temporary "masters" are lying.

Therefore that their masters are weak.

And since I have been asked to speak about colonization and civilization, let us go straight to the principal lie that is the source of all the others.

Colonization and civilization?

In dealing with this subject, the commonest curse is to be the dupe in good faith of a collective hypocrisy that cleverly misrepresents problems, the better to legitimize the hateful solutions provided for them.

In other words, the essential thing here is to see clearly, to think clearly—that is, dangerously—and to answer clearly the innocent first question: what, fundamentally, is colonization? To agree on what it is not: neither evangelization, nor a philanthropic enterprise, nor a desire to push back the frontiers of ignorance, disease, and tyranny, nor a project undertaken for the greater glory of God, nor an attempt to extend the rule of law. To admit once and for all, without flinching at the consequences, that the decisive actors here are the adventurer and the pirate, the wholesale grocer and the ship owner, the gold digger and the merchant, appetite and force, and behind them, the baleful projected shadow of a form of civilization which, at a certain point in its history, finds itself obliged, for internal reasons, to extend to a world scale the competition of its antagonistic economies.

Pursuing my analysis, I find that hypocrisy is of recent date; that neither Cortez discovering Mexico from the top of the great teocalli, nor Pizzaro before Cuzco (much less Marco Polo before Cambuluc), claims that he is the harbinger of a superior order; that they kill; that they plunder; that they have helmets, lances, cupidities; that the slavering apologists came later; that the chief culprit in this domain is Christian pedantry, which laid down the dishonest equations *Christianity = civilization, paganism = savagery,* from which

there could not but ensue abominable colonialist and racist consequences, whose victims were to be the Indians, the Yellow peoples, and the Negroes.

That being settled, I admit that it is a good thing to place different civilizations in contact with each other; that it is an excellent thing to blend different worlds; that whatever its own particular genius may be, a civilization that withdraws into itself atrophies; that for civilizations, exchange is oxygen; that the great good fortune of Europe is to have been a crossroads, and that because it was the locus of all ideas, the receptacle of all philosophies, the meeting place of all sentiments, it was the best center for the redistribution of energy.

But then I ask the following question: has colonization really *placed civilizations in contact*? Or, if you prefer, of all the ways of *establishing contact,* was it the best?

I answer *no.*

And I say that between *colonization* and *civilization* there is an infinite distance; that out of all the colonial expeditions that have been undertaken, out of all the colonial statutes that have been drawn up, out of all the memoranda that have been dispatched by all the ministries, there could not come a single human value.

First we must study how colonization works to *decivilize* the colonizer, to *brutalize* him in the true sense of the word, to degrade him, to awaken him to buried instincts, to covetousness, violence, race hatred, and moral relativism; and we must show that each time a head is cut off or an eye put out in Vietnam and in France they accept the fact, each time a little girl is raped and in France they accept the fact, each time a Madagascan is tortured and in France they accept the fact, civilization acquires another dead weight, a universal regression takes place, a gangrene sets in, a center of infection begins to spread; and that at the end of all these treaties that have been violated, all these lies that have been propagated, all these punitive expeditions that have been tolerated, all these prisoners who have been tied up and "interrogated," all these patriots who have been tortured, at the end of all the racial pride that has been encouraged, all the boastfulness that has been displayed, a poison has been distilled into the veins of Europe and, slowly but surely, the continent proceeds toward *savagery*.

And then one fine day the bourgeoisie is awakened by a terrific boomerang effect: the gestapos are busy, the prisons fill up, the torturers standing around the racks invent, refine, discuss.

People are surprised, they become indignant. They say: "How strange! But never mind—it's Nazism, it will pass!" And they wait, and they hope; and they hide the truth from themselves, that it is barbarism, the supreme barbarism, the crowning barbarism that sums up all the daily barbarisms; that it is Nazism, yes, but that before they were its victims, they were its accomplices; that they tolerated that Nazism before it was inflicted on them, that they absolved it, shut their eyes to it, legitimized it, because, until then, it had been applied only to non-European peoples; that they have cultivated that Nazism, that they are responsible for it, and that before engulfing the whole edifice of Western, Christian civilization in its reddened waters, it oozes, seeps, and trickles from every crack.

Yes, it would be worthwhile to study clinically, in detail, the steps taken by Hitler and Hitlerism and to reveal to the very distinguished, very humanistic, very Christian bourgeois of the twentieth century that without his being aware of it, he has a Hitler inside him, that Hitler *inhabits* him, that Hitler is his *demon,* that if he rails against him, he is being inconsistent and that, at bottom, what he cannot forgive Hitler for is not *the crime* in itself, *the crime against man,* it is not *the humiliation of man as such,* it is the crime against the white man, the humiliation of the white man, and the fact that he applied to Europe colonialist procedures which until then had been reserved exclusively for the Arabs of Algeria, the "coolies" of India, and the "niggers" of Africa.

And that is the great thing I hold against pseudo-humanism: that for too long it has diminished the rights of man, that its concept of those rights has been—and still is—narrow and fragmentary, incomplete and biased and, all things considered, sordidly racist.

I have talked a good deal about Hitler. Because he deserves it: he makes it possible to see things on a large scale and to grasp the fact that capitalist society, at its present stage, is incapable of establishing a concept of the rights of all men, just as it has proved incapable of establishing a system of individual ethics. Whether one likes it or not, at the end of the blind alley that is Europe, I mean the Europe of Adenauer, Schuman, Bidault, and a few others, there is Hitler. At the end of capitalism, which is eager to outlive its day, there is Hider. At the end of formal humanism and philosophic renunciation, there is Hitler.

And this being so, I cannot help thinking of one of his statements: "We aspire not to equality but to domination. The country of a foreign race must become once again a country of serfs, of agricultural laborers, or industrial workers. It is not a question of eliminating the inequalities among men but of widening them and making them into a law."

That rings clear, haughty, and brutal, and plants us squarely in the middle of howling savagery. But let us come down a step.

Who is speaking? I am ashamed to say it: it is the Western *humanist,* the "idealist" philosopher. That his name is Renan is an accident. That the passage is taken from a book entitled *La Reforme intellectuelle et morale,* that it was written in France just after a war which France had represented as a war of right against might, tells us a great deal about bourgeois morals.

> The regeneration of the inferior or degenerate races by the superior races is part of the providential order of things for humanity. With us, the common man is nearly always a declasse nobleman, his heavy hand is better suited to handling the sword than the menial tool. Rather than work, he chooses to fight, that is, he returns to his first estate. *Regere imperiopopulos,* that is our vocation. Pour forth this all-consuming activity onto countries which, like China, are crying aloud for foreign conquest, Turn the adventurers who disturb European society into a *vet sacrum,* a horde like those of the Franks, the Lombards, or

the Normans, and every man will be in his right role. Nature has made a race of workers, the Chinese race, who have wonderful manual dexterity and almost no sense of honor; govern them with justice, levying from them, in return for the blessing of such a government, an ample allowance for the conquering race, and they will be satisfied; a race of tillers of the soil, the Negro; treat him with kindness and humanity, and all will be as it should; a race of masters and soldiers, the European race. Reduce this noble race to working in the *ergastulum* like Negroes and Chinese, and they rebel. In Europe, every rebel is, more or less, a soldier who has missed his calling, a creature made for the heroic life, before whom you are setting *a task that is contrary to his race,* a poor worker, too good a soldier. But the life at which our workers rebel would make a Chinese or a fellah happy, as they are not military creatures in the least. *Let each one do what he is made for, and all will be well.*

Hitler? Rosenberg? No, Renan.

But let us come down one step further. And it is the long-winded politician. Who protests? No one, so far as I know, when M. Albert Sarraut, the former governor-general of Indochina, holding forth to the students at the Ecole Coloniale, teaches them that it would be puerile to object to the European colonial enterprises in the name of "an alleged right to possess the land one occupies, and some sort of right to remain in fierce isolation, which would leave unutilized resources to lie forever idle in the hands of incompetents."

And who is roused to indignation when a certain Rev. Barde assures us that if the goods of this world "remained divided up indefinitely, as they would be without colonization, they would answer neither the purposes of God nor the just demands of the human collectivity"?

Since, as his fellow Christian, the Rev. Muller, declares: "Humanity must not, cannot allow the incompetence, negligence, and laziness of the uncivilized peoples to leave idle indefinitely the wealth which God has confided to them, charging them to make it serve the good of all."

No one.

I mean not one established writer, not one academic, not one preacher, not one crusader for the right and for religion, not one "defender of the human person."

And yet, through the mouths of the Sarrauts and the Bardes, the Mullers and the Renans, through the mouths of all those who considered—and consider—it lawful to apply to non-European peoples "a kind of expropriation for public purposes" for the benefit of nations that were stronger and better equipped, it was already Hitler speaking!

What am I driving at? At this idea: that no one colonizes innocently, that no one colonizes with impunity either; that a nation which colonizes, that a civilization which justifies colonization—and therefore force—is already a sick civilization, a civilization which is morally diseased, which irresistibly, progressing from one consequence to another, one denial to another, calls for its Hitler, I mean its punishment.

Colonization: bridgehead in a campaign to civilize barbarism, from which there may emerge at any moment the negation of civilization, pure and simple.

Elsewhere I have cited at length a few incidents culled from the history of colonial expeditions.

Unfortunately, this did not find favor with everyone. It seems that I was pulling old skeletons out of the closet. Indeed!

Was there no point in quoting Colonel de Montagnac, one of the conquerors of Algeria: "In order to banish the thoughts that sometimes besiege me, I have some heads cut off, not the heads of artichokes but the heads of men."

Would it have been more advisable to refuse the floor to Count d'Herisson: "It is true that we are bringing back a whole barrelful of ears collected, pair by pair, from prisoners, friendly or enemy."

Should I have denied Saint-Arnaud the right to profess his barbarous faith: "We lay waste, we burn, we plunder, we destroy the houses and the trees."

Should I have prevented Marshal Bugeaud from systematizing all that in a daring theory and invoking the precedent of famous ancestors: "We must have a great invasion of Africa, like the invasions of the Franks and the Goths."

Lastly, should I have cast back into the shadows of oblivion the memorable feat of arms of General Gerard and kept silent about the capture of Ambike, a city which, to tell the truth, had never dreamed of defending itself: "The native riflemen had orders to kill only the men, but no one restrained them; intoxicated by the smell of blood, they spared not one woman, not one child.... At the end of the afternoon, the heat caused a light mist to arise: it was the blood of the five thousand victims, the ghost of the city, evaporating in the setting sun."

Yes or no, are these things true? And the sadistic pleasures, the nameless delights that send voluptuous shivers and quivers through Loti's carcass when he focuses his field glasses on a good massacre of the Annamese? True or not true? And if these things are true, as no one can deny, will it be said, in order to minimize them, that these corpses don't prove anything?

For my part, if I have recalled a few details of these hideous butcheries, it is by no means because I take a morbid delight in them, but because I think that these heads of men, these collections of ears, these burned houses, these Gothic invasions, this steaming blood, these cities that evaporate at the edge of the sword, are not to be so easily disposed of. They prove that colonization, I repeat, dehumanizes even the most civilized man; that colonial activity, colonial enterprise, colonial conquest, which is based on contempt for the native and justified by that contempt, inevitably tends to change him who undertakes it; that the colonizer, who in order to ease his conscience gets into the habit of seeing the other man as *an animal*, accustoms himself to treating him like an animal, and tends objectively to transform *himself into* an animal. It is this result, this boomerang effect of colonization that I wanted to point out.

Unfair? No. There was a time when these same facts were a source of pride, and when, sure of the morrow, people did not mince words. One last quotation; it is from a certain Carl Siger, author of an *Essai sur la colonisation* (Paris, 1907):

> The new countries offer a vast field for individual, violent activities which, in the metropolitan countries, would run up against certain prejudices, against a sober and orderly conception of life, and which, in the colonies, have greater freedom to develop and, consequently, to affirm their worth. Thus to a certain extent the colonies can serve as a safety valve for modern society. Even if this were their only value, it would be immense.

Truly, there are sins for which no one has the power to make amends and which can never be fully expiated.

But let us speak about the colonized.

I see clearly what colonization has destroyed: the wonderful Indian civilizations—and neither Deterding nor Royal Dutch nor Standard Oil will ever console me for the Aztecs and the Incas.

I see clearly the civilizations, condemned to perish at a future date, into which it has introduced a principle of ruin: the South Sea Islands, Nigeria, Nyasaland. I see less clearly the contributions it has made.

Security? Culture? The rule of law? In the meantime, I look around and wherever there are colonizers and colonized face to face, I see force, brutality, cruelty, sadism, conflict, and, in a parody of education, the hasty manufacture of a few thousand subordinate functionaries, "boys," artisans, office clerks, and interpreters necessary for the smooth operation of business.

I spoke of contact.

Between colonizer and colonized there is room only for forced labor, intimidation, pressure, the police, taxation, theft, rape, compulsory crops, contempt, mistrust, arrogance, self-complacency, swinishness, brainless elites, degraded masses.

No human contact, but relations of domination and submission which turn the colonizing man into a classroom monitor, an army sergeant, a prison guard, a slave driver, and the indigenous man into an instrument of production.

My turn to state an equation: colonization = "thingification."

I hear the storm. They talk to me about progress, about "achievements," diseases cured, improved standards of living.

*I* am talking about societies drained of their essence, cultures trampled underfoot, institutions undermined, lands confiscated, religions smashed, magnificent artistic creations destroyed, extraordinary *possibilities* wiped out.

They throw facts at my head, statistics, mileages of roads, canals, and railroad tracks.

*I* am talking about thousands of men sacrificed to the Congo-Océan. I am talking about those who, as I write this, are digging the harbor of Abidjan by hand. I am talking about millions of men torn from their gods, their land, their habits, their life—from life, from the dance, from wisdom.

*I* am talking about millions of men in whom fear has been cunningly instilled, who have been taught to have an inferiority complex, to tremble, kneel, despair, and behave like flunkeys.

They dazzle me with the tonnage of cotton or cocoa that has been exported, the acreage that has been planted with olive trees or grapevines.

*I* am talking about natural *economies* that have been disrupted—harmonious and viable *economies* adapted to the indigenous population—about food crops destroyed, malnutrition permanently introduced, agricultural development oriented solely toward the benefit of the metropolitan countries; about the looting of products, the looting of raw materials.

They pride themselves on abuses eliminated.

I too talk about abuses, but what I say is that on the old ones—very real—they have superimposed others—very detestable. They talk to me about local tyrants brought to reason; but I note that in general the old tyrants get on very well with the new ones, and that there has been established between them, to the detriment of the people, a circuit of mutual services and complicity.

They talk to me about civilization, I talk about proletarianization and mystification.

For my part, I make a systematic defense of the non-European civilizations.

Every day that passes, every denial of justice, every beating by the police, every demand of the workers that is drowned in blood, every scandal that is hushed up, every punitive expedition, every police van, every gendarme and every militiaman, brings home to us the value of our old societies.

They were communal societies, never societies of the many for the few.

They were societies that were not only ante-capitalist, as has been said, but also *anti-capitalist*.

They were democratic societies, always.

They were cooperative societies, fraternal societies.

I make a systematic defense of the societies destroyed by imperialism.

They were the fact, they did not pretend to be the idea; despite their faults, they were neither to be hated nor condemned. They were content to be. In them, neither the word *failure* nor the word *avatar* had any meaning. They kept hope intact.

Whereas those are the only words that can, in all honesty, be applied to the European enterprises outside Europe. My only consolation is that periods of colonization pass, that nations sleep only for a time, and that peoples remain.

This being said, it seems that in certain circles they pretend to have discovered in me an "enemy of Europe" and a prophet of the return to the pre-European past.

For my part, I search in vain for the place where I could have expressed such views; where I ever underestimated the importance of Europe in the history of human thought; where I ever preached a *return* of any kind; where I ever claimed that there could be a *return*.

The truth is that I have said something very different: to wit, that the great historical tragedy of Africa has been not so much that it was too late in making contact with the rest of the world, as the manner in which that contact was brought about; that Europe began to "propagate" at a time when it had fallen into the hands of the most unscrupulous financiers and captains of industry; that it was our misfortune to encounter that particular Europe on our path, and that Europe is responsible before the human community for the highest heap of corpses in history.

In another connection, in judging colonization, I have added that Europe has gotten on very well indeed with all the local feudal lords who agreed to serve, woven a villainous complicity with them, rendered their tyranny more effective and more efficient, and that it has actually tended to prolong artificially the survival of local pasts in their most pernicious aspects.

I have said—and this is something very different—that colonialist Europe has grafted modern abuse onto ancient injustice, hateful racism onto old inequality.

That if I am attacked on the grounds of intent, I maintain that colonialist Europe is dishonest in trying to justify its colonizing activity *a posteriori* by the obvious material progress that has been achieved in certain fields under the colonial regime—since *sudden change* is always possible, in history as elsewhere; since no one knows at what stage of material development these same countries would have been if Europe had not intervened; since the introduction of technology into Africa and Asia, their administrative reorganization, in a word, their "Europeanization," was (as is proved by the example of Japan) in no way tied to the European *occupation;* since the Europeanization of the non-European continents could have been accomplished otherwise than under the heel of Europe; since this movement of Europeanization was in progress; since it was even slowed down; since in any case it was distorted by the European takeover.

The proof is that at present it is the indigenous peoples of Africa and Asia who are demanding schools, and colonialist Europe which refuses them; that it is the African who is asking for ports and roads, and colonialist Europe which is niggardly on this score; that it is the colonized man who wants to move forward, and the colonizer who holds things back.

One of the values invented by the bourgeoisie in former times and launched throughout the world was *man*—and we have seen what has become of that. The other was the nation.

It is a fact: the *nation* is a bourgeois phenomenon.

Exactly; but if I turn my attention from *man* to *nations,* I note that here too there is great danger; that colonial enterprise is to the modern world what Roman imperialism was to the ancient world: the prelude to Disaster and the forerunner of Catastrophe. Come, now! The Indians massacred, the Moslem world drained of itself, the Chinese world defiled and perverted for a good century; the Negro world disqualified; mighty voices stilled forever; homes scattered to the wind; all this wreckage, all this waste, humanity reduced to a monologue, and you think all that does not have its price? The truth is that this policy *cannot but bring about the ruin of Europe itself,* and that Europe, if it is not careful, will perish from the void it has created around itself.

They thought they were only slaughtering Indians, or Hindus, or South Sea Islanders, or Africans. They have in fact overthrown, one after another, the ramparts behind which European civilization could have developed freely.

I know how fallacious historical parallels are, particularly the one I am about to draw. Nevertheless, permit me to quote a page from Edgar Quinet for the not inconsiderable element of truth which it contains and which is worth pondering.

Here it is:

> People ask why barbarism emerged all at once in ancient civilization. I believe I know the answer. It is surprising that so simple a cause is not obvious to everyone. The system of ancient civilization was composed of a certain number of nationalities, of countries which, although they seemed to be enemies, or were even ignorant of each other, protected, supported, and guarded one another. When the expanding Roman Empire undertook to conquer and destroy these groups of nations, the dazzled sophists thought they saw at the end of this road humanity triumphant in Rome. They talked about the unity of the human

spirit; it was only a dream. It happened that these nationalities were so many bulwarks protecting Rome itself… Thus when Rome, in its alleged triumphal march toward a single civilization, had destroyed, one after the other, Carthage, Egypt, Greece, Judea, Persia, Dacia, and Cisalpine and Transalpine Gaul, it came to pass that it had itself swallowed up the dikes that protected it against the human ocean under which it was to perish. The magnanimous Caesar, by crushing the two Gauls, only paved the way for the Teutons. So many societies, so many languages extinguished, so many cities, rights, homes annihilated, created a void around Rome, and in those places which were not invaded by the barbarians, barbarism was born spontaneously. The vanquished Gauls changed into Bagaudes. Thus the violent downfall, the progressive extirpation of individual cities, caused the crumbling of ancient civilization. That social edifice was supported by the various nationalities as by so many different columns of marble or porphyry.

When, to the applause of the wise men of the time, each of these living columns had been demolished, the edifice came crashing down; and the wise men of our day are still trying to understand how such mighty ruins could have been made in a moment's time.

And now I ask: what else has bourgeois Europe done? It has undermined civilizations, destroyed countries, ruined nationalities, extirpated "the root of diversity." No more dikes, no more bulwarks. The hour of the barbarian is at hand. The modern barbarian. The American hour. Violence, excess, waste, mercantilism, bluff, conformism, stupidity, vulgarity, disorder.

In 1913, Ambassador Page wrote to Wilson: "The future of the world belongs to us…. Now what are we going to do with the leadership of the world presently when it clearly falls into our hands?"

And in 1914: "What are we going to do with this England and this Empire, presently, when economic forces unmistakably put the leadership of the race in our hands?" This Empire.… And the others.…

And indeed, do you not see how ostentatiously these gentlemen have just unfurled the banner of anti-colonialism?

*"Aid to the disinherited countries,"* says Truman. "The time of the old colonialism has passed." That's also Truman.

Which means that American high finance considers that the time has come to raid every colony in the world. So, dear friends, here you have to be careful!

I know that some of you, disgusted with Europe, with all that hideous mess which you did not witness by choice, are turning—oh! in no great numbers—toward America and getting used to looking upon that country as a possible liberator.

"What a godsend!" you think.

"The bulldozers! The massive investments of capital! The roads! The ports!"

"But American racism!"

"So what? European racism in the colonies has inured us to it!"

And there we are, ready to run the great Yankee risk.

So, once again, be careful!

American domination—the only domination from which one never recovers. I mean from which one never recovers unscarred.

And since you are talking about factories and industries, do you not see the tremendous factory hysterically spitting out its cinders in the heart of our forests or deep in the bush, the factory for the production of lackeys; do you not see the prodigious mechanization, the mechanization of man; the gigantic rape of everything intimate, undamaged, undefiled that, despoiled as we are, our human spirit has still managed to preserve; the machine, yes, have you never seen it, the machine for crushing, for grinding, for degrading peoples?

So that the danger is immense.

So that unless, in Africa, in the South Sea Islands, in Madagascar (that is, at the gates of South Africa), in the West Indies (that is, at the gates of America), Western Europe undertakes on its own initiative a policy of *nationalities*, a new policy founded on respect for peoples and cultures—nay, more—unless Europe galvanizes the dying cultures or raises up new ones, unless it becomes the awakener of countries and civilizations (this being said without taking into account the admirable resistance of the colonial peoples primarily symbolized at present by Vietnam, but also by the Africa of the Rassemblement Democratique Africain),

Europe will have deprived itself of its last *chance* and, with its own hands, drawn up over itself the pall of mortal darkness.

Which comes down to saying that the salvation of Europe is not a matter of a revolution in methods. It is a matter of the Revolution—the one which, until such time as there is a classless society, will substitute for the narrow tyranny of a dehumanized bourgeoisie the preponderance of the only class that still has a universal mission, because it suffers in its flesh from all the wrongs of history, from all the universal wrongs: the proletariat.

# On Violence

## from *The Wretched of the Earth*

### By Frantz Fanon

• • • • • • • • • • • • • • • • • • • • • • • • • • • • • • • • • • • • • • •

## Editor's Introduction

Like his countryman, Aimé Césaire, Frantz Fanon delivers a damning condemnation on those who colonized the world, and instructions on how the colonized could liberate themselves physically and psychologically. Fanon's works appealed to Pan-African movements as well as Malcolm X, the Black Panther leaders, and many others who recognized his diagnosis. A psychiatrist, he advocated the role of violence in historic change as inevitable. This excerpt, "On Violence," should be compared with Césairé's reading, and any studies on white bias, internalized racism, and self-hatred.

### References

Fanon, Frantz. *The Wretched of the Earth*. Translated by Richard Philcox. New York: Grove Press, 2004.
_____. *Black Skin, White Masks.* Translated by Richard Philcox. New York: Grove Press, 2008.

National liberation, national reawakening, restoration of the nation to the people or Commonwealth, whatever the name used, whatever the latest expression, decolonization is always a violent event. At whatever level we study it—individual encounters, a change of name for a sports club, the guest list at a cocktail party, members of a police force or the board of directors of a state or private bank—decolonization is quite simply the substitution of one "species" of mankind by another. The substitution is unconditional, absolute, total, and seamless. We could go on to portray the rise of a new nation, the establishment of a new state, its diplomatic relations and its economic and political orientation. But instead we have decided to describe the kind of tabula rasa which from the outset defines any decolonization. What is singularly important is that it starts from the very first day with the basic claims of the colonized. In actual fact, proof of success lies in a social fabric that has been changed inside out. This change is extraordinarily important because it is desired, clamored for, and demanded. The need for this change exists in a raw, repressed, and reckless state in the lives and consciousness of colonized men and women. But the eventuality of such a change is also experienced as a terrifying future in the consciousness of another "species" of men and women: the *colons,* the colonists.

* * *

Decolonization, which sets out to change the order of the world, is clearly an agenda for total disorder. But it cannot be accomplished by the wave of a magic wand, a natural cataclysm, or a gentleman's agreement. Decolonization, we know, is an historical process: In other words, it can only be understood, it can only find its significance and become self coherent insofar as we can discern the history-making movement which gives it form and substance. Decolonization is the encounter between two congenitally antagonistic forces that in fact owe their singularity to the kind of reification secreted and nurtured by the colonial situation. Their first confrontation was colored by violence and their cohabitation—or rather the exploitation of the colonized by the colonizer—continued at the point of the bayonet and under cannon fire. The colonist and the colonized are old acquaintances. And consequently, the colonist is right when he says he "knows" them. It is the colonist who *fabricated* and *continues to fabricate* the colonized subject. The colonist derives his validity, i.e., his wealth, from the colonial system.

Decolonization never goes unnoticed, for it focuses on and fundamentally alters being, and transforms the spectator crushed to a nonessential state into a privileged actor, captured in a virtually grandiose fashion by the spotlight of History. It infuses a new rhythm, specific to a new generation of men, with a new language and a new humanity. Decolonization is truly the creation of new men. But such a creation cannot be attributed to a supernatural power: The "thing" colonized becomes a man through the very process of liberation.

Decolonization, therefore, implies the urgent need to thoroughly challenge the colonial situation. Its definition can, if we want to describe it accurately, be summed up in the well-known words: "The last shall be first." Decolonization is

verification of this. At a descriptive level, therefore, any decolonization is a success.

* * *

In its bare reality, decolonization reeks of red-hot cannonballs and bloody knives. For the last can be the first only after a murderous and decisive confrontation between the two protagonists. This determination to have the last move up to the front, to have them clamber up (too quickly, say some) the famous echelons of an organized society, can only succeed by resorting to every means, including, of course, violence.

You do not disorganize a society, however primitive it may be, with such an agenda if you are not determined from the very start to smash every obstacle encountered. The colonized, who have made up their mind to make such an agenda into a driving force, have been prepared for violence from time immemorial. As soon as they are born it is obvious to them that their cramped world, riddled with taboos, can only be challenged by out and out violence.

The colonial world is a compartmentalized world. It is obviously as superfluous to recall the existence of "native" towns and European towns, of schools for "natives" and schools for Europeans, as it is to recall apartheid in South Africa. Yet if we penetrate inside this compartmentalization we shall at least bring to light some of its key aspects. By penetrating its geographical configuration and classification we shall be able to delineate the backbone on which the decolonized society is reorganized.

The colonized world is a world divided in two. The dividing line, the border, is represented by the barracks and the police stations. In the colonies, the official, legitimate agent, the spokesperson for the colonizer and the regime of oppression, is the police officer or the soldier. In capitalist societies, education, whether secular or religious, the teaching of moral reflexes handed down from father to son, the exemplary integrity of workers decorated after fifty years of loyal and faithful service, the fostering of love for harmony and wisdom, those aesthetic forms of respect for the status quo, instill in the exploited a mood of submission and inhibition which considerably eases the task of the agents of law and order. In capitalist countries a multitude of sermonizers, counselors, and "confusion-mongers" intervene between the exploited and the authorities. In colonial regions, however, the proximity and frequent, direct intervention by the police and the military ensure the colonized are kept under close scrutiny, and contained by rifle butts and napalm. We have seen how the government's agent uses a language of pure violence. The agent does not alleviate oppression or mask domination. He displays and demonstrates them with the clear conscience of the law enforcer, and brings violence into the homes and minds of the colonized subject.

The "native" sector is not complementary to the European sector. The two confront each other, but not in the service of a higher unity. Governed by a purely Aristotelian logic, they follow the dictates of mutual exclusion: There is no conciliation possible, one of them is superfluous. The colonist's sector is a sector built to last, all stone and steel. It's a sector of lights and paved roads, where the trash cans constantly overflow with strange and wonderful garbage, undreamed-of leftovers. The colonist's feet can never be glimpsed, except perhaps in the sea, but then you can never get close enough. They are protected by solid shoes in a sector where the streets are clean and smooth, without a pothole, without a stone. The colonist's sector is a sated, sluggish sector, its belly is permanently full of good things. The colonist's sector is a white folks' sector, a sector of foreigners.

The colonized's sector, or at least the "native" quarters, the shanty town, the Medina, the reservation, is a disreputable place inhabited by disreputable people. You are born anywhere, anyhow. You die anywhere, from anything. It's a world with no space, people are piled one on top of the other, the shacks squeezed tightly together. The colonized's sector is a famished sector, hungry for bread, meat, shoes, coal, and light. The colonized's sector is a sector that crouches and cowers, a sector on its knees, a sector that is prostrate. It's a sector of niggers, a sector of towelheads. The gaze that the colonized

subject casts at the colonist's sector is a look of lust, a look of envy. Dreams of possession. Every type of possession: of sitting at the colonist's table and sleeping in his bed, preferably with his wife. The colonized man is an envious man. The colonist is aware of this as he catches the furtive glance, and constantly on his guard, realizes bitterly that: "They want to take our place." And its true there is not one colonized subject who at least once a day does not dream of taking the place of the colonist.

This compartmentalized world, this world divided in two, is inhabited by different species. The singularity of the colonial context lies in the fact that economic reality, inequality, and enormous disparities in lifestyles never manage to mask the human reality. Looking at the immediacies of the colonial context, it is clear that what divides this world is first and foremost what species, what race one belongs to. In the colonies the economic infrastructure is also a superstructure. The cause is effect: You are rich because you are white, you are white because you are rich. This is why a Marxist analysis should always be slightly stretched when it comes to addressing the colonial issue. It is not just the concept of the precapitalist society, so effectively studied by Marx, which needs to be reexamined here. The serf is essentially different from the knight, but a reference to divine right is needed to justify this difference in status. In the colonies the foreigner imposed himself using his cannons and machines. Despite the success of his pacification, in spite of his appropriation, the colonist always remains a foreigner. It is not the factories, the estates, or the bank account which primarily characterize the "ruling class." The ruling species is first and foremost the outsider from elsewhere, different from the indigenous population, "the others."

The violence which governed the ordering of the colonial world, which tirelessly punctuated the destruction of the indigenous social fabric, and demolished unchecked the systems of reference of the country's economy, lifestyles, and modes of dress, this same violence will be vindicated and appropriated when, taking history into their own hands, the colonized swarm into the forbidden cities. To blow the colonial world to smithereens is henceforth a clear image within the grasp and imagination of every colonized subject. To dislocate the colonial world does not mean that once the borders have been eliminated there will be a right of way between the two sectors. To destroy the colonial world means nothing less than demolishing the colonist's sector, burying it deep within the earth or banishing it from the territory.

Challenging the colonial world is not a rational confrontation of viewpoints. It is not a discourse on the universal, but the impassioned claim by the colonized that their world is fundamentally different. The colonial world is a Manichaean world. The colonist is not content with physically limiting the space of the colonized, i.e., with the help of his agents of law and order. As if to illustrate the totalitarian nature of colonial exploitation, the colonist turns the colonized into a kind of quintessence of evil.[1] Colonized society is not merely portrayed as a society without values. The colonist is not content with stating that the colonized world has lost its values or worse never possessed any. The "native" is declared impervious to ethics, representing not only the absence of values but also the negation of values. He is, dare we say it, the enemy of values. In other words, absolute evil. A corrosive element, destroying everything within his reach, a corrupting element, distorting everything which involves aesthetics or morals, an agent of malevolent powers, an unconscious and incurable instrument of blind forces. And Monsieur Meyer could say in all seriousness in the French National Assembly that we should not let the Republic be defiled by the penetration of the Algerian people. Values are, in fact, irreversibly poisoned and infected as soon as they come into contact with the colonized. The customs of the colonized, their traditions, their myths, especially their myths, are the very mark of this indigence and innate depravity. This is why we should place DDT, which destroys parasites, carriers of disease, on the same level as Christianity, which roots out heresy, natural impulses, and evil. The decline of yellow fever and the advances made by evangelizing form part of the same balance sheet. But triumphant reports by the missions in fact tell us how deep the seeds of alienation have been sown among the colonized. I am talking of Christianity and this should come as no surprise to anybody. The Church in the colonies is a white man's Church, a foreigners' Church. It does not call the colonized to the ways of God, but to the ways of the white man, to the ways of the master, the ways of the oppressor. And as we know, in this story many are called but few are chosen.

Sometimes this Manichaeanism reaches its logical conclusion and dehumanizes the colonized subject. In plain talk, he is reduced to the state of an animal. And consequently, when the colonist speaks of the colonized he uses zoological terms. Allusion is made to the slithery movements of the yellow race, the odors from the "native" quarters, to the hordes, the stink, the swarming, the seething, and the gesticulations. In his endeavors at description and finding the right word, the colonist refers constantly to the bestiary. The European seldom has a problem with figures of speech. But the colonized, who immediately grasp the intention of the colonist and the exact case being made against them, know instantly what he is thinking. This explosive population growth, those hysterical masses, those blank faces, those shapeless, obese bodies, this headless, tailless cohort, these children who seem not to belong to anyone, this indolence sprawling under the sun, this vegetating existence, all this is part of the colonial vocabulary. General de Gaulle speaks of "yellow multitudes," and Monsieur Mauriac of the black, brown, and yellow hordes that will soon invade our shores. The colonized know all that and roar with laughter every time they hear themselves called an animal by the other. For they know they are not animals. And at the very moment when they discover their humanity, they begin to sharpen their weapons to secure its victory.

As soon as the colonized begin to strain at the leash and to pose a threat to the colonist, they are assigned a series of good souls who in the "Symposiums on Culture" spell out the specificity

---

1 We have demonstrated in *Black Skin, White Masks* the mechanism of this Manichaean world.

and richness of Western values. But every time the issue of Western values crops up, the colonized grow tense and their muscles seize up. During the period of decolonization the colonized are called upon to be reasonable. They are offered rock-solid values, they are told in great detail that decolonization should not mean regression, and that they must rely on values which have proved to be reliable and worthwhile. Now it so happens that when the colonized hear a speech on Western culture they draw their machetes or at least check to see they are close to hand. The supremacy of white values is stated with such violence, the victorious confrontation of these values with the lifestyle and beliefs of the colonized is so impregnated with aggressiveness, that as a counter measure the colonized rightly make a mockery of them whenever they are mentioned. In the colonial context the colonist only quits undermining the colonized once the latter have proclaimed loud and clear that white values reign supreme. In the period of decolonization the colonized masses thumb their noses at these very values, shower them with insults and vomit them up.

Such an occurrence normally goes unseen because, during decolonization, certain colonized intellectuals have established a dialogue with the bourgeoisie of the colonizing country. During this period the indigenous population is seen as a blurred mass. The few "native" personalities whom the colonialist bourgeois have chanced to encounter have had insufficient impact to alter their current perception and nuance their thinking. During the period of liberation, however, the colonialist bourgeoisie frantically seeks contact with the colonized "elite." It is with this elite that the famous dialogue on values is established. When the colonialist bourgeoisie realizes it is impossible to maintain its domination over the colonies it decides to wage a rearguard campaign in the fields of culture, values, and technology, etc. But what we should never forget is that the immense majority of colonized peoples are impervious to such issues. For a colonized people, the most essential value, because it is the most meaningful, is first and foremost the land: the land, which must provide bread

and, naturally, dignity. But this dignity has nothing to do with "human" dignity. The colonized subject has never heard of such an ideal. All he has ever seen on his land is that he can be arrested, beaten, and starved with impunity; and no sermonizer on morals, no priest has ever stepped in to bear the blows in his place or share his bread. For the colonized, to be a moralist quite plainly means silencing the arrogance of the colonist, breaking his spiral of violence, in a word ejecting him outright from the picture. The famous dictum which states that all men are equal will find its illustration in the colonies only when the colonized subject states he is equal to the colonist. Taking it a step further, he is determined to fight to be more than the colonist. In fact, he has already decided to take his place. As we have seen, it is the collapse of an entire moral and material universe. The intellectual who, for his part, has adopted the abstract, universal values of the colonizer is prepared to fight so that colonist and colonized can live in peace in a new world. But what he does not see, because precisely colonialism and all its modes of thought have seeped into him, is that the colonist is no longer interested in staying on and coexisting once the colonial context has disappeared. It is no coincidence that, even before any negotiation between the Algerian government and the French government, the so-called "liberal" European minority has already made its position clear: it is clamoring for dual citizenship, nothing less. By sticking to the abstract the colonist is being forced to make a very substantial leap into the unknown. Let us be honest, the colonist knows perfectly well that no jargon is a substitute for reality.

The colonized subject thus discovers that his life, his breathing and his heartbeats are the same as the colonist's. He discovers that the skin of a colonist is not worth more than the "native's." In other words, his world receives a fundamental jolt. The colonized's revolutionary new assurance stems from this. If, in fact, my life is worth as much as the colonist's, his look can no longer strike fear into me or nail me to the spot and his voice can no longer petrify me. I am no longer uneasy in his presence. In reality, to hell with him. Not only does his presence no longer bother me, but I am already preparing to waylay him in such a way that soon he will have no other solution but to flee.

The colonial context, as we have said, is characterized by the dichotomy it inflicts on the world. Decolonization unifies this world by a radical decision to remove its heterogeneity, by unifying it on the grounds of nation and sometimes race. To quote the biting words of Senegalese patriots on the maneuvers of their president, Senghor: "We asked for the Africanization of the top jobs and all Senghor does is Africanize the Europeans." Meaning that the colonized can see right away if decolonization is taking place or not: The minimum demand is that the last become the first.

But the colonized intellectual introduces a variation on this demand and in fact, there seems to be no lack of motivation to fill senior positions as administrators, technicians, and experts. The colonized, however, equate this nepotism with acts of sabotage and it is not unusual to hear them declare: "What is the point of being independent then…?"

Wherever an authentic liberation struggle has been fought, wherever the blood of the people has been shed and the armed phase has lasted long enough to encourage the intellectuals to withdraw to their rank and file base, there is an effective eradication of the superstructure borrowed by these intellectuals from the colonialist bourgeois circles. In its narcissistic monologue the colonialist bourgeoisie, by way of its academics, had implanted in the minds of the colonized that the essential values—meaning Western values—remain eternal despite all errors attributable to man. The colonized intellectual accepted the cogency of these ideas and there in the back of his mind stood a sentinel on duty guarding the Greco-Roman pedestal. But during the struggle for liberation, when the colonized intellectual touches base again with his people, this artificial sentinel is smashed to smithereens. All the Mediterranean values, the triumph of the individual, of enlightenment and Beauty turn into pale, lifeless trinkets. All those discourses appear a jumble of dead words. Those values which seemed to ennoble the soul prove worthless because they have nothing in common with the real-life struggle in which the people are engaged.

And first among them is individualism. The colonized intellectual learned from his masters that the individual must assert himself. The colonialist bourgeoisie hammered into the colonized mind the notion of a society of individuals where each is locked in his subjectivity, where wealth lies in thought. But the colonized intellectual who is lucky enough to bunker down with the people during the liberation struggle, will soon discover the falsity of this theory. Involvement in the organization of the struggle will already introduce him to a different vocabulary. "Brother," "sister," "comrade" are words outlawed by the colonialist bourgeoisie because in their thinking my brother is my wallet and my comrade, my scheming. In a kind of auto-da-fe, the colonized intellectual witnesses the destruction of all his idols: egoism, arrogant recrimination, and the idiotic, childish need to have the last word. This colonized intellectual, pulverized by colonialist culture, will also discover the strength of the village assemblies, the power of the people's commissions and the extraordinary productiveness of neighborhood and section committee meetings. Personal interests are now the collective interest because in reality *everyone* will be discovered by the French legionnaires and consequently massacred or else *everyone* will be saved. In such a context, the "every man for himself" concept, the atheist's form of salvation, is prohibited.

Self-criticism has been much talked about recently, but few realize that it was first of all an African institution. Whether it be in the *djemaas* of North Africa or the palavers of West Africa, tradition has it that disputes which break out in a village are worked out in public. By this I mean collective self-criticism with a touch of humor because everyone is relaxed, because in the end we all want the same thing. The intellectual sheds all that calculating, all those strange silences, those ulterior motives, that devious thinking and secrecy as he gradually plunges deeper among the people. In this respect then we can genuinely say that the community has already triumphed and exudes its own light, its own reason.

But when decolonization occurs in regions where the liberation struggle has not yet made its impact sufficiently felt, here are the same smart alecks, the sly, shrewd intellectuals whose behavior and ways of thinking, picked up from their rubbing shoulders with the colonialist bourgeoisie, have remained intact. Spoiled children of yesterday's colonialism and today's governing powers, they oversee the looting of the few national resources. Ruthless in their scheming and legal pilfering they use the poverty, now nationwide, to work their way to the top through import-export holdings, limited companies, playing the stock market, and nepotism. They insist on the nationalization of business transactions, i.e., reserving contracts and business deals for nationals. Their doctrine is to proclaim the absolute need for nationalizing the theft of the nation. In this barren, national phase, in this so-called period of austerity, their success at plundering the nation swiftly sparks anger and violence from the people. In the present international and African context, the poverty-stricken and independent population achieves a social consciousness at a rapidly accelerating pace. This, the petty individualists will soon find out for themselves.

In order to assimilate the culture of the oppressor and venture into his fold, the colonized subject has had to pawn some of his own intellectual possessions. For instance, one of the things he has had to assimilate is the way the colonialist bourgeoisie thinks. This is apparent in the colonized intellectual's inaptitude to engage in dialogue. For he is unable to make himself inessential when confronted with a purpose or idea. On the other hand, when he operates among the people he is constantly awestruck. He is literally disarmed by their good faith and integrity. He is then constantly at risk of becoming a demagogue. He turns into a kind of mimic man who nods his assent to every word by the people, transformed by him into an arbiter of truth. But the fellah, the unemployed and the starving do not lay claim to truth. They do not say they represent the truth because they are the truth in their very being.

During this period the intellectual behaves objectively like a vulgar opportunist. His maneuvering, in fact, is still at work. The people would never think of rejecting him or cutting the ground from under his feet. What the people want is for everything to be pooled together. The colonized intellectual's insertion into this human tide will find itself on hold because of his curious obsession with detail. It is not that the people are opposed to analysis. They appreciate clarification, understand the reasoning behind an argument and like to see where they are going. But at the start of his cohabitation with the people the colonized intellectual gives priority to detail and tends to forget the very purpose of the struggle—the defeat of colonialism. Swept along by the many facets of the struggle, he tends to concentrate on local tasks, undertaken zealously but almost always too pedantically. He does not always see the overall picture. He introduces the notion of disciplines, specialized areas and fields into that awesome mixer and grinder called a people's revolution. Committed to certain frontline issues he tends to lose sight of the unity of the movement and in the event of failure at the local level he succumbs to doubt, even despair. The people, on the other hand, take a global stance from the very start. "Bread and land: how do we go about getting bread and land?" And this stubborn, apparently limited, narrow-minded aspect of the people is finally the most rewarding and effective working model.

The question of truth must also be taken into consideration. For the people, only fellow nationals are ever owed the truth. No absolute truth, no discourse on the transparency of the soul can erode this position. In answer to the lie of the colonial situation, the colonized subject responds with a lie. Behavior toward fellow nationalists is open and honest, but strained and indecipherable toward the colonists. Truth is what hastens the dislocation of the colonial regime, what fosters the emergence of the nation. Truth is what protects the "natives" and undoes the foreigners. In the colonial context there is no truthful behavior. And good is quite simply what hurts *them* most.

We have seen therefore that the Manichaeanism that first governed colonial society is maintained intact during the period of decolonization. In fact the colonist never ceases to be the enemy, the antagonist, in plain words public enemy number

1. The oppressor, ensconced in his sector, creates the spiral, the spiral of domination, exploitation and looting. In the other sector, the colonized subject lies coiled and robbed, and fuels as best he can the spiral which moves seamlessly from the shores of the colony to the palaces and docks of the metropolis. In this petrified zone, not a ripple on the surface, the palm trees sway against the clouds, the waves of the sea lap against the shore, the raw materials come and go, legitimating the colonist's presence, while more dead than alive the colonized subject crouches for ever in the same old dream. The colonist makes history. His life is an epic, an odyssey. He is invested with the very beginning: "We made this land." He is the guarantor for its existence: "If we leave, all will be lost, and this land will return to the Dark Ages." Opposite him, listless beings wasted away by fevers and consumed by "ancestral customs" compose a virtually petrified background to the innovative dynamism of colonial mercantilism.

The colonist makes history and he knows it. And because he refers constantly to the history of his metropolis, he plainly indicates that here he is the extension of this metropolis. The history he writes is therefore not the history of the country he is despoiling, but the history of his own nation's looting, raping, and starving to death. The immobility to which the colonized subject is condemned can be challenged only if he decides to put an end to the history of colonization and the history of despoliation in order to bring to life the history of the nation, the history of decolonization.

A world compartmentalized, Manichaean and petrified, a world of statues: the statue of the general who led the conquest, the statue of the engineer who built the bridge. A world cocksure of itself, crushing with its stoniness the backbones of those scarred by the whip. That is the colonial world. The colonial subject is a man penned in; apartheid is but one method of compartmentalizing the colonial world. The first thing the colonial subject learns is to remain in his place and not overstep its limits. Hence the dreams of the colonial subject are muscular dreams, dreams of action, dreams of

aggressive vitality. I dream I am jumping, swimming, running, and climbing. I dream I burst out laughing, I am leaping across a river and chased by a pack of cars that never catches up with me. During colonization the colonized subject frees himself night after night between nine in the evening and six in the morning.

The colonized subject will first train this aggressiveness sedimented in his muscles against his own people. This is the period when black turns on black, and police officers and magistrates don't know which way to turn when faced with the surprising surge of North African criminality. We shall see later what should be made of this phenomenon.[2] Confronted with the colonial order the colonized subject is in a permanent state of tension. The colonist's world is a hostile world, a world which excludes yet at the same time incites envy. We have seen how the colonized always dream of taking the colonist's place. Not of becoming a colonist, but of replacing him. This hostile, oppressive and aggressive world, bulldozing the colonized masses, represents not only the hell they would like to escape as quickly as possible but a paradise within arm's reach guarded by ferocious watchdogs.

The colonized subject is constantly on his guard: Confused by the myriad signs of the colonial world he never knows whether he is out of line. Confronted with a world configured by the colonizer, the colonized subject is always presumed guilty. The colonized does not accept his guilt, but rather considers it a kind of curse, a sword of Damocles. But deep down the colonized subject acknowledges no authority. He is dominated but not domesticated. He is made to feel inferior, but by no means convinced of his inferiority. He patiently waits for the colonist to let his guard down and then jumps on him. The muscles of the colonized are always tensed. It is not that he is anxious or terrorized, but he is always ready to change his role as game for that of hunter. The colonized subject is a persecuted man who is forever dreaming of becoming the persecutor. The symbols of society

---

2 *Colonial Wars and Mental Disorders*, chapter 5.

such as the police force, bugle calls in the barracks, military parades, and the flag flying aloft, serve not only as inhibitors but also as stimulants. They do not signify: "Stay where you are." But rather "Get ready to do the right thing." And in fact if ever the colonized subject begins to doze off or forget, the colonist's arrogance and preoccupation with testing the solidity of the colonial system will remind him on so many occasions that the great showdown cannot be postponed indefinitely. This impulse to take the colonist's place maintains a constant muscular tonus. It is a known fact that under certain emotional circumstances an obstacle actually escalates action.

The relationship between colonist and colonized is one of physical mass. Against the greater number the colonist pits his force. The colonist is an exhibitionist. His safety concerns lead him to remind the colonized out loud: "Here I am the master." The colonist keeps the colonized in a state of rage, which he prevents from boiling over. The colonized are caught in the tightly knit web of colonialism. But we have seen how on the inside the colonist achieves only a pseudo-petrification. The muscular tension of the colonized periodically erupts into bloody fighting between tribes, clans, and individuals.

At the individual level we witness a genuine negation of common sense. Whereas the colonist or police officer can beat the colonized subject day in and day out, insult him and shove him to his knees, it is not uncommon to see the colonized subject draw his knife at the slightest hostile or aggressive look from another colonized subject. For the colonized subject's last resort is to defend his personality against his fellow countryman. Internecine feuds merely perpetuate age-old grudges entrenched in memory. By throwing himself muscle and soul into his blood feuds, the colonized subject endeavors to convince himself that colonialism has never existed, that everything is as it used to be and history marches on. Here we grasp the full significance of the all too familiar "head-in-the-sand" behavior at a collective level, as if this collective immersion in a fratricidal bloodbath suffices to mask the obstacle and postpone the inevitable alternative, the inevitable emergence of the armed struggle against colonialism. So one of the ways the colonized subject releases his muscular tension is through the very real collective self-destruction of these internecine feuds. Such behavior represents a death wish in the face of danger, a suicidal conduct which reinforces the colonist's existence and domination and reassures him that such men are not rational. The colonized subject also manages to lose sight of the colonist through religion. Fatalism relieves the oppressor of all responsibility since the cause of wrong-doing, poverty, and the inevitable can be attributed to God. The individual thus accepts the devastation decreed by God, grovels in front of the colonist, bows to the hand of fate, and mentally readjusts to acquire the serenity of stone.

In the meantime, however, life goes on and the colonized subject draws on the terrifying myths that are so prolific in underdeveloped societies as inhibitions for his aggressiveness: malevolent spirits who emerge every time you put one foot wrong, leopard men, snake men, six-legged dogs, zombies, a whole never-ending gamut of animalcules or giants that encircle the colonized with a realm of taboos, barriers, and inhibitions far more terrifying than the colonialist world. This magical superstructure that permeates the indigenous society has a very precise function in the way the libido works. One of the characteristics, in fact, of underdeveloped societies is that the libido is primarily a matter for the group and family. Anthropologists have amply described societies where the man who dreams he has sexual intercourse with a woman other than his own must publicly confess his dream and pay the penalty in kind or in several days' work to the husband or the injured family party—which proves, by the way, that so-called prehistorical societies attach great importance to the unconscious.

In scaring me, the atmosphere of myths and magic operates like an undeniable reality. In terrifying me, it incorporates me into the traditions and history of my land and ethnic group, but at the same time I am reassured and granted a civil status, an identification. The secret sphere in underdeveloped countries is a collective sphere that falls exclusively within the realm of magic. By entangling me in this inextricable web where gestures are repeated with a secular limpidity, my very own world, our very own world, thus perpetuates itself. Zombies, believe me, are more terrifying than colonists. And the problem now is not whether to fall in line with the armor-plated world of colonialism, but to think twice before urinating, spitting, or going out in the dark.

The magical, supernatural powers prove to be surprisingly ego boosting. The colonist's powers are infinitely shrunk, stamped by foreignness. There is no real reason to fight them because what really matters is that the mythical structures contain far more terrifying adversaries. It is evident that everything is reduced to a permanent confrontation at the level of phantasy.

In the liberation struggle, however, this people who were once relegated to the realm of the imagination, victims of unspeakable terrors, but content to lose themselves in hallucinatory dreams, are thrown into disarray, re-form, and amid blood and tears give birth to very real and urgent issues. Giving food to the mujahideen, stationing lookouts, helping deprived families and taking over from the slain or imprisoned husband—such are the practical tasks the people are asked to undertake in the liberation struggle.

In the colonial world, the colonized's affectivity is kept on edge like a running sore flinching from a caustic agent. And the psyche retracts, is obliterated, and finds an outlet through muscular spasms that have caused many an expert to classify the colonized as hysterical. This overexcited affectivity, spied on by invisible guardians who constantly communicate with the core of the personality, takes an erotic delight in the muscular deflation of the crisis.

Another aspect of the colonized's affectivity can be seen when it is drained of energy by the ecstasy of dance. Any study of the colonial world therefore must include an understanding of the phenomena of dance and possession. The colonized's way of relaxing is precisely this muscular orgy during which the most brutal aggressiveness and impulsive violence are channeled, transformed, and spirited away. The dance circle is a permissive circle. It protects and empowers. At a fixed time and a fixed date men and women assemble in a given place, and under the solemn gaze of the tribe launch themselves into a seemingly disarticulated, but in fact extremely ritualized, pantomime where the exorcism, liberation, and expression of a community are grandiosely and spontaneously played out through shaking of the head, and back and forward thrusts of the body. Everything is permitted in the dance circle. The hillock, which has been climbed as if to get closer to the moon, the river bank, which has been descended whenever the dance symbolizes ablution, washing, and purification, are sacred places. Everything is permitted, for in fact the sole purpose of the gathering is to let the supercharged libido and the stifled aggressiveness spew out volcanically. Symbolic killings, figurative cavalcades, and imagined multiple murders, everything has to come out. The ill humors seep out, tumultuous as lava flows.

One step further and we find ourselves in deep possession. In actual fact, these are organized seances of possession and dispossession: vampirism, possession by djinns, by zombies, and by Legba, the illustrious god of voodoo. Such a disintegration, dissolution or splitting of the personality, plays a key regulating role in ensuring the stability of the colonized world. On the way there these men and women were stamping impatiently, their nerves "on edge." On the way back, the village returns to serenity, peace, and stillness.

During the struggle for liberation there is a singular loss of interest in these rituals. With his back to the wall, the knife at his throat, or to be more exact the electrode on his genitals, the colonized subject is bound to stop telling stories.

After years of unreality, after wallowing in the most extraordinary phantasms, the colonized subject, machine gun at the ready, finally confronts the only force which challenges his very being: colonialism. And the young colonized subject who grows up in an atmosphere of fire and brimstone has no scruples mocking zombie ancestors, two-headed horses, corpses woken from the dead, and djinns who, taking advantage of a yawn, slip inside the body. The colonized subject discovers reality and transforms it through his praxis, his deployment of violence and his agenda for liberation.

We have seen that this violence throughout the colonial period, although constantly on edge, runs on empty. We have seen it channeled through the emotional release of dance or possession. We have seen it exhaust itself in fratricidal struggles. The challenge now is to seize this violence as it realigns itself. Whereas it once reveled in myths and contrived ways to commit collective suicide, a fresh set of circumstances will now enable it to change directions.

From the point of view of political tactics and History, the liberation of the colonies poses a theoretical problem of crucial importance at the current time: When can it be said that the situation is ripe for a national liberation movement? What should be the first line of action? Because decolonization comes in many shapes, reason wavers and abstains from declaring what is a true decolonization and what is not. We shall see that for the politically committed, urgent decisions are needed on means and tactics, i.e., direction and organization. Anything else is but blind voluntarism with the terribly reactionary risks this implies.

# Color-Blindness
## and White Privilege

# The Central Frames of Color-Blind Racism

By Eduardo Bonilla-Silva

• • • • • • • • • • • • • • • • • • • • • • • • • • • • • • • • • • • • • • • • • • • • • • •

## Editor's Introduction

In this detailed text, the author identifies many negatives associated with the concept of a color-blind society, and reveals how racism can continue, often unchallenged, in such an environment. Among the many issues covered include the common notion that the past was worse, and that people today do not really "see" color anymore, or use blatant racial epithets. However, Eduardo Bonilla-Silva points out that even in a supposedly color-blind society, people are still "otherized" by using terms such as "you people" or even "illegals" to denote subordinate status. Complex in scope, this selection uncovers what the author identifies to be "The Central Frames of Color-Blind Racism."

### References

Bonilla-Silva, Eduardo. *Racism Without Racists, Third Edition*. Lanham, MA: Rowman & Littlefield, 2010.

> The master defense against accurate social perception and change is always and in every society the tremendous conviction of rightness about any behavior form which exists.
>
> —John Dollard, *Class and Caste in a Southern Town*

If Jim Crow's racial structure has been replaced by a "new racism," what happened to Jim Crow racism? What happened to beliefs about blacks' mental, moral, and intellectual inferiority, to the idea that "it is the [black man's] own fault that he is a lower-caste... a lower-class man" or the assertion that blacks "lack initiative, are shiftless, have no sense of time, or do not wish to better themselves";[1] in short, what happened to the basic claim that blacks are subhuman?[2] Social analysts of all stripes agree that most whites no longer subscribe to these tenets. However, this does not mean the "end of racism,"[3] as a few conservative commentators have suggested. Instead, a new powerful ideology has emerged to defend the contemporary racial order: the ideology of color-blind racism. Yet, color-blind racism is a curious racial ideology. Although it engages, as all ideologies do, in "blaming the victim," it does so in a very indirect, "now you see it, now you don't" style that matches the character of the new racism. Because of the slipperiness of color-blind racism, in this chapter I examine its central frames and explain how whites use them in ways that justify racial inequality.

## The Frames of Color-Blind Racism

Ideologies are about "meaning in the service of power."[4] They are expressions at the symbolic level of the fact of dominance. As such, the ideologies of the powerful are central in the production and reinforcement of the status quo. They comfort rulers and charm the ruled much like an Indian snake handler. Whereas rulers receive solace by believing they are not involved in the terrible ordeal of creating and maintaining inequality, the ruled are charmed by the almost magic qualities of a hegemonic ideology.[5]

The central component of any dominant racial ideology is its frames or *set paths for interpreting information*. These set paths operate as cul-de-sacs because after people filter issues through them, they explain racial phenomena following a predictable route. Although by definition dominant frames must misrepresent the world (hide the fact of dominance), this does not mean that they are totally without foundation. (For instance, it is true that people of color in the United States are much better off today than at any other time in history. However, it is also true—facts hidden by color-blind racism—that because people of color still experience *systematic* discrimination and remain appreciably behind whites in many important areas of life, their chances of catching up with whites are very slim.) Dominant racial frames, therefore, provide the intellectual road map used by rulers to navigate the always rocky road of domination and, as I will show in chapter 6, derail the ruled from their track to freedom and equality.

Analysis of the interviews with college students and DAS respondents revealed that color-blind racism has four central frames and that these frames are used by an overwhelming majority of the white respondents. The four frames are *abstract liberalism, naturalization, cultural racism,* and *minimization of racism.* Of the four frames, abstract liberalism is the most important, as it constitutes the foundation of the new racial ideology. It is also the hardest to understand (What is *racial* about opposing busing or affirmative action, policies that clearly interfere with our American individualism?). Thus, I dedicate more space in this chapter to its discussion and to how it plays out in the color-blind drama.

In order to adequately understand the *abstract liberalism* frame, first we need to know what is liberalism. According to John Gray, liberalism, or "liberal humanism," is at the core of modernity; of the philosophical, economic, cultural, and political challenge to the feudal order. Although he acknowledges that liberalism has no "essence," he points out that it has a "set of distinctive features," namely, individualism, universalism, egalitarianism, and meliorism (the idea that people and institutions can be improved).[6] All these components were endorsed and placed at the core of the constitutions of emerging nation-states by a new set of actors: the bourgeoisies of early modern capitalism. When the bourgeoisie lauded freedom, they meant "free trade, free selling and buying"; when they applauded "individualism," they had in mind "the bourgeois... the middle-class owner of property"; 'The ideas of religious liberty and freedom of conscience merely gave expression to the sway of free competition within the domain of knowledge."[7]

Hence, classical liberalism was the philosophy of a nascent class that as an aspiring ruling class expressed its needs (political as well as economic) as general societal goals. But the bourgeois goals were not extended to the populace in their own midst until the twentieth century.[8] Moreover, the liberal project was never inclusive of the countries that Spain, Portugal, France, Britain, the Netherlands, Italy, and later on, Germany used as outposts for raw materials and racialized workers (e.g., slaves). Although contemporary commentators debate the merits of liberal humanism as it pertains to current debates about race-based policies, muticulturalism, and "equality of results,"[9] many seem oblivious to the fact that *"European humanism* (and liberalism) *usually meant that only Europeans were human,*"[10] Philosophers such as Kant stated that the differences between blacks and whites were "to be as great in regard to mental capacities as in colour." Voltaire, the great French philosopher, said on the same subject that "only a blind man is permitted to doubt that Whites, Blacks, and Albinoes... are totally different races." Lastly, even the father of modern liberalism, John Stuart Mill, author of *On Liberty*, justified 19th-century colonialism and supported slavery in antiquity and in certain 19th-century colonial situations.[11] To be clear, my intent here is not to vilify the founders of liberalism, but to point out that modernity, liberalism, and racial exclusion were all part of the same historical movement.

The liberal tradition informed the American Revolution, the U.S. Constitution, and "the leading American liberal thinker of this period, Thomas Jefferson."[12] And in the United States as in Europe, the exclusion of the majority of white men and all white women from the rights of citizenship and the classification of Native Americans and African Americans as subpersons accompanied the development of the new liberal nation-state.[13] Specifically, racially based policies such as slavery, the removal of Native Americans from their lands and their banishment to reservations, the superexploitation and degrading utilization of Mexicans and various Asian groups as contract laborers, Jim Crow, and many other policies were part of the United States' "liberal" history from 1776 until the 1960s.

Nevertheless, I would be remiss if I failed to acknowledge that, in both Europe and the United States, disenfranchised groups and progressive politicians used the liberal rhetoric to advance social and legal reforms (e.g., the Civil Rights Movement, the National Organization of Women, Liberal parties in Europe).[14] Thus liberalism, when extended to its seemingly logical conclusions ("Life, liberty, and the pursuit of happiness for *all*") and connected to social movements, can be progressive. My point, however, is less about social-reform liberalism (although I contend many reform organizations and many white reform-minded individuals[15] have adopted color-blind

racism) than about how central elements of liberalism have been *rearticulated* in post-Civil Rights America to rationalize racially unfair situations.

**The frame of *abstract liberalism* involves using ideas associated with political liberalism (e.g., "equal opportunity," the idea that force should not be used to achieve social policy) and economic liberalism (e.g., choice, individualism) in an *abstract* manner to explain racial matters.** By framing race-related issues in the language of liberalism, whites can appear "reasonable" and even "moral," while opposing almost all practical approaches to deal with de facto racial inequality. For instance, the principle of equal opportunity, central to the agenda of the Civil Rights Movement and whose extension to people of color was vehemently opposed by most whites, is invoked by whites today to oppose affirmative-action policies because they supposedly represent the "preferential treatment" of certain groups. This claim necessitates ignoring the fact that people of color are *severely* underrepresented in most good jobs, schools, and universities and, hence, it is an abstract utilization of the idea of "equal opportunity." Another example is regarding each person as an "individual" with "choices" and using this liberal principle as a justification for whites having the right of choosing to live in segregated neighborhoods or sending their children to segregated schools. This claim requires ignoring the multiple institutional and state-sponsored practices behind segregation and being unconcerned about these practices' negative consequences for minorities.

***Naturalization* is a frame that allows whites to explain away racial phenomena by suggesting they are natural occurrences.** For example, whites can claim "segregation" is natural because people from all backgrounds "gravitate toward likeness." Or that their taste for whiteness in friends and partners is just "the way things are." Although the above statements can be interpreted as "racist" and as contradicting the colorblind logic, they are actually used to reinforce the myth of nonracialism. How? By suggesting these preferences are almost biologically driven and typical of all groups in society, preferences for primary associations with members of one's race are rationalized as nonracial because *"they* (racial minorities) do it too."

**Cultural racism is a frame that relies on culturally based arguments such as "Mexicans do not put much emphasis on education" or "blacks have too many babies" to explain the standing of minorities in society.** This frame has been adequately discussed by many commentators and does not require much discussion.[16] During slavery and Jim Crow a central rationale for excluding racial minorities was their presumed biological inferiority. Even as late as 1940, a white newspaper editor in Durham, North Carolina, could confidently state that:

> A Negro is different from other people in that he's an unfortunate branch of the human family who hasn't been able to make out of himself all he is capable of. He is not capable of being rushed because of the background of the jungle. Part of his human nature can't be rushed; it gets him off his balance.... You can't wipe away inbred character in one year or a hundred years, it must be nursed along. We look upon him for his lack of culture, as being less reliable, in business and unsafe socially. His passions are aroused easily.[17]

Today only white supremacist organizations spout things such as this in open forums. Yet, these biological views have been replaced by cultural ones that, as I will show, are as effective in defending the racial status quo.[18] For example, George McDermott, one of the white middle-class residents interviewed by Katherine Newman in her *Declining Fortunes,* stated:

> I believe in morality: I believe in ethics: I believe in hard work: I believe in all the old values. I don't believe in handouts.... So that the whole welfare system falls into that [category].... The idea of fourteen-year-old kids getting pregnant and then having five children

by the time they're twenty is absurd! It's ridiculous! And that's what's causing this country to go downhill

And as Newman poignantly comments, "George does not see himself as racist. Publicly he would subscribe to the principle everyone in this society deserves a fair shake."[19] Color-blind racism is racism without racists!

**Minimization of racism is a frame that suggests discrimination is no longer a central factor affecting minorities' life chances ("It's better now than in the past" or "There is discrimination, but there are plenty of jobs out there").** This frame allows whites to accept facts such as the racially motivated murder of James Byrd Jr. in Jasper, Texas,[20] the brutal police attack on Rodney King, the Texaco case,[21] the 2005 lawsuit by black workers alleging that Tyson Foods maintained a "Whites Only" bathroom in one of their Alabama plants, the neglect and slow response by government officials toward a mostly black population during Hurricane Katrina, and many other cases and still accuse minorities of being "hypersensitive," of using race as an "excuse," or of "playing the infamous race card." More significantly, this frame also involves regarding discrimination exclusively as all-out racist behavior, which, given the way "new racism" practices operate in post-Civil Rights America (chapter 1), eliminates the bulk of racially motivated actions by individual whites and institutions by fiat.

Before proceeding to illustrate how whites use these frames, I need to clarify a few points about the data and how I present them. First, whites used these frames in combination rather than in pure form. This is understandable, since informal expressions of ideology are a constructive effort, a process of building arguments in situ. Therefore, the examples of how whites use a particular frame may be mixed with other frames. Second, the frames were verbalized by participants in various emotional tones, ranging from sympathy to absolute disgust and outrage toward minorities. This suggests whites with differing levels of sympathy toward minorities resort to the *same* frames when constructing their accounts of racial matters. I attempt to represent this range of emotion in the quotes. Third, because the college student and DAS samples represent two different populations, I present quotes from the two studies separately in the text. I do so to better identify differences in style or content among the two populations. Fourth, the quotes in the chapter were selected to embrace the variety of ways in which the frames are used by respondents. This implies that many outrageously racist quotes were left out for the sake of representing the variance in the samples. Fifth, the interviews were transcribed to be as close to what the respondents uttered as possible. Thus the transcripts include nonlexical expressions (umm, ahh, umhmm), pauses (indicated by ellipses when they are short and by a number in seconds in parentheses representing the duration of the pause, when they are longer than five seconds), emphases (indicated by *italics* or, for notations of the respondent tone, by italic letters in brackets), self-corrections (denoted by a short line,—), and other important discursive matters (laughs and changes in tone are indicated with italic letters in brackets). Whenever I have added words they appear in brackets; the interviewers' interventions appear in brackets and in italic letters. However, to improve its readability, I edited the material lightly.

## Abstract Liberalism: Unmasking Reasonable Racism[22]

Because of the curious way in which liberalism's principles are used in the post-Civil Rights era, other analysts label modern racial ideology "laissez-fare racism" or "competitive racism" or argue that modern racism is essentially a combination of the "American Creed" with antiblack resentment.[23] The importance of this frame is evident in that whites use it on issues ranging from affirmative action and interracial friendship and marriage to neighborhood and residential segregation. Because of the pivotal role played by this frame in organizing whites' racial views, I provide numerous examples below.

## Rationalizing Racial Unfairness in the Name of Equal Opportunity

An archetype of how white students use the notion of equal opportunity in an abstract manner to oppose racial fairness is Sue, a student at SU.

When asked if minority students should be provided unique opportunities to be admitted into universities, Sue stated:

> I don't think that they should be provided with unique opportunities. I think that they should have the same opportunities as everyone else. You know, it's up to them to meet the standards and whatever that's required for entrance into universities or whatever. I don't think that just because they're a minority that they should, you know, not meet the requirements, you know.

Sue, like most whites, ignored the effects of past and contemporary discrimination on the social, economic, and educational status of minorities. Therefore, by supporting equal opportunity for everyone without a concern for the savage inequalities between whites and blacks, Sue's stance safeguards white privilege. Sue even used the notion of equal opportunity to avoid explaining why blacks tend to perform worse than whites academically: "I don't know… urn, like I said, I don't see it as a group thing. I see it more as an individual [thing] and I don't know why as a whole they don't do better. I mean, as I see it, they have the same opportunity and everything. They *should* be doing equal."

College students are not the only ones who use this abstract notion of equal opportunity to justify their racial views. For example, Eric, a corporate auditor in his forties, and a very affable man who seemed more tolerant than most members of his generation (e.g., he had dated a black woman for three years, recognized that discrimination happens "a lot" and identified multiple examples, and even said that "the system is… is white"), erupted in anger when asked if reparations were due to blacks for the injuries caused by slavery and Jim Crow: "Oh tell them to shut up, OK! I had nothing to do with the whole situation. The opportunity is there, there is no reparation involved and let's not dwell on it. I'm very opinionated about that!" After suggesting that Jews and Japanese are the ones who really deserve reparation, Eric added, "But something that happened three God-damned generations ago, what do you want us to do about it now? Give them opportunity, give them scholarships, but reparations?"

Was Eric just a white with a "principled opposition" to government intervention (see chapter 1 for analysts who make this claim)? This does not seem to be the case since Eric, like most whites, made a distinction between government spending on behalf of victims of child abuse, the homeless, and battered women (whom whites deem as legitimate candidates for assistance) and government spending on blacks (whom whites deem as unworthy candidates for assistance). This finding was consistent with DAS survey results. For instance, whereas 64.3 percent of whites agreed that "we should expand the services that benefit the poor," only 39.6 percent (as opposed to 84 percent of blacks) agreed with the proposition "The government should make every effort to improve the social and economic position of blacks living in the United States." Furthermore, whereas 75.2 percent of white respondents approved of increasing federal spending for the environment and 59.7 percent for social security, only 31.7 percent approved such increases for programs to assist blacks. And when the question dealt with government programs that were not perceived as "racial" in any way,[24] the proportion of whites supporting the program increased even more.

### "The Most Qualified …": A Meritocratic Way of Defending White Privilege

Another tenet of liberalism whites use to explain racial matters is the Jeffersonian idea of "the cream rises to the top," or meritocracy (reward by merit). And whites seem unconcerned that the color of the "cream" that usually "rises" is white. For example, Diane, a student at SU, expressed her dissatisfaction about providing blacks unique opportunities to be admitted into universities: "I don't think you should admit anyone. It's gotta be, you've gotta be on the level to do it. If they were prepared beforehand to handle the college level to succeed in it, then there you go, anyone can." Diane then added, "They've gotta have the motivation to do well before you get there, I mean, I can't imagine being unprepared to go [to college] like just barely getting by in high school and then coming here to take the classes, you just can't go, 'OK, we want to put minorities in here so put anyone in, you know.'" Diane also used the notion of meritocracy to explain her opposition to affirmative action.

> That's so hard. I still believe in merit, you know, I still believe in equality, you know. If you did have two people with the same qualifications, one's minority and one's not, you know, I'd want to interview them and just maybe a personality stands out that works with the job, I don't know. Just find something other than race to base it on, you know? Let that not be a factor if they qualify.

How could Diane maintain these views and remain "reasonable"? Diane could say these things and seem reasonable because she believes discrimination is not the reason why blacks are worse off than whites. Instead, she relied on the cultural racism frame to explain blacks' status. This view can be seen too in her response to a question on why blacks fare worse academically than whites: "I don't know why. Mine was a personal motivation so, you know, I don't know. I don't want to say they weren't personally motivated to get good grades, but that's what it was for me," Diane expanded on this matter and said, "maybe some of them don't have parents to push them or… maybe the schools are not equal" She also speculated, "maybe, you know, they've got in their mind that they can't succeed because they're a minority and they don't try, you know, no one there to tell them 'You can do it, it doesn't matter who you are.'"

Whites from the Detroit metro area used the meritocratic frame as extensively as college students. For instance Jim, a thirty-year-old computer software salesperson from a privileged background, explained in the following way his opposition to affirmative action:

> I think it's unfair top to bottom on everybody and the whole process. It often, you know, discrimination itself is a bad word, right? But you discriminate everyday. You wanna buy a beer at the store and there are six kind a beers you can get, from Natural Light to Sam Adams, right? And you look at the price and you look at the kind of beer, and you… *it's a choice.* And a lot of that you have laid out in front of you, which one you get? Now, should the government sponsor Sam Adams and make it cheaper than Natural Light because it's brewed by someone in Boston? That doesn't make much sense, right? Why would we want that or make Sam Adams eight times as expensive because we want people to buy Natural Light? And it's the same thing about getting into school or getting into some place. And universities it's easy, and universities is a hot topic now, and I could bug you, you know, Midwestern University I don't think has a lot of racism in the admissions process. And I think Midwestern University would, would agree with that pretty strongly. So why not just pick people that are going to do well at Midwestern University, pick people by their merit? I think we should stop the whole idea of choosing people based on their color. It's bad to choose someone based on their color; why do we, why do we enforce it in an institutional process?

Since Jim posited hiring decisions are like market choices (choosing between competing brands of beer), he embraced a laissez-faire position on hiring. The problem with Jim's view is that discrimination in the labor market is alive and well (e.g., it affects black and Latino job applicants 30 to 50 percent of the time) and that most jobs (as many as 80 percent) are obtained through informal networks.[25] Jim himself acknowledged that being white is an advantage in America because "there's more people in the world who are white and are racist against people that are black than vice versa." However, Jim also believes that although blacks "perceive or feel" like there is a lot of discrimination, he does not believe there is much discrimination out there. Hence, by upholding a strict laissez-faire view on hiring and, at the same time, ignoring the significant impact of past and contemporary discrimination in the labor market, Jim can safely voice his opposition to affirmative action in an apparently race-neutral way.

### "Nothing Should Be Forced Upon People": Keeping Things the Way They Are

A central tenet of liberal democracies is that governments should intervene in economic and social matters as little as possible because the "invisible hand of the market" eventually balances states of disequilibrium. A corollary of this tenet, and part of the American mythology, is the idea that social change should be the outcome of a rational and democratic process and not of the government's coercive capacity.[26] During the Jim Crow era, the belief that racial change should happen through a slow, evolutionary process in "peoples' hearts" rather than through governmental actions was expressed in the phrase "you cannot legislate morality."[27] This old standpoint has been curiously reformulated in the modern era to justify keeping racial affairs the way they are. These ideas appeared occasionally in discussions on affirmative action, but most often in discussions about school and residential integration in America.

Sonny, a student at MU, explained in typical fashion her position on whether school segregation is the fault of government, whites, or blacks. As almost all the students, Sonny first stated her belief that school integration is in principle a good thing to have: "In principle, yeah, I think that's a good idea because like with, like with people interacting, they will understand each other better in future generations." But Sonny also, as most students, was not too fond of government attempts to remedy school segregation or, in her words, "I, I don't—I mean, it should be done if people want to do it. If people volunteer for it, and they want that part of their lives, then they should do it, but the government should not force people to bus if they don't want that." When asked to clarify her stance on this matter, she added, "I don't think the government should impose any legislation thinking that it will change people's hearts because people have to change them on their own. You can't force them to say 'Well, OK, now that I have to bus my kid there, I like it.'"

DAS respondents were as adamant as students in arguing that it is not the government's business to remedy racial problems. For example, Lynn, a human resources manager in her early fifties, explained why there has been so little school integration since the 1954 *Brown v. Board of Education* decision:

> I don't and that's another one. *I do not believe in busing.* The reason I don't believe in busing, you know, I said I don't. I didn't encourage my children to play with the neighborhood kids. I still felt that going to school in your community was the key to developing a child's sense of community and I still believe that. One of the reasons, another reason I moved from where I was [was] that I didn't want my children to be bused. I didn't want to have them got on a bus, especially me working. So I don't think that is an answer. I think the answer is education and helping people learn to make a life for themselves and, you know, any type of social program that interacts, that provides interaction

between races I think is excellent. But I'm just not a busing person.

Lynn wants equal opportunity in education as well as community schools, a position that sounds perfectly reasonable. However, one would expect Lynn to support doing something to make sure that communities throughout America are diverse, a policy that other things being equal would guarantee school integration. Yet, Lynn took a very strong laissez-faire, antigovernment intervention stance on this matter. Lynn answered as follows the question, "America has lots of all-white and all-black neighborhoods. What do you think of this situation?"

> I don't have a problem with all-white and all-black neighborhoods if that's the choice of the people, the *individuals.* But, if it's *forced* either way, if I'm a black person and I've come into the neighborhood and I want to live here and selectively denied that option, that's wrong. But, again, there still has to be some type of social interaction for growth and if the social interaction takes place then, the cross-integration will take place, I think.

When pressed about what she thought could be done specifically to increase the mixing of the races in neighborhoods, Lynn restated that this could only be achieved "through educating (people) and encouraging businesses." Lynn was not alone in having this abstract view on school and neighborhood integration. Only one of the white respondents who opposed busing in the interviews (69.7 percent of whites opposed busing in the survey) provided a specific proposal that if implemented would increase residential as well as school integration.[28]

### Individual Choice or an Excuse for Racial Unfairness and Racially Based Choices?

Individualism[29] today has been recast as a justification for opposing policies to ameliorate racial inequality because they are "group based" rather than "case by case." In addition, the idea of individual choice is used to defend whites' right to live and associate primarily with whites (segregation) and for choosing whites exclusively as their mates. The problem with how whites apply the notion of individualism to our present racial conundrum is that a relation of domination-subordination still ordains race relations in the United States (see chapters 1 and 4 in my *White Supremacy and Racism in the Post-Civil Rights Era*). Thus, if minority groups face group-based discrimination and whites have group-based advantages, demanding individual treatment for all can only benefit the advantaged group.[30] And behind the idea of people having the right of making their own "choices" lays the fallacy of racial pluralism—the false assumption that all racial groups have the same power in the American polity. Because whites have more power, their unfettered, so-called individual choices help reproduce a form of white supremacy in neighborhoods, schools, and society in general.

Lynn, a human resources manager, used the notion of individualism in a very curious way. Although Lynn expressed her support for affirmative action because "there's still a lot of discrimination," she thinks that "there isn't as much discrimination as there used to be." Lynn also acknowledged white males have advantages in society and said "the white male is pretty much instilled" and "very much represses... um, people and other minorities." Nevertheless, when it came to the possibility of affirmative action affecting her, Lynn said:

> Um, because affirmative action is based on a group as a whole, but when it comes down to the individual, like if affirmative action were against me one time, like it would anger me. I mean, because, you know, I as an individual got ripped off and, you know, getting a job.

DAS respondents also used individualism to justify their racial views and race-based preferences.

For example, Mandi, a registered nurse in her thirties, said she had no problems with neighborhood segregation. She justified her potentially problematic position by saying that people have the right to choose where and with whom they live.

> Umm, I think that people select a neighborhood to live in that they are similar to and people, you know, whatever similarities they *find [louder voice]*, you know, it's race, economical level, religion, or, you know, whatever. When you are looking at somebody you don't know what, what denomination they are or what political preference they have, but you can tell right off in race. I think that they choose to live in a neighborhood that is their race.

## Naturalization: Decoding the Meaning of "That's the Way It Is"

A frame that has not yet been brought to the fore by social scientists is whites' naturalization of race-related matters. Although the naturalization frame was the least used frame of color-blind racism by respondents in these two projects, about 50 percent of DAS respondents and college students used it, particularly when discussing school or neighborhood matters, to explain the limited contact between whites and minorities, or to rationalize whites' preferences for whites as significant others. The word "natural" or the phrase "that's the way it is" is often interjected to normalize events or actions that could otherwise be interpreted as racially motivated (residential segregation) or racist (preference for whites as friends and partners). But, as social scientists know quite well, few things that happen in the social world are "natural," particularly things pertaining to racial matters. Segregation as well as racial preferences are produced through social processes and that is the delusion/illusion component of this frame.

The importance and usefulness of this frame can be illustrated with Sara, a student at MU who used the frame on three separate occasions. Sara, for example, used the frame to answer the question on black self-segregation.

> Hmm. I don't really think it's a segregation. I mean, I think people, you know, spend time with people that they are like, not necessarily in color, but you know, their ideas and values and, you know, maybe their class has something to do with what they're used to. But I don't really think it's a segregation. I don't think I would have trouble, you know, approaching someone of a different race or color. I don't think it's a problem. It's just that the people that I do hang out with are just the people that I'm with all the time. They're in my organizations and stuff like that.

Sara also used the naturalization frame to explain the paltry level of school integregation in the United States.

> Well, I also think that, you know, where you are in school has to do with the neighborhood that you grow up in and, like, I grew up in mainly all-white communities so that community was who I was going to school with. And if that community had been more black, then that would be, I guess, more integrated and that would be just fine. I don't know if there's any way you can change the places in which people live because I think there *are* gonna be white communities and there are gonna be black communities and, you know, I don't know how you can get two communities like in the same school system.

The interviewer followed up Sara's answer with the question, "Why do you think there are white communities and black communities?" Sara's answer was: "Maybe like I said before, if people like to be with people that they're similar with and it means, you know—well, I don't think it has anything to do with color. I think it has to do with where they…," Sara did not complete her thought as a light seems to have clicked on in her mind. She then proceeded to change her answer and acknowledged that race has a bearing on how people select neighborhoods: "Well, I guess it does *[laughs]*." The interviewer asked Sara if she thought her parents would move into an almost all-black neighborhood. Sara employed all sorts of rhetorical maneuvers (see chapter 3) to defend her parents by conveying the idea that racial considerations would have never been a criterion for selecting a neighborhood.

Finally Liz, a student at SU, suggested that self segregation is a universal process or, in her own words: "I do think they segregate themselves, but I don't necessarily think it's on purpose. I think it's that, you know, *we all try to stay with our own kind* so, therefore, you know, *they get along better with their own people* or whatnot [my emphasis]." By universalizing segregation as a natural phenomenon, Liz was able to justify even her own racial preference for white mates. When asked if she had ever been attracted to minority people, Liz said:

> Um no, just because I wasn't really attracted to them, you know, I'm more attracted to someone that's like kinda more like me. But, you know, and I wouldn't say that, I mean, I like if he's good looking or not, you know, it's not that, it's just I'm more attracted to someone white, I don't know why *[laughs]*.

DAS respondents naturalized racial matters too, but in general did it in a more crude fashion. For instance, Bill, a manager in a manufacturing firm, explained the limited level school integration:

> I don't think it's anybody's fault. Because people tend to group with their own people. Whether it's white or black or upper-middle class or lower class or, you now, upper class, you know, Asians. People tend to group with their own.

Doesn't mean if a black person moves into your neighborhood, they shouldn't go to your school. They should and you should mix and welcome them and everything else, but you can't force people together. If people want to be together, they should intermix more. *[Interviewer: OK. So the lack of mixing is really just kind of an individual lack of desire?]* Well, individuals, its just the way it is. You know, people group together for lots of different reasons: social, religious. Just as animals in the wild, you know. Elephants group together, cheetahs group together. You bus a cheetah into an elephant herd because they should mix? You can't force that *[laughs].*

Bill's unflattering and unfitting metaphor comparing racial segregation to the separation of species, however, was not the only crude way of using the naturalization frame. For example, Earl, a small-time contractor in his fifties, explained segregation in a matter-of-fact way.

I think you're never going to change that! I think it's just kind of, you know, it's going to end up that way.... Every race sticks together and that's the way it should be, you know. I grew up in a white neighborhood, you know, most of the blacks will live in the black neighborhood. *[Interviewer: So you don't think there's anything wrong?]* No. Well, they can move, they still have the freedom to move anywhere they want anyway.

A significant number of DAS respondents naturalized racial matters in a straightforward manner. For example, Jim, a thirty-year-old computer software salesperson for a large company, naturalized school segregation as follows:

Eh, you know, it's more of the human nature's fault. It's not the government's fault, right? The government doesn't tell people where to live. So as people decide where to live or where to move into or where they wanna feel comfortable, [they] move to where they feel comfortable. We all kinda hang out with people that are like us. I mean, you look at Detroit, we have a Mexican village, why do we have a Mexican village? Why aren't Mexican people spread out all over on metro Detroit? Well, they like being near other Mexican people; that way they could have a store that suited them close by the, you know, those sort of things probably together. So, it's more human nature that I would blame for it.

Despite whites' belief that residential and school segregation, friendship, and attraction are natural and raceless occurrences, social scientists have documented how racial considerations affect all these issues. For example, residential segregation is created by white buyers searching for white neighborhoods and aided by realtors, bankers, and sellers.[31] As white neighborhoods develop, white schools follow—an outcome that further contributes to the process of racial isolation. Socialized in a "white habitus" (see chapter 5) and influenced by the Eurocentric culture, it is no wonder whites interpret their racialized choices for white significant others as "natural." They are the "natural" consequence of a white socialization process.[32]

### "They Don't Have It Altogether": Cultural Racism

Pierre-André Taguieff has argued that modern European racism does not rely on an essentialist interpretation of minorities' endowments.[33] Instead, it presents their presumed cultural practices as fixed features (hence he labels it as the "biologization of racism") and uses that as the rationale for justifying racial inequality. Thus, Europeans may no longer believe Africans, Arabs,

Asian Indians, or blacks from the West Indies are biologically inferior, but they assail them for their presumed lack of hygiene, family disorganization, and lack of morality.[34] This cultural racism frame is very well established in the United States. Originally labeled as the "culture of poverty"[35] in the 1960s, this tradition has resurfaced many times since, resurrected by conservative scholars such as Charles Murray and Lawrence Mead, liberals such as William Julius Wilson, and even radicals such as Cornel West.[36] The essence of the American version of this frame is "blaming the victim," arguing that minorities' standing is a product of their lack of effort, loose family organization, and inappropriate values.

Since there is little disagreement among social scientists about the centrality of this frame in the post-Civil Rights era, I focus my attention on highlighting what this frame allows whites to accomplish. I begin my illustration of this frame with two, clear-cut examples of college students who used it. The students agreed with the premise of the question, "Many whites explain the status of blacks in this country as a result of blacks lacking motivation, not having the proper work ethic, or being lazy. What do you think?" The first student is Kara, an MU student.

> I think, to some extent, that's true. Just from, like, looking at the black people that I've met in my classes and the few that I knew before college, not like they're—I don't want to say waiting for a handout, but to some extent, that's kind of what I'm like hinting at. Like, almost like they feel like they were discriminated against hundreds of years ago, now what are you gonna give me? You know, or maybe even it's just their background, that they've never, like maybe they're the first generation to be in college, so they feel like just that is enough for them.

The second quote is from Kim, a student at SU:

Yeah, I totally agree with that. I don't think, you know, they're all like that, but, I mean, it's just that if it wasn't that way, why would there be so many blacks living in the projects? You know, why would there be so many poor blacks? If they worked hard, they could make it just as high as anyone else could. You know, I just think that's just, you know, they're raised that way and they see what their parents are like so they assume that's the way it should be. And they just follow the roles their parents had for them and don't go anywhere.

When cultural racism is used in combination with the "minimization of racism" frame, the results are ideologically deadly. If people of color say they experience discrimination, whites, such as Kara and Kim, do not believe them and claim they use discrimination as an "excuse" to hide the central reason why they are behind whites in society: their presumed "laziness."

Although Kara and Kim used the cultural racism frame in a crude form, most students did not. They articulated their culture of poverty views in a gentler, at times even "compassionate," way. For example, Ann, a student at WU, inserted the frame in her answer to a question about why blacks as a group fare worse than whites academically.

> Um, I guess I would have to say primarily family structure. Maybe it's not [being] able to support the child and, you know, in school and really encourage. It might be that it's a single-parent family and it's necessary [for them] to get out and get a job, you know, a full-time job and work a part-time job and still try to go to school. Maybe it's not encouraged as much for, like long term, it's mainly survival. I don't know, something, income; if the family is really skimping by it would be really far fetched, well, it wouldn't be probably necessarily the first thing that a child from [such] a family would think of, you know, expensive

college rather than paying the rent, you know what I mean *[laughs]*? So, I mean, you know, the priorities are different.

Although Ann's arguments seem "reasonable" (poor people may have a different set of priorities than other people based on their economic situation), her explanation is wanting because it avoids mentioning the institutional effects of discrimination in the labor, housing, and educational markets and the well-documented[37] impact that discrimination has on middle- and upper-middle-class blacks. More significantly, Ann's failure to recognize how old- and new-fashioned discrimination affects blacks' life chances is not an argumentative slip, but the way in which most whites construe the situation of blacks, as evidenced by how respondents in both samples used similar arguments in answering questions about blacks' status.

This kinder and gentler way of using the cultural frame was the preferred choice of students. For example, Jay, a student at WU, explained as follows why blacks have a worse overall standing than whites:

> Hmm, I think it's due to lack of education. I think because if they didn't grow up in a household that afforded them the time to go to school and they had to go out and get jobs right away, I think it is just a cycle [that] perpetuates things, you know. I mean, I can't say that blacks can't do it because, obviously, there are many, many of them [that] have succeeded in getting good jobs and all that.

Jay, as most whites, admits to the "exceptional black." However, Jay immediately goes back to the gentle cultural argument:

> So it's possible that the cycle seems to perpetuate itself because—I mean, let's say they go out and get jobs and they settle down much earlier than they would normally if they had gone to school and then they have kids at a

young age and they—these kids—have to go and get jobs and so.

How did DAS respondents use this cultural frame? They relied on this frame as often as students did but were significantly more likely to use it in a straightforward and crude manner. The following two cases exemplify how most DAS respondents used this frame. First is Isaac, an engineer in his fifties. In response to the question comparing blacks' and whites' overall standing, Isaac argued that few blacks have the education to work as engineers. This led to the following exchange between Isaac and the interviewer:

> *Interviewer:* So you feel maybe there's a lack of interest in education that black people have?
> *Isaac:* They want to get a short cut to make money. There's no urgency to get education. They want to make, to get money faster than whites. They don't want to take the time to get educated, they want to get money fast. *Interviewer:* So they also don't put the time into developing their educational skills?
> *Isaac:* Yeah the way you learn, the way you grow, is the way you become.
> *Interviewer:* Some people say that minorities are worse off than whites because they lack motivation, are lazy, or do not have the proper values to succeed in our society. What do you think?
> *Isaac:* Right now I think our minorities are lazy. They don't have the patience to keep going.

Ian, the manager of information security at an automotive company, explained why blacks are worse off than whites as follows:

> The majority of 'em just don't strive to do anything, to make themselves better. Again, I've seen that all the way through. "I do this today, I'm fine, I'm happy with it, I don't need anything better." Never,

never, never striving or giving extra to,
to make themselves better.

Ian's perception of blacks as lazy emerged from his understanding of blacks as culturally deficient. This view was clearly expressed in his response to the question, "Do you think that the races are naturally different?"

> Well I think that genes have something, some play in this, but I think a lot of it is past history of the people and the way they're brought up. You look at Chinese, if you're gonna get ahead in China, you've gotta be very intellectual and you've gotta be willing to, uh, to fight for everything that you're gonna get. Ja-Japan is the same way. For a kid just to get into college, they gonna take two years of going through entrance exams to get in. Then you kinda look at the blacks' situation. It's like, "Well, because of slavery, I ought to be given this for nothing, so I don't have to work for it, just give it to me." So culture and their upbringing is the big part of this.

Although Ian came close to the old biological view ("Well, I think genes have something, some play in this"), overall he made use of the cultural frame to explain blacks' status (Asians do well because they "gotta be intellectual," whereas blacks believe that because of slavery they do not have to work).

## Minimization of Racism: Whites' Declining Significance of Race Thesis

When William Julius Wilson published *The Declining Significance of Race* in 1978, he made many whites in academia feel good about themselves. Wilson's main claim—that class rather than race was the central obstacle for black mobility—was an argument that had been brewing among whites for quite a while. Yet, whites believe that discrimination exists. For example, when white and black respondents in the DAS

survey were given the statement, "Discrimination against blacks is no longer a problem in the United States," a high proportion of *both* groups (82.5 percent of whites and 89.5 percent of blacks) "disagreed" or "strongly disagreed" with that statement. Although whites and blacks believe discrimination is still a problem, they dispute its salience as a factor explaining blacks' collective standing. Thus, in response to the more specific statement, "Blacks are in the position that they are today as a group because of present day discrimination," only 32.9 percent of whites "agreed" or "strongly agreed" (compared to 60.5 percent of blacks). This means that in general whites believe discrimination has all but disappeared, whereas blacks believe that discrimination—old and new—is alive and well.

College students were more likely than DAS respondents to give lip service to the existence of discrimination. Because students for this study were taking social science courses at the time of the interviews, they may have become sensitized to the significance of discrimination as well as to the new character of contemporary discrimination. However, despite this sensitization, few believed discrimination and institutionalized racism are the reasons minorities lag behind whites in this society. In general, the students articulated their declining significance of race thesis in three ways. A plurality (18 of 41) used an indirect strategy of denial set by one of the following two phrases, "I am not black" or "I don't see discrimination" (see chapter 3 for an analysis of the functions of these phrases), others (9 of 41) minimized racism directly, and yet others (7 of 41) argued minorities make things look racial when they are not.

The following example illustrates how students used the indirect strategy of denial. The response of Mary, a student at SU, to the statement, "Many blacks and other minorities claim that they do not get access to good jobs because of discrimination and that when they get the jobs they are not promoted at the same speed as their white peers," was:

> I think before you really start talking about hiring practices and promotion

practices, you have to look at credentials. I mean, you know, I've only really had one job. I worked for a general contractor so it was basically me in the office all day with him, my boss. But I, in fact, you have to look at credentials. I mean, I don't know if, you know, a white person gets a job over a minority, I can't sit here and say "Well, that's discrimination" because I don't know what the factors were. This person got a master's degree versus a bachelor's degree, or more in-depth training than this person, you know? I mean, I definitely do not doubt that [discrimination] happens, that minorities get passed over for promotions and that they are not hired based on their race. I have absolutely no doubt that it happens. I think that before you can sit there and start calling a lot of things discrimination, you need to look into the background, the credentials behind it.

Rather than stating "I don't believe minorities experience discrimination," Mary suggested they may not get jobs or promotions because they lack the credentials. And although Mary, as most whites, recognizes discrimination exists ("I definitely do not doubt that [discrimination] happens"), she clearly believes most claims are bogus ("I think that before you can sit there and start calling a lot of things discrimination, you need to look into the background, the credentials behind it").

The next example is of students who minimized the significance of racism directly. Andy, a student at WU, answered a question on whether discrimination is the central reason why blacks are behind whites today by saying, "I think they do." Yet his answer was wanting, since he could not provide a meaningful explanation of how discrimination affects minorities' life chances. More importantly, Andy's answers to the other questions minimized the salience of racism. For instance, his answer to the question of whether or not discrimination affects the chances of minorities getting jobs and promotions was, "I think that there's probably less than it used to be, but that it still happens. It's just in isolated places or, you know, it happens in different places, but in most jobs, I think it probably does not happen." When asked to elaborate, Andy stated he believes the reason why blacks do not get good jobs is, "if anything, it's probably education" because "you can't apply for certain jobs without a lot of education."

The last example is of students who argued blacks make situations racial that are not. Janet, an SU student, answered all the questions on discrimination by denying that discrimination is a salient factor in minorities' life chances and suggesting alternative interpretations. For instance, Janet's answer to the same question, on whether or not discrimination is the central reason why blacks lag behind whites was: "I would say it depends on the individual I'm sure there are some… that do and others [that] don't, so.…" When asked to clarify, she said, "Right. But I would say for the most part, most of them don't unless they make it out to be the case." When the interviewer asked Janet if she thought most claims of discrimination by minorities were a perception issue, she replied: "If they looked at it as a different way or something, they might see—might not see it as racism, you see what I'm saying? [*Interviewer: You are saying that they are seeing more than is actually out there?*] Right." When asked about discrimination in jobs, Janet answered in a blunt fashion.

I would say that's a bunch of crap [*laughs*]. I mean, if they're qualified, they'll hire you and if you are not qualified, then you don't get the job. It's the same way with, once you get the job, if you are qualified for a promotion, you'll get the promotion. It's the same way with white, blacks, Asians, whatever. If you do the job, you'll get the job.

DAS respondents used similar argumentative strategies to deny the significance of discrimination. The strategy they used the most was direct minimization (18 of 66), followed by outright denial (13 of 66), stating that minorities make things racial (11 of 66), and indirect minimization

The remaining respondents (20 of 66) include a few who sincerely believe discrimination is important (see chapter 7) and others who denied the centrality of discrimination in their own peculiar way.

The first case exemplifies DAS respondents who minimized the significance of discrimination directly. Joann, a poor white woman in her fifties who works in a large chain store, answered the direct discrimination question by stating, "I don't see any in the store." When asked about discrimination against minorities in general, Joann said:

> I don't think it's as bad as it was. It probably needs improvement. What [society] needs is a knowledgeable crew and I think that is the truth there. I think that the work will have to be done up continually until we're all one big happy family. [Interviewer: Do you foresee that happening?] It wouldn't surprise me. My great granddaughter might marry a black, I don't know. I have no idea!

The next case is an example of respondents who denied discrimination outright. It is worth pointing out that all the DAS respondents who used this strategy were from working- or lower-class backgrounds. Scott, a twenty-three-year-old drafter for a mechanical engineering company, answered the direct question on discrimination as follows:

> I don't—nowadays I don't, I don't really feel that way, I really don't at all. Maybe like when I was younger I would notice it, but right now I don't really feel that there's too much segregation anymore. If it is because of the person, you know, from their past experience. And, I mean, if you got a record, you're not gonna go too far, you know. So then they might feel like "Just being held back just because, you know, just 'cause I'm black."

The interviewer followed up Scott's answer with the question, "So you don't think that discrimination is a factor in most blacks lives nowadays?" His answer was: "It might be just because of their past and their attitudes toward life. But if you just took it as everyday life and just went with it, no, I don't feel it at all, I don't see it. I don't practice it and my friends, all my friends [don't] practice it"

Next are examples of respondents who argued blacks make things racial that are not. Sandra, a retail salesperson in her early forties, explained her view on discrimination as follows:

> I think if you are looking for discrimination, I think it's there to be *found*. But if you make the best of any situation, and if *you don't use it as an excuse*. I think sometimes it's an excuse because people felt they deserved a job, whatever! I think if things didn't go their way I know a lot of people have tendency to use prejudice or racism as whatever as an *excuse*. I think in some ways, *yes* there is people who are prejudiced. It's not only blacks, it's about Spanish, or women. In a lot of ways there [is] a lot of *reverse* discrimination. It's just what you wanna make of it.

Finally, I provide an example of respondents who used the indirect minimization strategy. Dave, an engineer in his forties who owns a smalltime employment agency, answered the direct question on discrimination by saying: "[laughs] I don't know any blacks so I don't know. But, in general, I probably have to say it's true." When asked for clarification, Dave stated:

> Oh that's a hard one to just, well, I guess it comes down to stereotypes though like I said earlier. It just—some people may try to say that some blacks don't work as hard as whites. So, in looking for a job they may feel like they didn't get the job because they have been discriminated against because they were

black, that's very possible. That may not really be, but as a person, they make the assumption.

Dave explained blacks' inferior status as compared to whites by suggesting that it "really comes down to individuals" and that he has "especially noted that if you want a job, there's jobs out there." In this reply Dave intimates his belief that racial discrimination is not a factor in the labor market since "there's jobs out there."

The last case is of DAS respondents who did not fit the overall strategies and used sui generis arguments to deny the significance of racial discrimination. Henrietta, a transsexual school teacher in his fifties, said the following in response to the question on discrimination:

> [9-second pause] Trying to be an unbiased observer because as a transsexual I am discriminated against. I think if people act responsible they will not be discriminated against. People who are acting irresponsible, in other words, demanding things, ah, "I need this" or "You did this because of my skin color" yeah, then they will be discriminated against. People who are intelligent present themselves in a manner that is appropriate for the situation and will not be discriminated against.

Thus, Henrietta suggests that blacks who experience discrimination deserve so because they act irresponsibly or complain too much.

## Conclusion

In this chapter I illustrated how whites use the four central frames of color-blind racism, namely, abstract liberalism, naturalization, cultural racism, and minimization of racism. These frames are central to the views of whites, young (college-student sample) and old (DAS respondents), and serve them as an interpretive matrix from where to extract arguments to explain a host of racial issues. More significantly, together these frames form an impregnable yet elastic wall that barricades whites from the United States' racial reality. The trick is in the way the frames bundle with each other, that is, in the wall they form. Whites, for example, would have a tough time using the abstract liberalism frame if they could not resort to the minimization of racism frame as well. Precisely because they use these frames the way children use building blocks, whites can say things such as "I am all for equal opportunity, that's why I oppose affirmative action" and also say "Everyone has almost the same opportunities to succeed in this country because discrimination and racism are all but gone." And if anyone dares to point out that in this land of milk and honey there is a tremendous level of racial inequality—a fact that could deflate the balloon of color blindness—they can argue this is due to minorities' schools, lack of education, family disorganization, or lack of proper values and work ethic. In short, whites can blame minorities (blacks in particular) for their own status.

But what if someone pokes holes in whites' color-blind story by pointing out that whites live mostly in white neighborhoods, marry and befriend mostly whites, interact mostly with whites in their jobs, and send their children to white schools or, if they attend mixed schools, make sure they take most of their classes with white children. Whites have two discursive options to avoid the potentially devastating effects of these arguments. They can resort to the abstract liberalism frame and say something like "I support integration, but I do not believe in forcing people to do anything that they do not want to do" or "People have the right to make their own individual choices and no one can interfere." Alternatively, they can naturalize the whiteness in which they live ("Blacks like living with blacks, and whites like living with whites... it's a natural thing"). As I documented in this chapter, whites mix and match arguments as they see fit. Therefore, someone can say, "Segregation is a natural thing" but also say that "I believe that no one has the right of preventing people from moving into a neighborhood." These frames then form a formidable wall because they provide whites a seemingly nonracial way of stating their racial views without appearing irrational or rabidly racist.

But if the ideological wall of color-blind racism were not pliable, a few hard blows would suffice to bring it down. That is why the flexibility of the frames is so useful Color-blind racism's frames are pliable because they do not rely on absolutes ("All blacks are..." or "Discrimination ended in 1965"). Instead, color-blind racism gives some room for exceptions ("Not all blacks are lazy, but most are") and allows for a variety of ways of holding on to the frames—from crude and straightforward to gentle and indirect. Regarding the former, almost every white respondent in these studies mentioned the exceptional black ("Well, Robert, my black friend, is not like that"), agreed in principle with racially progressive notions ("I believe that school integration is great because we can learn so much from each other" or "Gee, I wish I could see the day when we have the first black president"), or even joined Martin Luther King Jr. in the dream of color blindness ("In two or three generations race will disappear and we will all just be Americans"). Regarding the latter, whites used the color-blind frames in crude ways displaying resentment and anger toward minorities ("Blacks are God-damned lazy") or in compassionate ways ("It is terrible the way they live in those neighborhoods, with those schools, without fathers, with crime just around the corner... it saddens me whenever I see all that on TV").

The pliability of the color-blind wall is further enhanced by the style of color blindness. For instance, if whites find themselves in a rhetorical bind, such as having disclosed a personal taste for whiteness or a dislike for blackness, they can always utter a disclaimer such as, "I am not prejudiced," or "If I ever fall in love with a black person, the race thing will never be an obstacle for us getting together," They can tiptoe around the most dangerous racial minefields because the stylistic elements of color blindness provide them the necessary tools to get in and out of almost any discussion. I examine these tools in detail in the next chapter.

# Notes

1. John Dollard, *Caste and Class in a Southern Town*, 2d ed. (New York: Doubleday, 1949).

2. For discussions on the "defensive beliefs" that supported Jim Crow, see Dollard, *Caste and Class*; Gunnar Myrdal, *An American Dilemma: The Negro Problem and Modern Democracy* (New York: Harper Brothers, 1944); Allison Davis et al., *Deep South* (Chicago: University of Chicago Press, 1941); and Charles S. Johnson, *Patterns of Negro Segregation* (New York: Harper Brothers, 1943).

3. This is taken from the title of conservative commentator Dinesh D'Souza's book, *The End of Racism: Principles for a Multiracial Society* (New York: Free Press, 1995). This book is, among other things, a crude example of color-blind racism.

4. J. B. Thompson, *Studies in the Theory of Ideology* (Cambridge, UK: Polity, 1984).

5. All ideologies aspire to be hegemonic, to rule the hearts of rulers and ruled. However, only those that incorporate elements of the "common sense" of the oppressed (albeit in partial and refracted manner) can truly become hegemonic.

6. See John Gray, *Liberalism* (Minneapolis: University of Minnesota Press, 1986).

7. All these quotes are from *The Communist Manifesto*. See David McLellan, ed., *Karl Marx: Selected Writings* (London: Oxford University Press, 1982). For a detailed intellectual assault at the farce of liberalism, see Karl Marx and Frederick Engels, *The German Ideology* (New York: International, 1985).

8. For a marvelous discussion of this point and of "racial capitalism," see Cedric J. Robinson, *Black Marxism: The Making of the Black Radical Tradition* (Chapel Hill: University of North Carolina Press, 2000).

9. Good examples of this trend, are Andrea T. Baumeister, *Liberalism and the "Politics of Difference"* (Edinburgh: Edinburgh University Press, 2000), and Patrick Neal, *Liberalism and Its Discontents* (New York: New York University Press, 1997). Although Baumeister skillfully shows the tensions in traditional liberal discourse that foreshadow some of today's debates and provides a reasonable philosophical resolution based on "value pluralism," she fails to point out the exclusionary character of liberalism and the Enlightenment. Neal's account

produces two interesting modifications of liberalism: the idea that liberal states cannot be neutral and the notion of "modus vivendi liberalism," which entails an open liberal approach to social issues. Yet, like Baumeister, Neal is silent about the racism of the founding fathers of liberalism and the meaning of their racial exclusions for today's liberal project.

10. Charles W. Mills, *The Racial Contract* (Ithaca, N.Y.: Cornell University Press, 1997), 27.

11. The quotes by Kant and Voltaire as well as the views of Mill on slavery and colonialism can be found in chapter 2 of David Theo Goldberg, *Racist Culture* (Cambridge, UK: Blackwell, 1993). See also Zygmunt Bauman, *Modernity and Ambivalence* (Ithaca, N.Y.: Cornell University Press, 1991).

12. Richard Bellamy, "Liberalism," in *Contemporary Political Ideologies*, edited by Roger Eatwall and Anthony Wright (Boulder, Colo.: Westview, 1993), 23–49.

13. See Dana D. Nelson, *National Citizenship: Capitalist Citizenship and the Imagined Fraternity of White Men* (Durham, N.C.: Duke University Press, 1998), and chapter 5 in Howard Zinn, *A People's History of the United States* (New York: HarperCollins, 1980).

14. From a social movements perspective, "liberal groups are those that attempt to reform social systems for the purpose of giving all groups equal opportunities," Margaret L. Andersen, *Thinking about Women: Sociological Perspectives on Sex and Gender* (New York: Macmillan, 1988), 299.

15. For a scathing critique of color-blind "radicals" such as Todd Gitlin, Michael Tomasky, Richard Rorty, Jim Sleeper, Barbara Epstein, and Eric Hobsbawm, see chapter 4 in Robin D. G. Kelley, *Yo' Mama's Disfunktional: Fighting the Culture Wars in Urban America* (Boston: Beacon, 1997).

16. The classic statement on the subject still is William Ryan, *Blaming the Victim* (New York: Vintage, 1976).

17. Charles S. Johnson, *Racial Attitudes: Interviews Revealing Attitudes of Northern and Southern White Persons, of a Wide Range of Occupational and Educational Levels, toward Negroes* (Nashville, Tenn.: Social Science Institute, Fisk University, 1946), 153.

18. It is important to note that cultural racism was part and parcel of European and American racisms. My point is that this theme has supplanted biological racism in importance and effectiveness.

19. Katherine S. Newman, *Declining Fortunes: The Withering of the American Dream* (New York: Basic, 1993), 168.

20. James Byrd was a black man murdered by three white supremacist ex-convicts in 1998 in Jasper, Texas.

21. High-level Texaco executives were caught on tape saying some racially insensitive things about blacks and other minorities a few years back, which led them to settle a lawsuit brought by minority employees accusing the company of racial discrimination in pay and promotion.

22. I borrow the phrase "reasonable racism" from Jody David Armour, *Negrophobia and Reasonable Racism* (New York: New York University Press, 1997).

23. The former label is used in the works of Lawrence Bobo and his coauthors (see introduction) and the latter by Philomena Essed, in *Diversity: Gender, Color, and Culture* (Amherst: University of Massachusetts Press, 1996).

24. When the question at hand could be perceived as racial, white support declined significantly. Thus, for example, only 21 percent of whites agreed with the proposition to increase welfare spending.

25. The specific citations for these facts can be found in the introduction, or the reader can consult my chapter, coauthored with Amanda E. Lewis, 'The 'New Racism': Toward an Analysis of the U.S. Racial Structure, 1960–1990s," in *Race, Nationality, and Citizenship*, edited by Paul Wong (Boulder, Colo.: Westview, 1999).

26. Bringing about social change in this country has never been a rational, civilized feat, particularly when racial considerations have been involved. Force and resistance have accompanied the most significant changes in America's political and racial order. We used force to achieve our independence from Britain, to keep the Union together, and to end state-sanctioned Jim Crow. An excellent little book on this subject is Irving J. Sloan, *Our Violent Past: An American Chronicle* (New York: Random House, 1970).

27. Southern sociologist Howard W. Odum took William Graham Sumner's idea of "mores" and suggested that racial conflicts must be solved through an evolutionary approach that he labeled "racial adjustments." In a similar vein, northern sociologist Robert E. Park argued that race contacts went through "race

cycles" that ended in racial assimilation. See Howard W. Odum, *American Social Problems* (New York: Holt, 1939), and Robert E. Park, *Race and Culture* (Glencoe, 111.: Free Press, 1950).

28. One respondent suggested a tax incentive policy to stimulate residential integration.

29. Despite its elitist origins in American history (see chapter 5 in Zinn, *A People's History of the United States)*, the notion of individualism has been used by social reform movements such as the Jacksonian democracy movement of the nineteenth century, the Civil Rights Movement of the 1950s and 1960s ("one man, one vote"), and the Woman's Suffrage Movement of the early 20th century ("one person, one vote") to advance truly inclusive democratic agendas.

30. David Ingram, *Group Rights: Reconciling Equality and Difference* (Lawrence: University Press of Kansas, 2000).

31. For a review, see chapter 4 in my *White Supremacy and Racism in the Post-Civil Rights Era* (Boulder, Colo.: Rienner, 2001).

32. *On all these matters, see Beverly Daniel Tatum, "Why Are All the Black Kids Sitting Together in the Cafeteria?: And Other Conversations about Race" (New York: Basic, 1997).*

33. Most of the work of this important French scholar has not been published in English. A few of his pieces have appeared in *Telos* and, fortunately, the University of Minnesota Press translated his *La Force du prejuge: Essai sur le racisme et ses doubles.* Pierre-And re Taguieff, *The Force of Prejudice: Racism and Its Doubles* (Minneapolis: University of Minnesota Press, 2001). See also Pierre-Andre Taguieff, ed., *Face au racisme, Tome II: Analyse, hypotheses, perspectives* (Paris: La Decouverte, 1991).

34. See my "'This Is a White Country': The Racial Ideology of the Western Nations of the World-System," *Research in Politics and Society* 6, no. 1 (1999): 85–102.

35. The culture of poverty argument was formally developed by anthropologist Oscar Lewis. His claim was that the poor develop a culture based on adaptations to their poverty status, which is then transmitted from generation to generation and becomes an obstacle for moving out of poverty. Although Lewis formulated his thesis as a class-based one, because the characters in his famous books, *The Children of Sanchez* (1961) and *La Vida* (1965), were Mexican and Puerto Rican, respectively, it was almost impossible not to interpret his argument as especially pertinent for understanding minorities' well-being in America. Lewis's argument was roundly condemned by many of his contemporaries, but it stuck in scholarly policy circles as well as among conservative politicians and a few "liberals" such as Senator Patrick Moynihan.

36. Charles A. Murray, *Losing Ground: American Social Policy, 1950–1980* (New York: Basic, 1984); Lawrence M. Mead, *Beyond Entitlement: The Social Obligations of Citizenship* (New York: Free Press, 1986); William Julius Wilson, *The Truly Disadvantaged: The Inner City, the Underclass, and Public Policy* (Chicago: University of Chicago Press, 1987); Cornel West, *Race Matters* (Boston: Beacon, 1993).

37. See Sharon Collins, *Black Corporate Executives: The Making and Breaking of a Black Middle Class* (Philadelphia: Temple University Press, 1997); Ellis Cose, *The Rage of a Privileged Class* (New York: HarperCollins, 1995); and Joe R. Feagin and Melvin Sikes, *Living with Racism: The Black Middle Class Experience* (Boston: Beacon, 1994).

Naturalization
Abstract Liberalism
Cultural Racism
Minimization of Racism
Meritocracy

# White Privilege

## Unpacking the Invisible Knapsack

By Peggy Mcintosh

● ● ● ● ● ● ● ● ● ● ● ● ● ● ● ● ● ● ● ● ● ● ● ● ● ● ● ● ● ● ● ● ● ● ● ● ● ● ● ● ● ● ● ● ●

## Editor's Introduction

Often cited but seldom presented in its full form, this now-classic treatise on white privilege is embraced widely as a tool for anti-racist educators. As noted in the Beverly Tatum selection, whites seldom realize how they benefit from the invisible forms of privilege, but this article by Peggy McIntosh is one of the first written by a white person addressing this topic. Perhaps more than any other issue in the United States, the assumption that all are equal under the Constitution is refuted by institutionalized racism, unofficial policies at companies to follow non-whites while they shop, and a host of other considerations. Students should engage in open discussion on this matter and realize that the definition of racism as a system of privileges enjoyed knowingly and unknowingly by whites is vital to disseminating notions of a color-blind society.

### References

McIntosh, Peggy. "White Privilege: Unpacking the Invisible Knapsack," Independent School, vol. 49, no. 2, 1990.

Through work to bring materials from Women's Studies into the rest of the curriculum, I have often noticed men's unwillingness to grant that they are over-privileged, even though they may grant that women are disadvantaged. They may say they will work to improve women's status, in the society, the university, or the curriculum, but they can't or won't support the idea of lessening men's. Denials which amount to taboos surround the subject of advantages which men gain from women's disadvantages. These denials protect male privilege from being fully acknowledged, lessened or ended.

Thinking through unacknowledged male privilege as a phenomenon, I realized that, since hierarchies in our society are interlocking, there was most likely a phenomenon of white privilege that was similarly denied and protected. As a white person, I realized I had been taught about racism as something that puts others at a disadvantage, but had been taught not to see one of its corollary aspects, white privilege, which puts me at an advantage.

I think whites are carefully taught not to recognize white privilege, as males are taught not to recognize male privilege. So I have begun in an untutored way to ask what it is like to have white privilege. I have come to see white privilege as an invisible package of unearned assets that I can count on cashing in each day, but about which I was "meant" to remain oblivious. White privilege is like an invisible weightless knapsack of special provisions, maps, passports, codebooks, visas, clothes, tools and blank checks.

Describing white privilege makes one newly accountable. As we in Women's Studies work to reveal male privilege and ask men to give up some of their power, so one who writes about white privilege must ask, "Having described it, what will I do to lessen or end it?"

After I realized the extent to which men work from a base of unacknowledged privilege, I understood that much of their oppressiveness was unconscious. Then I remembered the frequent charges from women of color that white women whom they encounter are oppressive. I began to understand why we are justly seen as oppressive, even when we don't see ourselves that way. I began to count the ways in which I enjoy unearned skin privilege and have been conditioned into oblivion about its existence.

My schooling gave me no training in seeing myself as an oppressor, as an unfairly advantaged person, or as a participant in a damaged culture. I was taught to see myself as an individual whose moral state depended on her individual moral will. My schooling followed the pattern my colleague Elizabeth Minnich has pointed out: whites are taught to think of their lives as morally neutral, normative, and average, and also ideal, so that when we work to benefit others, this is seen as work which will allow "them" to be more like "us."

I decided to try to work on myself at least by identifying some of the daily effects of white privilege in my life. I have chosen those conditions which I think in my case *attach somewhat more to skin-color privilege* than to class, religion, ethnic status, or geographic location, though of course all these other factors are intricately intertwined. As far as I can see, my African American co-workers, friends, and acquaintances with whom I come into daily or frequent contact in this particular time, place and line of work cannot count on most of these conditions.

1. I can if I wish arrange to be in the company of people of my race most of the time.
2. If I should need to move, I can be pretty sure of renting or purchasing housing in an area which I can afford and in which I would want to live.
3. I can be pretty sure that my neighbors in such a location will be neutral or pleasant to me.
4. I can go shopping alone most of the time, pretty well assured that I will not be followed or harassed.
5. I can turn on the television or open to the front page of the paper and see people of my race widely represented.
6. When I am told about our national heritage or about "civilization," I am shown that people of my color made it what it is.
7. I can be sure that my children will be given curricular materials that testify to the existence of their race.
8. If want to, I can be pretty sure of finding a publisher for this piece on white privilege.
9. I can go into a music shop and count on finding the music of my race represented, into a supermarket and find the staple foods that fit with my cultural traditions, into a hairdresser's shop and find someone who can cut my hair.
10. Whether I use checks, credit cards or cash, I can count on my skin color not to work against the appearance of financial reliability.
11. I can arrange to protect my children most of the time from people who might not like them.
12. I can swear, or dress in second-hand clothes, or not answer letters, without having people attribute these choices to the bad morals, the poverty, or the illiteracy of my race.
13. I can speak in public to a powerful male group without putting my race on trial.
14. I can do well in a challenging situation without being called a credit to my race.

15. I am never asked to speak for all the people of my racial group.

16. I can remain oblivious of the language and customs of persons of color who constitute the world's majority without feeling in my culture any penalty for such oblivion.

17. I can criticize our government and talk about how much I fear its policies and behavior without being seen as a cultural outsider.

18. I can be pretty sure that if I ask to talk to "the person in charge," I will be facing a person of my race.

19. If a traffic cop pulls me over or if the IRS audits my tax return, I can be sure I haven't been singled out because of my race.

20. I can easily buy posters, postcards, picture books, greeting cards, dolls, toys, and children's magazines featuring people of my race.

21. I can go home from most meetings of organizations I belong to feeling somewhat tied in, rather than isolated, out-of-place, outnumbered, unheard, held at a distance, or feared.

22. I can take a job with an affirmative action employer without having co-workers on the job suspect that I got it because of race.

23. I can choose public accommodations without fearing that people of my race cannot get in or will be mistreated in the places I have chosen.

24. I can be sure that if I need legal or medical help, my race will not work against me.

25. If my day, week, or year is going badly, I need not ask of each negative episode or situation whether it has racial overtones.

26. I can choose blemish cover or bandages in "flesh" color and have them more less match my skin.

I repeatedly forgot each of the realizations on this list until I wrote it down. For me, white privilege has turned out to be an elusive and fugitive subject. The pressure to avoid it is great, for in facing it I must give up the myth of meritocracy. If these things are true, this is not such a free country; one's life is not what one makes it; many doors open for certain people through no virtues of their own.

In unpacking this invisible knapsack of white privilege, I have listed conditions of daily experience that I once took for granted. Nor did I think of any of these prerequisites as bad for the holder. I now think that we need a more finely differentiated taxonomy of privilege, for some of these varieties are only what one would want for everyone in a just society, and others give license to be ignorant, oblivious, arrogant and destructive.

I see a pattern running through the matrix of white privilege, a pattern of assumptions that were passed on to me as a white person. There was one main piece of cultural turf; it was my own turf, and I was among those who could control the turf. *My skin color was an asset for any move I was educated to want to make.* I could think of myself as belonging in major ways and of making social systems work for me. I could freely disparage, fear, neglect, or be oblivious to anything outside of the dominant cultural forms. Being of the main culture, I could also criticize it fairly freely.

In proportion as my racial group was being made confident, comfortable, and oblivious, other groups were likely being made inconfident, uncomfortable, and alienated. Whiteness protected me from many kinds of hostility, distress and violence, which I was being subtly trained to visit, in turn, upon people of color.

For this reason, the word "privilege" now seems to me misleading. We usually think of privilege as being a favored state, whether earned or conferred by birth or luck. Yet some of the conditions I have described here work systematically to overempower certain groups. Such privilege simply *confers dominance* because of one's race or sex.

I want, then, to distinguish between earned strength and unearned power conferred systemically. Power from unearned privilege can look like strength when it is in fact permission to escape or to dominate. But not all of the privileges on my list are inevitably damaging. Some, like the expectation that neighbors will be decent to you, or that your race will not count against you in court, should be the norm in a just society. Others, like the privilege to ignore less powerful people, distort the humanity of the holders as well as the ignored groups.

We might at least start by distinguishing between positive advantages, which we can work to spread, and negative types of advantage, which unless rejected will always reinforce our present hierarchies. For example, the feeling that one belongs within the human circle, as Native Americans say, should not be seen as privilege for a few. Ideally it is an *unearned entitlement*. At present, since only a few have it, it is an *unearned advantage* for them. This paper results from a process of coming to see that some of the power that I originally saw as attendant on being a human being in the United States consisted in unearned advantage and conferred dominance.

I have met very few men who are truly distressed about systemic, unearned male advantage and conferred dominance. And so one question for me and others like me is whether we will be like them, or whether we will get truly distressed, even outraged, about unearned race advantage and conferred dominance, and, if so, what will we do to lessen them. In any case, we need to do more work in identifying how they actually affect our daily lives. Many, perhaps most, of our white students in the U.S. think that racism doesn't affect them because they are not people of color, they do not see "whiteness" as a racial identity. In addition, since race and sex are not the only advantaging systems at work, we need similarly to examine the daily experience of having age advantage, or ethnic advantage, or physical ability, or advantage related to nationality, religion, or sexual orientation.

Difficulties and dangers surrounding the task of finding parallels are many. Since racism, sexism, and heterosexism are not the same, the advantages associated with them should not be seen as the same. In addition, it is hard to disentangle aspects of unearned advantage which rest more on social class, economic class, race, religion, sex, and ethnic identity than on other factors. Still, all of the oppressions are interlocking, as the Combahee River Collective Statement of 1977 continues to remind us eloquently.

One factor seems clear about all of the interlocking oppressions. They take both active forms, which we can see, and embedded forms, which as a member of the dominant group one is taught not to see. In my class and place, I did not see myself as a racist because I was taught to recognize racism only in individual acts of meanness by members of my group, never in invisible systems conferring unsought racial dominance on my group from birth.

Disapproving of the systems won't be enough to change them. I was taught to think that racism could end if white individuals changed their attitudes. But a "white" skin in the United States opens many doors for whites whether or not we approve of the way dominance has been conferred on us. Individual acts can palliate, but cannot end, these problems.

To redesign social systems, we need first to acknowledge their colossal unseen dimensions. The silences and denials surrounding privilege are the key political tool here. They keep the thinking about equality or equity incomplete, protecting unearned advantage and conferred dominance by making these taboo subjects. Most talk by whites about equal opportunity seems to me now to be about equal opportunity to try to get into a position of dominance while denying that *systems* of dominance exist.

It seems to me that obliviousness about white advantage, like obliviousness about male advantage, is kept strongly inculturated in the United States so as to maintain the myth of meritocracy, the myth that democratic choice is equally available to all. Keeping most people unaware that freedom of confident action is there for just a small number of people props up those in power and serves to keep power in the hands of the same groups that have most of it already.

Although systemic change takes many decades, there are pressing questions for me and I imagine for some others like me if we raise our daily consciousness on the perquisites of being light-skinned. What will we do with such knowledge? As we know from watching men, it is an open question whether we will choose to use unearned advantage to weaken hidden systems of advantage, and whether we will use any of our arbitrarily awarded power to try to reconstruct power systems on a broader base.

*This is an authorized excerpt of McIntosh's original white privilege article, "White Privilege and Male Privilege: A Personal Account of Coming to See Correspondences through Work in Women's Studies," Working Paper 189 (1988), Wellesley Centers for Women, Wellesley College, MA.

# Defining Racism

## "Can We Talk?"

### By Beverly Daniel Tatum

## Editor's Introduction

Just as the other selections in this anthology deal with specific issues and broader terms, Beverly Tatum asserts that racism "[is] a system of privileges based on race."[1] This excerpt should be read closely and compared with the Peggy McIntosh article on white privilege. The concepts of color-blind society also arise, and thus, another good match for Eduardo Bonilla-Silva's discourse on racism without racists.

One of Tatum's goals is to open the discussion on race and make it clear that racism is alive and well in American society. However, once awareness is reached, as well as recognition, change can begin, albeit slowly.

### Notes

Tatum, Beverly Daniel. *"Why Are All the Black Kids Sitting Together in the Cafeteria?" and Other Conversations About Race.* New York: Basic Books, 2003, 7.

Early in my teaching career, a White student I knew asked me what I would be teaching the following semester. I mentioned that I would be teaching a course on racism. She replied, with some surprise in her voice, "Oh, is there still racism?" I assured her that indeed there was and suggested that she sign up for my course. Fifteen years later, after exhaustive media coverage of events such as the Rodney King beating, the Charles Stuart and Susan Smith cases, the O. J. Simpson trial, the appeal to racial prejudices in electoral politics, and the bitter debates about

affirmative action and welfare reform, it seems hard to imagine that anyone would still be unaware of the reality of racism in our society. But in fact, in almost every audience I address, there is someone who will suggest that racism is a thing of the past. There is always someone who hasn't noticed the stereotypical images of people of color in the media, who hasn't observed the housing discrimination in their community, who hasn't read the newspaper articles about documented racial bias in lending practices among well-known banks, who isn't aware of the racial tracking pattern at the local school, who hasn't seen the reports of rising incidents of racially motivated hate crimes in America—in short, someone who hasn't been paying attention to issues of race. But if you are paying attention, the legacy of racism is not hard to see, and we are all affected by it.

The impact of racism begins early. Even in our preschool years, we are exposed to misinformation about people different from ourselves. Many of us grew up in neighborhoods where we had limited opportunities to interact with people different from our own families. When I ask my college students, "How many of you grew up in neighborhoods where most of the people were from the same racial group as your own?" almost every hand goes up. There is still a great deal of social segregation in our communities. Consequently, most of the early information we receive about "others"—people racially, religiously, or socio-economically different from ourselves—does not come as the result of firsthand experience. The secondhand information we do receive has often been distorted, shaped by cultural stereotypes, and left incomplete.

Some examples will highlight this process. Several years ago one of my students conducted a research project investigating preschoolers' conceptions of Native Americans. Using children at a local day care center as her participants, she asked these three- and four-year-olds to draw a picture of a Native American. Most children were stumped by her request. They didn't know what a Native American was. But when she rephrased the question and asked them to draw a picture of an Indian, they readily complied. Almost every picture included one central feature: feathers. In fact, many of them also included a weapon—a knife or tomahawk—and depicted the person in violent or aggressive terms. Though this group of children, almost all of whom were White, did not live near a large Native American population and probably had had little if any personal interaction with American Indians, they all had internalized an image of what Indians were like. How did they know? Cartoon images, in particular the Disney movie *Peter Pan* were cited by the children as

their number-one source of information. At the age of three, these children already had a set of stereotypes in place. Though I would not describe three-year-olds as prejudiced, the stereotypes to which they have been exposed become the foundation for the adult prejudices so many of us have.

Sometimes the assumptions we make about others come not from what we have been told or what we have seen on television or in books, but rather from what we have *not* been told. The distortion of historical information about people of color leads young people (and older people, too) to make assumptions that may go unchallenged for a long time. Consider this conversation between two White students following a discussion about the cultural transmission of racism:

"Yeah, I just found out that Cleopatra was actually a Black woman"

"What?"

The first student went on to explain her newly learned information. The second student exclaimed in disbelief, "That can't be true. Cleopatra was beautiful!"

What had this young woman learned about who in our society is considered beautiful and who is not? Had she conjured up images of Elizabeth Taylor when she thought of Cleopatra? The new information her classmate had shared and her own deeply ingrained assumptions about who is beautiful and who is not were too incongruous to allow her to assimilate the information at that moment.

Omitted information can have similar effects. For example, another young woman, preparing to be a high school English teacher, expressed her dismay that she had never learned about any Black authors in any of her English courses. How was she to teach about them to her future students when she hadn't learned about them herself? A White male student in the class responded to this discussion with frustration in his response journal, writing "Its not my fault that Blacks don't write books" Had one of his elementary, high school, or college teachers ever told him that there were no Black writers? Probably not. Yet because he had never been exposed to Black authors, he had drawn his own conclusion that there were none.

Stereotypes, omissions, and distortions all contribute to the development of prejudice. *Prejudice* is a preconceived judgment or opinion, usually based on limited information. I assume that we all have prejudices, not because we want them, but simply because we are so continually exposed to misinformation about others. Though I have often heard students or workshop participants describe someone as not having "a prejudiced bone in his body," I usually suggest that they look again. Prejudice is one of the inescapable consequences of living in a racist society. Cultural racism—the cultural images and messages that affirm the assumed superiority of Whites and the assumed inferiority of people of color—is like among in the air. Sometimes it is so thick it is visible, other times it is less apparent, but always, day in and day out, we are breathing it in. None of us would introduce ourselves as "smog-breathers" (and most of us don't want to be described as prejudiced), but if we live in a smoggy place, how can we avoid breathing the air? If we live in an environment in which we are bombarded with stereotypical images in the media, are frequently exposed to the ethnic jokes of friends and family members, and are rarely informed of the accomplishments of oppressed groups, we will develop the negative categorizations of those groups that form the basis of prejudice.

People of color as well as Whites develop these categorizations. Even a member of the stereotyped group may internalize the stereotypical categories about his or her own group to some degree. In fact, this process happens so frequently that it has a name, *internalized oppression*. Some of the consequences of believing the distorted messages about ones own group will be discussed in subsequent chapters.

Certainly some people are more prejudiced than others, actively embracing and perpetuating negative and hateful images of those who are different from themselves. When we claim to be free of prejudice, perhaps what we are really saying is that we are not hate-mongers. But none of us is completely innocent. Prejudice is an integral part of our socialization, and it is not our fault. Just as the preschoolers my student interviewed are not to blame for the negative messages they internalized, we are not at fault for the stereotypes, distortions, and omissions that shaped our thinking as we grew up.

To say that it is not our fault does not relieve us of responsibility, however. We may not have polluted the air, but we need to take responsibility, along with others, for cleaning it up. Each of us needs to look at our own behavior. Am I perpetuating and reinforcing the negative messages so pervasive in our culture, or am I seeking to challenge them? If I have not been exposed to positive images of marginalized groups, am I seeking them out, expanding my own knowledge base for myself and my children? Am I acknowledging and examining my own prejudices, my own rigid categorizations of others, thereby minimizing the adverse impact they might have on my interactions with those I have categorized? Unless we engage in these and other conscious acts of reflection and reeducation, we easily repeat the process with our children. We teach what we were taught. The unexamined prejudices of the parents are passed on to the children. It is not our fault, but it is our responsibility to interrupt this cycle.

## Racism: A System of Advantage Based on Race

Many people use the terms *prejudice* and *racism* interchangeably. I do not, and I think it is important to make a distinction. In his book *Portraits of White Racism,* David Wellman argues convincingly that limiting our understanding of racism to prejudice does not offer a sufficient explanation for the persistence of racism. He defines racism as a "system of advantage based on race." In illustrating this definition, he provides example after example of how Whites defend their racial advantage—access to better schools, housing, jobs—even when they do not embrace overtly prejudicial thinking. Racism cannot be fully explained as an expression of prejudice alone.

This definition of racism is useful because it allows us to see that racism, like other forms of oppression, is not only a personal ideology based on racial prejudice, but a *system* involving cultural messages and institutional policies and practices as well as the beliefs and actions of individuals. In the context of the United States, this system clearly operates to the advantage of Whites and to the disadvantage of people of color. Another related definition of racism, commonly used by antiracist educators and consultants, is "prejudice plus power." Racial prejudice when combined with social power—access to social, cultural, and economic resources and decision-making—leads to the institutionalization of racist policies and practices. While I think this definition also captures the idea that racism is more than individual beliefs and attitudes, I prefer Wellman's definition because the idea of systematic advantage and disadvantage is critical to an understanding of how racism operates in American society.

In addition, I find that many of my White students and workshop participants do not feel powerful. Defining racism as prejudice plus power has little personal relevance. For some, their response to this definition is the following: "I'm not really prejudiced, and I have no power, so racism has nothing to do with me." However, most White people, if they are really being honest with themselves, can see that there are advantages to being White in the United States. Despite the current rhetoric about affirmative action and "reverse racism," every social indicator, from salary to life expectancy, reveals the advantages of being White.

The systematic advantages of being White are often referred to as White privilege. In a now well-known article, "White Privilege: Unpacking the Invisible Knapsack," Peggy McIntosh, a White feminist scholar, identified a long list of societal privileges that she received simply because she was White. She did not ask for them, and it is important to note that she hadn't always noticed that she was receiving them. They included major and minor advantages. Of course she enjoyed greater access to jobs and housing. But she also was able to shop in department stores without being followed by suspicious salespeople and could always find appropriate hair care products and makeup in any drugstore. She could send her child to school confident that the teacher would not discriminate against him on the basis of race. She could also be late for meetings, and talk with her mouth full, fairly confident that these behaviors would not be attributed to the fact that she was White. She could express an opinion in a meeting or in print and not have it labeled the "White" viewpoint. In other words, she was more often than not viewed as an individual, rather than as a member of a racial group.

This article rings true for most White readers, many of whom may have never considered the benefits of being White. It's one thing to have enough awareness of racism to describe the ways that people of color are disadvantaged by it. But this new understanding of racism is more elusive. In very concrete terms, it means that if a person of color is the victim of housing discrimination, the apartment that would otherwise have been rented to that person of color is still available for a White person. The White tenant is, knowingly or unknowingly, the beneficiary of racism, a system of advantage based on race. The unsuspecting tenant is not to blame for the prior discrimination, but she benefits from it anyway.

For many Whites, this new awareness of the benefits of a racist system elicits considerable pain, often accompanied by feelings of anger and guilt. These uncomfortable emotions can hinder further discussion. We all like to think that we deserve the good things we have received, and that others, too, get what they deserve. Social psychologists call this tendency a "belief in a jus world." Racism directly contradicts such notions of justice.

Understanding racism as a system of advantage based on race is antithetical to traditional notions of an American meritocracy. For those who have internalized this myth, this definition generates considerable discomfort. It is more comfortable simply to think of racism as a particular form of prejudice. Notions of power or privilege do not have to be addressed when our understanding of racism is constructed in that way.

The discomfort generated when a systemic definition of racism is introduced is usually quite visible in the workshops I lead. Someone in the group is usually quick to point out that this is not the definition you will find in most dictionaries. I reply, "Who wrote the dictionary?" I am not being facetious with this response. Whose interests are served by a "prejudice only" definition of racism? It is important to understand that the system of advantage is perpetuated when we do not acknowledge its existence.

## Racism: For Whites Only?

Frequently someone will say, "You keep talking about White people. People of color can be racist, too." I once asked a White teacher what it would mean to her if a student or parent of color accused her of being racist. She said she would feel as though she had been punched in the stomach or called a "low-life scum." She is not alone in this feeling. The word *racist* holds a lot of emotional power. For many White people, to be called racist is the ultimate insult. The idea that this term might only be applied to Whites becomes highly problematic for after all, can't people of color be "low-life scum" too?

Of course, people of any racial group can hold hateful attitudes and behave in racially discriminatory and bigoted ways. We can all cite examples of horrible hate crimes which have been perpetrated by people of color as well as Whites. Hateful behavior is hateful behavior no matter who does it. But when I am asked, "Can people of color be racist?" I reply, "The answer depends on your definition of racism." If one defines racism as racial prejudice, the answer is yes. People of color can and do have racial prejudices. However, if one defines racism as a system of advantage based on race, the answer is no. People of color are not racist because they do not systematically benefit from racism. And equally important, there is no systematic cultural and institutional support or sanction for the racial bigotry of people of color. In my view, reserving the term *racist* only for behaviors committed by Whites in the context of a White-dominated society is a way of acknowledging the ever-present power differential afforded Whites by the culture and institutions that make up the system of advantage and continue to reinforce notions of White superiority (Using the same logic, I reserve the word *sexist* for men. Though women can and do have gender-based prejudices, only men systematically benefit from sexism.)

Despite my best efforts to explain my thinking on this point, there are some who will be troubled, perhaps even incensed, by my response. To call the racially motivated acts of a person of color acts of racial bigotry and to describe similar acts committed by Whites as racist will make no sense to some people, including some people of color. To those, I will respectfully say, "We can agree to disagree." At moments like these, it is not agreement that is essential, but clarity. Even if you don't like the definition of racism I am using, hopefully you are now clear about what it is. If I also understand how you are using the term, our conversation can continue—despite our disagreement.

Another provocative question I'm often asked is "Are you saying all Whites are racist?" When asked this question, I again remember that White teacher's response, and I am conscious that perhaps the question I am really being asked is, "Are you saying all Whites are bad people?" The answer to that question is of course not. However, all White people, intentionally or unintentionally, do benefit from racism. A more relevant question is what are White people as individuals doing to interrupt racism? For many White people, the image of a racist is a hood-wearing Klan member or a name-calling Archie Bunker figure. These images represent what might be called *active racism*, blatant, intentional acts of racial bigotry and discrimination. *Passive racism* is more subtle and can be seen in the collusion of laughing when a racist joke is told, of letting exclusionary hiring practices go unchallenged, of accepting as appropriate the omissions of people of color from the curriculum, and of avoiding difficult race-related issues. Because racism is so ingrained in the fabric of American institutions, it is easily self-perpetuating. All that is required to maintain it is business as usual.

I sometimes visualize the ongoing cycle of racism as a moving walkway at the airport. Active racist behavior is equivalent to walking fast on the conveyor belt. The person engaged in active racist behavior has identified with the ideology of White supremacy and is moving with it. Passive racist behavior is equivalent to standing still on the walkway. No overt effort is being made, but the conveyor belt moves the bystanders along to the same destination as those who are actively walking. Some of the bystanders may feel the motion of the conveyor belt, see the active racists ahead of them, and choose to turn around, unwilling to go to the same destination as the White supremacists. But unless they are walking actively in the opposite direction at a speed faster than the conveyor belt—unless they are actively antiracist—they will find themselves carried along with the others.

So, not all Whites are actively racist. Many are passively racist. Some, though not enough, are actively antiracist. The relevant question is not whether all Whites are racist, but how we can move more White people from a position of active or passive racism to one of active antiracism? The task of interrupting racism is obviously not the task of Whites alone. But the fact of White privilege means that Whites have greater access to the societal institutions in need of transformation. To whom much is given, much is required.

It is important to acknowledge that while all Whites benefit from racism, they do not all benefit equally. Other factors, such as socioeconomic status, gender, age, religious affiliation, sexual orientation, mental and physical ability, also play a role in our access to social influence and power. A White woman on welfare is not privileged to the same extent as a wealthy White heterosexual man. In her case, the systematic disadvantages of sexism and classism intersect with her White privilege, but the privilege is still there. This point was brought home to me in a 1994 study conducted by a Mount Holyoke graduate student, Phyllis Wentworth. Wentworth interviewed a group of female college students, who were both older than their peers and were the first members of their families to attend college, about the pathways that lead them to college. All of the women interviewed were White, from working-class backgrounds, from families where women were expected to graduate from high school and get married or get a job. Several had experienced abusive relationships and other personal difficulties prior to coming to college. Yet their experiences were punctuated by "good luck" stories of apartments obtained without a deposit, good jobs offered without experience or extensive reference checks, and encouragement provided by willing mentors.

While the women acknowledged their good fortune, none of them discussed their Whiteness. They had not considered the possibility that being White had worked in their favor and helped give them the benefit of the doubt at critical junctures. This study clearly showed that even under difficult circumstances, White privilege was still operating.

It is also true that not all people of color are equally targeted by racism. We all have multiple identities that shape our experience. I can describe myself as a light-skinned, well-educated, heterosexual, able-bodied, Christian African American woman raised in a middle-class suburb. As an African American woman, I am systematically disadvantaged by race and by gender, but I systematically receive benefits in the other categories, which then mediate my experience of racism and sexism. When one is targeted by multiple isms—racism, sexism, classism, heterosexism, ableism, anti-Semitism, ageism—in whatever combination, the effect is intensified. The particular combination of racism and classism in many communities of color is life-threatening. Nonetheless, when I, the middle-class Black mother of two sons, read another story about a Black man's unlucky encounter with a White police officer's deadly force, I am reminded that racism by itself can kill.

## The Cost of Racism

Several years ago, a White male student in my psychology of racism course wrote in his journal at the end of the semester that he had learned a lot about racism and now understood in a way he never had before just how advantaged he was. He also commented that he didn't think he would do anything to try to change the situation. After all, the system was working in his favor. Fortunately, his response was not typical. Most of my students leave my course with the desire (and an action plan) to interrupt the cycle of racism. However, this young man's response does raise an important question. Why should Whites who are advantaged by racism *want* to end that system of advantage? What are the *costs* of that system to them?

A *Money* magazine article called "Race and Money" chronicled the many ways the American economy was hindered by institutional racism. Whether one looks at productivity lowered by racial tensions in the workplace, or real estate equity lost through housing discrimination, or the tax revenue lost in underemployed communities of color, or the high cost of warehousing human talent in prison, the economic costs of racism are real and measurable.

As a psychologist, I often hear about the less easily measured costs. When I ask White men and women how racism hurts them, they frequently talk about their fears of people of color, the social incompetence they feel in racially mixed situations, the alienation they have experienced between parents and children when a child marries into a family of color, and the interracial friendships they had as children that were lost in adolescence or young adulthood without their ever understanding why. White people are paying a significant price for the system of advantage. The cost is not as high for Whites as it is for people of color, but a price is being paid. Wendell Berry, a White writer raised in Kentucky, captures this psychic pain in the opening pages of his book, *The Hidden Wound:*

> If white people have suffered less obviously from racism than black people, they have nevertheless suffered greatly; the cost has been greater perhaps than we can yet know. If the white man has inflicted the wound of racism upon black men, the cost has been that he would receive the mirror image of that wound into himself. As the master, or as a member of the dominant race, he has felt little compulsion to acknowledge it or speak of it; the more painful it has grown the more deeply he has hidden it within himself. But the wound is there, and it is a profound disorder, as great a damage in his mind as it is in his society.

The dismantling of racism is in the best interests of everyone.

## A Word About Language

Throughout this chapter I have used the term *White,* to refer to Americans of European descent. In another era, I might have used the term *Caucasian.* I have used the term *people of color* to refer to those groups in America that are and have been historically targeted by racism. This includes people of African descent, people of Asian descent, people of Latin American descent, and indigenous peoples (sometimes referred to as Native Americans or American Indians)." Many people refer to these groups collectively as non-Whites. This term is particularly offensive because it defines groups of people in terms of what they are not. (Do we call women "non-men?") I also avoid using the term *minorities* because it represents another kind of distortion of information which we need to correct. So-called minorities represent the majority of the world's population. While the term *people of color* is inclusive, it is not perfect. As a workshop participant once said, White people have color, too. Perhaps it would be more accurate to say "people of more color," though I am not ready to make that change. Perhaps fellow psychologist Linda James Myers is on the right track. She refers to two groups of people, those of acknowledged African descent and those of unacknowledged African descent, reminding us that we can all trace the roots of our common humanity to Africa.

I refer to people of acknowledged African descent as Black. I know that *African American* is also a commonly used term, and I often refer to myself and other Black people born and raised in America in that way. Perhaps because I am a child of the 1960s "Black and beautiful" era, I still prefer *Black*. The term is more inclusive than *African American,* because there are Black people in the United States who are not African American—Afro-Caribbeans, for example—yet are targeted by racism, and are identified as Black.

When referring to other groups of color, I try to use the terms that the people themselves want to be called. In some cases, there is no clear consensus. For example, some people of Latin American ancestry prefer *Latino,* while others prefer *Hispanic* or, if of Mexican descent, *Chicano.* The terms *Latino* and *Hispanic* are used interchangeably here. Similarly, there are regional variations in the use of the terms *Native American, American Indian,* and *Indian. American Indian* and *Native people* are now more widely used than *Native American,* and the language used here reflects that. People of Asian descent include Pacific Islanders, and that is reflected in the terms *Asian/Pacific Islanders* and *Asian Pacific Americans.* However, when quoting others I use whichever terms they use.

My dilemma about the language to use reflects the fact that race is a social construction. Despite myths to the contrary, biologists tell us that the only meaningful racial categorization is that of human. Van den Berghe defines race as "a group that is socially defined but on the basis of *physical* criteria," including skin color and facial features.

*Racial identity development,* a central focus of this book, usually refers to the process of defining for oneself the personal significance and social meaning of belonging to a particular racial group. The terms *racial identity* and *ethnic identity* are often used synonymously, though a distinction can be made between the two. An ethnic group is a socially defined group based on *culture* criteria, such as language, customs, and shared history.

An individual might identify as a member of an ethnic group (Irish or Italian, for example) but might not think of himself in racial terms (as White). On the other hand, one may recognize the personal significance of racial group membership (identifying as Black, for instance) but may not consider ethnic identity (such as West Indian) as particularly meaningful.

Both racial and ethnic categories are socially constructed, and social definitions of these categories have changed over time. For example, in his book *Ethnic Identity: The Transformation of White America,* Richard Alba points out that the high rates of intermarriage and the dissolution of other social boundaries among European ethnic groups in the United States have reduced the significance of ethnic identity for these groups. In their place, he argues, a new ethnic identity is emerging, that of European American.

Throughout this [work], I refer primarily to racial identity. It is important, however, to acknowledge that ethnic identity and racial identity sometimes intersect. For example, dark-skinned Puerto Ricans may identify culturally as Puerto Rican and yet be categorized racially by others as Black on the basis of physical appearance. In the case of either racial or ethnic identity, these identities remain most salient to individuals of racial or ethnic groups that have been historically disadvantaged or marginalized.

The language we use to categorize one another racially is imperfect. These categories are still evolving as the current debate over Census classifications indicates. The original creation of racial categories was in the service of oppression. Some may argue that to continue to use them is to continue that oppression. I respect that argument. Yet it is difficult to talk about what is essentially a flawed and problematic social construct without using language that is itself problematic. We have to be able to talk about it in order to change it. So this is the language I choose.

## Study Terms

Prejudice
Cultural Racism
Internalized Oppression
Racism
Racial Prejudice
White Privilege
Active Racism
Passive Racism
Racial Identity Development
Ethnic Identity
Ethnic Group

# Afro-Latin America

# The Leather Strap

By Jorge Amado

•••••••••••••••••••••••••••••••••••••••••••••

## Editor's Introduction

Situated in the late 1960s or early 1970s, Brazil was in the midst of a twenty-one-year military dictatorship. The conservative element in Brazilian society emanated from the strong influence of the Catholic Church and the government that sought to restrict land reforms and curtail socialist movements during the Cold War. One conflict, however, is the presence of Afro-Brazilian religions, such as *candomblé*, in Salvador de Bahia, a legacy of the slave trade that officially ended in 1888. Other themes that arise from this excerpt by Jorge Amado are issues of mixed race, religious prejudices, self-hatred, and internalized racism. Today in Brazil a new element of religious discrimination toward the Afro-Brazilian faiths is evident from the growth of evangelical and Pentecostal churches that actively seek to weaken the Catholic traditions and "pagan idolatry."

## References

Amado, Jorge. *The War of the Saints.* Translated by Gregory Rabassa. New York: Dial Press, 2005.
Chestnut, R. Andrew. *Competitive Spirits: Latin America's New Religious Economy.* New York: Oxford University Press, 2007.

### Adalgisa at the Street Door
### with the Five Wounds of Christ

Adalgisa's yell shook the foundations of the Avenida da Ave-Maria: "Inside, right now, filthy brat! Slut!"

Manela scurried off, fleeing her aunt so that when Adalgisa lifted her arm for the slap, the girl was nowhere to be seen. She must have gone through the always wide-open door of Damiana's house. To Adalgisa it even looked like a brothel, with all that coming and going of people, in and out.

Damiana was a candy-maker, and in the morning she prepared pots of dough for the cakes of cassava, corn, and sweet manioc that an insolent troop of black urchins peddled from door to door in the afternoons to regular customers. A masterful sweets-maker, Sweet-Rice Damiana was famous—oh! Damiana's sweet rice, just thinking about it makes your mouth water—not just in the Barbalho district; her clientele was spread throughout the four corners of the city.

During June, the month of the festivals of Saint John and Saint Peter, she couldn't fill all the orders for corn and coconut mush, tamales, and honey-corn cakes. It was a happy, hard-working house. Comparing it to a brothel showed an excess of ill will, but Adalgisa wasn't one for halfway measures. Besides, Adalgisa knew nothing about brothels, outside or in. If she chanced to pass a woman of pleasure on the street, she would spit to the side to show her disgust and disapproval. She considered herself a lady, not just an ordinary woman: Ladies have principles, and they demonstrate them.

An expert in amplified speech, she didn't lower her voice but yelled so the neighbor woman would hear her:

"I swear by the Five Wounds of Christ that I'm going to put an end to that love affair if it's the last thing I do in my life! God will give me the strength to stand up to such lowlifes trying to take a young girl down the wrong road, the road to perdition! The Lord is with me—I'm not afraid, nothing can touch me, that nigger business won't get anywhere with me. I'm cut from better cloth, don't need to mix with any common people. I'll get the sin out of that girl if it costs me what health I've got left."

Adalgisa was always complaining about her fragile health, because in spite of her healthy appearance, she was subject to recurring migraines, continuing headaches that often persisted day and night, turning her mood bitter, driving her out of her mind. She blamed her acquaintances and relatives, not to mention the whole neighborhood, but especially her niece and her husband, for all the migraine attacks that persecuted and plagued her. Dona Adalgisa Perez Correia, of touted Spanish blood on her father's side and whispered African blood on her mother's, was the nightmare, the terror of her street.

## Adalgisa's Hips, and the Rest of Her Body

It wasn't even a street: The Avenida da Ave-Maria was nothing but a blind alley, a cul-de-sac, to use Professor Joao Batista de Lima e Silva's pedantic phrase. Still a bachelor in his forties, the professor lived in the last little house on the alley, also the smallest. Whenever he heard Adalgisa's ill-tempered echoes, he went to the window, lowered his reading glasses, and rested his eyes on his irritable neighbor's hips.

Adalgisa was certainly irritating—but she was a knockout in looks. Everything has its compensation. In the mediocre setting of the alley, bereft of lawns and gardens, of trees and flowers, the real compensation was Adalgisa's derriere, which reaffirmed the beauty of the universe. The fanny of a Venus, Aphrodite's bottom, worthy of a painting by Goya—so meditated the professor. He, too, exaggerated somewhat, as can be seen.

The rest of Adalgisa's body was nothing to be sneezed at either—quite to the contrary, the professor allowed, feasting his eyes: full, firm breasts, long legs, black braids encircling an oblong Spanish face with eyes of fury, burning dramatically. A pity she had such an aggressive demeanor. On the day Adalgisa lost her arrogant, mocking, and disdainful ways, her air of superiority, on the day Adalgisa left the Five Wounds of Christ in peace and smiled without rancor, without affectation—oh! on that day her beauty would transfix the heart, inspire the poets' verses.

From her father's side, the Perez y Perezes, Adalgisa got her pious and penitent behavior, displayed in Holy Week processions in Seville, carrying the cross of Christ. She acknowledged only that side of her family, not wishing to know anything about her mother's. She took no pride in her Goya hips, and if she knew about Venus, beautiful but missing both arms, she'd never heard tell of Aphrodite.

## The Junior Partner

The angry cavalcade of threats reached its peak of rage when Adalgisa recognized, sitting behind the wheel of the taxi parked by the entrance to the alley, Miro. The mangy dog was waving at her, that cynical, cheeky, insolent pauper! But then, noticing that she was also being observed by the professor, a solid citizen, teacher, journalist, she nodded courteously, feeling obliged to explain her fury and bad manners:

"I'm bearing my cross, paying for my sins," she said. "That's what comes of raising other people's children: blame and mortification. That wretched girl is leaving me all skin and bones, ruining my health, driving me to my grave. Never seen anything like it, a girl barely seventeen."

"That's youth." The professor tried to make excuses without knowing exactly what Manela's crime was. He suspected that she'd been fooling around with her boyfriend—could she have actually done it already? A girl of seventeen? The aunt was blind; she hadn't noticed that Manela was all woman, headstrong and wiggly, an appetizing body, ready for bed. Wasn't she a candidate for Miss Something-or-Other? "You've got to be patient with young people."

"More patient than I've been?" Adalgisa was horrified. "You don't know the half of it, professor! If I were to tell you—"

If Manela still hadn't, the professor thought, she was wasting her time. Drugstores sold the Pill without requiring any prescription. Freed from the fears of pregnancy, the girls of today live it up, in a wild hurry, their tails on fire. They don't follow Adalgisa's ideal of chastity and honor.

As everyone was tired of hearing, Adalgisa had had no gentlemen friends until she met Danilo, her first and the only one, the man who had led her to the altar a virgin and pure. Well, a virgin, maybe—pure is more doubtful. There's no morality capable of passing through a yearlong engagement unscathed; a few daring things, minimal as they might be, always end up happening: a hand on the breast, a tool between the thighs. Danilo Correia was a modest but enterprising clerk in the notary office of the Wilson Guimaraes Vieira, and a former soccer star; he was the worthy opponent of the professor at checkers and backgammon, fortunate husband, exclusive master of those sumptuous hips and the rest of Adalgisa's body, that chaste, virtuous woman—what a pity! the professor thought.

Actually, Professor Joao Batista de Lima e Silva was mistaken. He knew Adalgisa was chaste, but he hadn't guessed she was prudish. Danilo at the very most was a junior partner. The one who actually mastered Adalgisa's body, who determined the rules in her bed, was Christ our Lord.

## Historical Note

This is a solemn promise. In a little while we'll return to the burning and controversial subject of Adalgisa's prudishness, her Catholic bed, governed by her father confessor each Sunday in the confessional of the Church of Sant'Ana, before ten o'clock mass and holy communion. We will also get to the Spartan personality of her confessor, the Reverend Father Jose Antonio Hernandez, a Falangist, incorruptible, master of the fires of hell, missionary to Brazil—*me cago en Dios,* what a painful, rotten mission!—custodian of Adalgisa's purity. When we do, we will recount, with all the necessary details, the bitter vicissitudes of the clerk Danilo Correia, her noncompliant victim.

First, however, the figure of Manela must come to the fore, now only barely glimpsed as she disappeared from her aunt's sight into the wide-open door of fat Damiana's house. From Damiana's house emerged the appetizing smell of spices mixed with coconut milk and grated lemon cooking in the oven: vanilla and clove, cinnamon, ginger, almonds, and cashew nuts.

In Professor Joao Batista's ponderings, doubts about Manela have been raised. Why did her aunt Adalgisa want to punish her? Was she still a virgin, or did she already know the taste of what's good? Was she or wasn't she running for Miss Something-or-Other? It's important to clear up such uncertainties because a few pages back it was announced that it was to free Manela from captivity that Oya Yansan, the *iaba* who has no fear of the dead and whose very cry lights up the craters of volcanos on the summits of mountains, was visiting the City of Bahia, her sack of thunder and lightning strapped over her shoulder. So in the end, what was the question of Manela?

Her name was Manela, just as it's written—not Manuela, as was asked whenever her name was seen or heard, as if to correct a spelling mistake or mispronunciation. It was a name she inherited from her Italian ancestor, whose memory was kept within the family because the beauty of that first Manela, a scandalous and fatal beauty, had become legendary. Two dashing and foolish lieutenant colonels, in disrespect of orders, had fought a duel over this earlier Manela; one governor of a province had conceived a passion and killed himself for her; one priest on his way to the honors of a bishopric had committed a sacrilege, reneged on his eminence, tossed his cassock aside, and run off to live with her.

In order to familiarize oneself with the extensive and lively chronicle of Manela Belini, with the precise details of names and dates, titles and offices, a reading of the chapter in *Supplement to the History of the Province of Bahia,* by Professor Luis Henrique Dias Tavares, is recommended. It records the triumphs of this diva in the theater, who sang operatic arias for ecstatic audiences; the deadly duel with swords in which the honor of La Belini was bathed in blood—only a few drops, but sufficient; the rumors about the governor's suicide; and the concubinage with the priest, which resulted in the Bahian family and the tradition of the name Manela. It's pleasant reading, in spite of the title.

Luis Henrique Dias Tavares, historian, is the alter ego of the fiction writer Luis Henrique, or Luis Henrique *tout court,* as his colleague and intimate friend Joao Batista de Lima e Silva would say. The fiction writer used the episode of the priest to create a charming picaresque novel. It's difficult to say who deserves greater praise, the historian or the novelist—it would be best to read both.

Eufrasio Belini do Espirito Santo, the descendant of the sacrilege, liked retelling stories about his great-grandmother during rounds of beer and conversation—a gorgeous Italian woman she was, whose hair blew in the wind. The day he had a daughter he gave her the name Manela. He was a romantic and a reveler.

Our Manela did not come from Seville; nor did she participate in any Procession of the Dead Lord on Good Fridays. No, her procession was that of Bomfim Thursday or if you will, the washing festival, the waters of Oxala, the most important festival in Bahia, unique in all the world. Nor did our Manela wrap herself in atonement and penitence, cover herself with a black mantilla, or recite the litany to the sinister sound of rattles: *"Mea culpa! Mea culpa!"* Her aunt Adalgisa so repented, pounding her chest. But Manela came wrapped in joy and merriment, dressed in the dazzling traditional white dress of a Baiana, a Bahian woman. On her head, balanced over her torso, she carried the jug of scented water for washing the Church of Bomfim, and she went along dancing and singing Carnival songs to the irresistible sounds of the music truck.

That year, for the first time, Manela took her place among the Baianas on Bomfim Thursday. In order to walk in the procession—unbeknownst to her aunt, needless to say—she had played hookey from her English class in the intersession program at the Americans' institute. She played hookey in a proper fashion, however, because the day before the procession the class had unanimously informed Bob Burnet, the teacher, of their decision not to attend that day in order to take part in the washing festival Curious about Bahian customs, young Bob not only went along with the idea but proposed that he keep them company, and he did so with his well-known thoroughness: he *samba-ed* ceaselessly under the burning January sun, bloating himself with beer. He was what you'd call a nice guy.

Manela changed her clothes at the house of her other aunt, Gildete, who lived nearby in Tororo. Manela's parents, Dolores and Eufrasio, had died in an automobile accident several years ago, while returning in the early morning hours from a wedding party in Feira de Sant'Ana. Eufrasio, who was behind the wheel, hadn't had time to get out of the way of a truck loaded with cases of beer. After the funeral, Adalgisa had taken charge of thirteen-year-old Manela, while Gildete took charge of Marieta, Manela's sister, who was a year younger. Although Gildete was a widow and mother of three children, she had wanted to keep both girls, but Adalgisa wouldn't allow it: The sister of Dolores, she was just as much an aunt to the girls as Eufrasio's sister was. She took on her responsibilities, fulfilled her duty. God had not given her children, so she dedicated herself to making a lady out of Manela—a lady of principle.

Adalgisa kept to herself her opinion of the fate that had been awarded Marieta, relegated as she had been to an environment whose customs she considered censurable—and Adalgisa never passed up an occasion to censure them. Gildete was the widow of a shopkeeper at the market and a public schoolteacher. She was not a lady, although she was a very good person. So that we keep everything out in the open, it's worth quickly mentioning the general opinion of all their friends and acquaintances, who agreed that in the lottery of orphanhood, it was Marieta who had won the grand prize.

On Bomfim Thursday, Manela had arrived at the steps of the Church of the Conceicao da Praia, the dwelling of Yemanja, to begin the revelry. She'd come early in the morning in the company of Aunt Gildete, Marieta, and Cousin Violeta, and they mingled with dozens of Baianas as they waited for the procession to form. What do we mean, dozens? Actually, there were hundreds of Baianas gathered on the steps of the church, all in the elegance of their ritualistic white costume: the wide skirt, the starched petticoat, the smock of lace and embroidery, the low-heeled sandals, On their arms and necks they displayed silver *balanganda* bracelets and necklaces, jewelry and armbands in the colors of their saints. The pot, jug, or jar on the turban atop their heads carried scented water for their obligation. *Maes de santo* and *filhas de santo* of all Afro-Bahian nations were there—Nago, Jeje, Ijexa, Angola, Congo—and copper-colored beauties of the mulatto nations, full of coquetry and merriment. Manela, perhaps the prettiest of all, was blooming with excitement. Up on the trucks the *atabaque* drums were throbbing, calling the people together. Suddenly music

exploded from a Carnival truck, and the dancing began.

The procession wound all the way from the Church of the Conceicao da Praia, along the Lacerda Elevator, up to the Church of Bomfim on Sacred Hill, for a distance of six miles, more or less, depending on the quantity of devotion and cane liquor consumed by the participants. Thousands of people—the procession was a sea of people—it stretched out of sight. Cars, trucks, carriages, and donkeys festooned with flowers and sprigs, carrying full barrels on their backs; all ensured there would be no lack of scented water for the ceremony. In the trucks were lively groups, whole families, *samba* clubs, and *afoxes*. Musicians clutched their instruments: guitars, accordions, ukeleles, tambourines, *capoeira berimbaus*. Popular singers and composers were there, like Tiao the Chauffeur, River Man, Chocolate, and Paulinho Camafeu. The voices of Jeronimo, of Moraes Moreira were heard. In riding breeches, white jacket, dandified, kinky cotton hair, Batatinha, "Small Potatoes," smiled while crossing the street. People shook his hand, shouted his name, "Batatinha!" embraced him. A blond—American, Italian, from Sao Paulo?—ran over and kissed him on his black and beautiful face.

Rich and poor mingled, rubbing elbows. In the mixed-blood city of Bahia, all shades of color exist in the flesh of its inhabitants, ranging from a black so dark it's blue, to milky white, the color of snow, and in between the infinite gamut of mulattos. Who isn't a devotee of Our Lord of Bomfim, with his countless miracles; who doesn't cling to Oxala, bearing the unfailing *ebos*?

Also present were the commanding general of the region, the admiral of the naval base, the brigadier of the air force, the president of the Assembly, the presiding judge of the Superior Court, the president of the Honorable Chamber of Aldermen, bankers, cacao barons, entrepreneurs, executives, senators, and deputies. Some paraded in black limousines. Others, however— the governor, the mayor, and the head of the tobacco industry, Mario Portugal—followed on foot along with the people. There followed a mob of demagogues—that is, candidates in the upcoming elections—canvassing every mile, butting in, distributing fliers and embraces, kisses, smiles, and pats on the back to potential voters.

The procession swayed to the music from the trucks: religious hymns, folk songs, Carnival *sambas,* and *frevos.* The accompaniment swelled along the way, the multitude expanded; people clambered down the hillsides, the Sao Joaquim market emptied out, latecomers disembarked from ferryboats and launches or arrived in sloops. When the front of the procession reached the foot of Sacred Hill, a voice well known and loved rose from the music truck of Dodo and Osmar—a hush descended over everyone, the procession halted, and Caetano Veloso intoned the hymn to Our Lord of Bomfim.

Then the march up the hillside resumed to the beating of the drums, to the singing of the *afoxes* about the waters of Oxala. The mass of people headed for the Church of Bomfim, which had been closed by a decision of the Curia. In years past, the procession would wash the whole church and honor Oxala on the altar of Jesus. Someday it will go back to being that way. Today the Baianas occupied the steps and the entrance to the church; the washing began, and the obligation of the *candomble* is fulfilled: *"Exe-e-babd!"*

Our Lord of Bomfim arrived in Bahia from Portugal during colonial times riding on the mournful Catholic vow of a shipwrecked Portuguese sailor; Oxala arrived from the coast of Africa, during the time of the traffic in blacks, riding on the bloody back of a slave. Today they hovered over the procession, Our Lord and Oxala, fused in the breasts of the Baianas, plunged into the scented water, and mingled. Together they are a single uniquely Brazilian divinity.

## The Two Aunts

That Bomfim Thursday was decisive in Manela's life. The procession, a happy time of singing and dancing, the ceremonious Baianas, the square on Sacred Hill festooned with paper streamers and decorated with fronds of coconut palms, the washing of the steps of the basilica, the possessed women receiving the enchanted ones, the sacred ritual, and having lunch with her cousins at a table of love, eating and drinking, dende oil running from her mouth down her chin, her hands licked, cold beer, *batidas* and the warmth of cane liquor, cinnamon and clove, prancing around the square with her sister, her cousin, and the boys, parties in family homes and the public dance in the street, the music trucks, the lighting of the footlights, the colored bulbs on the facade of the church, she wandering amid the crowd with Miro beside her, leading her by the hand. With a sense of lightness, Manela felt capable of taking flight, a free swallow in the euphoria of the festival.

That morning, when she had first arrived at the Church of the Conceicao da Praia, she had been a poor, unhappy girl—oppressed, lacking a will of her own, always on the defensive: timid, deceiving, disheartened, submissive. Yes, Auntie. I heard, Auntie. I'm coming, Auntie. Well behaved. She'd attended the procession because Gildete had demanded it with an ultimatum of fearsome threats:

"If you're not here bright and early," her aunt had said, "I'm coming to get you, and I'm a woman capable of slapping that so-and-so right in the face if she so much as dares say you can't come with me. Where did anyone ever hear tell of such a thing? She thinks she's carrying the king in her belly, but she's nothing but a stuck-up bitch. I don't know how Danilo puts up with all that crap—it takes balls."

Hands on hips, on a war footing, Gildete finished:

"I've got some accounts to settle with that busybody, going around talking about me, treating me like a street walker or some hoodooer. She'll pay me for that someday."

Yet, big-hearted, cordial, loving, a piece of coconut sweet, Aunt Gildete held no rancor; the threatened revenge, the promised vengeance, never went beyond words. On the rare occasion when she lost her temper, she would become transformed, capable of uttering the worst absurdities.

Wasn't Gildete the one who had stormed wildly into the office of the secretary of education like a crazy woman, when the government attempted to cancel student lunches in order to save money? "Calm down, my dear teacher!"—that was all the secretary had said to her. He lost his composure in fear of physical assault as he faced Gildete's robust figure, itching for a fight, her harsh accusations defending the poor children, her imperious figure—and he hastily left the room. Panicky stenographers tried to restrain her, but Gildete had pushed them away; all determination, ignoring protests and warnings, she crossed through anterooms until she got to the sanctum sanctorum where the secretary issued his orders. Her photograph later appeared in the newspapers with an expose about the plan to do away with elementary school lunches—it had been a carefully guarded secret until then—resulting in such a wave of protests, including the threat of a strike and a demonstration, that the measure was canceled, and Gildete even escaped a negative report in her service file. Instead of a reprimand, she was praised; for the governor took advantage of what had happened to get rid of the secretary, whose political loyalty he had doubted anyway. The governor attributed the authorship of the disastrous idea to the secretary, then threw him to the wolves.

Along with the praise came a certain notoriety: Newton Macedo Campos, a combative opposition deputy, referred to the incident in a speech in the State Assembly, praising Gildete to the skies, calling her an "ardent patriot and distinguished citizen, paladin of children, paragon of teachers." In addition the union tried to coopt her for its leadership, but she refused: She enjoyed the praise but had no ambitions to be a paladin or a paragon.

On Bomfim Thursday, Manela turned her weakness into strength and did as Gildete had instructed her. Early in the morning, she set out for Gildete's, taking advantage of the fact that Adalgisa was gone for the morning—she and Danilo had left to attend the seventh-day mass for the wife of one of his co-workers. Manela carried her English books and notebooks so that when she came home for lunch, they would think she had been off at her class. To be back for lunch, Manela planned to check her watch, leave the procession in time to pick up her dress and her

books, and catch the bus—the whole thing was well orchestrated in her mind. Trembling inside, astounded by her own audacity, she had changed her clothes had put on the petticoat and wide skirt, her breasts naked under the Baiana smock—oh, if Aunt Adalgisa ever saw such a thing!

To say that Manela wasn't sorry she had come, that she was in love, would be to say very little. By the time she finally did take the road back home that day, poorly timed rather than according to her schedule, she was a different Manela. The real Manela, the one who'd hidden herself away ever since the death of her parents, had almost extinguished herself in fear of punishment—the punishment of God who, omnipresent, sees everything and makes note of all for a settling of final accounts on the Day of Judgment. And she had lived in fear of the punishment of Aunt Adalgisa, who reared and educated her. Auntie, ever watchful and nosy, had collected her dues for whatever she saw or found out with a good tongue-lashing and the leather strap, too!

As the twig is bent, so grows the tree. Manela had been thirteen and a half when she came to live with her aunt and uncle, so she wasn't that young. But according to Adalgisa, her parents had brought her up very poorly: She was a teenager full of wiles and will, accustomed to bad company, consorting with trash, loose with her schoolmates at movie matinees, only pretending to take part in programs for children, running off to festivals on the square. Why, her parents had even taken her to *candomble* temples, that was how irresponsible…

Adalgisa had taken her in hand, put a leash on her. She'd laid down strict hours: She couldn't let her set foot on the street, and as for festivals and movies, she could go only if accompanied by her aunt and uncle. *Candombles?* Not even to be mentioned: Adalgisa had a horror of *candombles*—a *sacred* horror, the adjective imposes itself. A short rein and a strong wrist would bring Manela under control. Adalgisa would punish her with no misgivings or pity. She was fulfilling her duty as an adoptive mother—and one day, established in life, Manela would thank her for it.

## The Hour of Noon

"*Exe-e-baba!*" The palms of her open hands at chest level, Manela greeted Oxolufa, Qxala the elder, as he arrived at the entrance to the Church of Bomfim. Bending over in front of Aunt Gildete, she watched Gildete quiver, close her eyes, and bend her body over her knees, possessed. Leaning on her broom as an improvised *paxoro*, Gildete came out doing the dance of the enchanted one: Oxala, old, debilitated, but free from captivity at last, from the jail where he'd been punished without any trial or sentence, was celebrating his freedom. When he showed himself on the square, the bells were ringing, announcing the hour of noon.

Noon was the hour when Manela was expected back at the Avenida da Ave-Maria for lunch, dressed again as a student, skirt and blouse, her breasts held in by a brassiere, carrying the schoolbag with her English text and her notebooks, as if she were coming from her class at the institute. Good afternoon, Auntie, how was the mass?

But she must have forgotten, or decided not to, and when she heard the bells, it was no longer any use if she remembered, because at half-past noon on the dot, Uncle Danilo was sitting at the table and Aunt Adalgisa was serving him his repast. Whenever Manela happened to be late, her prepared plate would grow cold waiting in the kitchen. That day Adalgisa didn't even fix up the cold plate, and she herself barely tasted the beef stew with dwarf beans—she stopped with the first forkful, choking with surprise and indignation. Her mouth was as bitter as bile, her head was bursting, mute. She did not want to believe what her eyes had seen—she'd rather go blind.

## The Waters of Oxalá

Anyone who moves backward is a crab, Aunt Gildete had stated the night before, using proverbial phrases, popular tales, and folk wisdom to sum up her diatribe against Adalgisa. Returning to her normal self, sitting with her nieces, stroking the head of her daughter Violeta who was crouching at her feet, she'd mentioned the legend

of the waters of Oxala and recounted it—if you'd like to hear it, I'll tell it to you. She cleared her throat and spoke what follows, perhaps a word more, a word less:

"The ancients tell, I heard from my granny, a Grunci black woman, that Oxala went out one day through the lands of his kingdom and the kingdoms of his three sons, Xango, Oxossi, and Ogum, to find out how the people were getting along, with the intention of correcting injustices and punishing evildoers. In order not to be recognized, he covered his body with the rags of a beggar and set out, asking questions. He didn't get very far; accused of vagrancy, he was taken to jail and beaten. Just on suspicion they tossed him into the clink where, forgotten, he spent years on end in solitude and filth.

"One day, happening to pass by the miserable jail, Oxossi recognized his missing father, who had been given up for dead. Quickly freed, he was loaded down with honors, and before he returned to the royal palace, Oxala was bathed and perfumed. Singing and dancing, the women brought water and balm and bathed him. The most beautiful among them warmed his bed, his heart, and his parts for him.

"'I have learned with my own flesh the conditions under which the people of my kingdom live, and of the kingdoms of my sons. Here, there, everywhere, whim and violence reign, rules of obedience and silence: I carry the marks on my body. The waters that put out the fire and washed the wounds are going to extinguish despotism and fear. The lives of the people are going to change.' Oxala was true to his word, he put his power as king into play. That's the story of the waters of Oxala. It passed from mouth to mouth, crossed the ocean, and so it reached our Bahian capital city. A lot of people who walk along in the procession, carrying jugs and jars of scented water to wash the floor of the church, don't know why they're doing it. Now you know, and you can pass it on to your children and grandchildren when you have them; it's a pretty good story, and it bears a lesson."

Oxala didn't manage to change the lives of the people—that was easy to see. Even so, we have to recognize that no word spoken against violence and tyranny is entirely vain and useless: Somebody who hears it just might overcome fear and start to rebel Just look at Manela following the path of Oxala in front of the Church of Bomfim, just at that moment when she should have been hightailing it home.

## The *Ekede*

When the noon bells rang, in her affliction at the lost hour, Manela clung to Our Lord of Bomfim, for whom nothing is impossible. On the upper floor of the sacristy was a whole tier filled with thanks and exvotos, the awesome museum of miracles, attesting to and proving the power of the patron saint.

At the same time that she was invoking a divine protection—Have I mercy, my Lord of Bomfim!—with an instinctive hereditary gesture, Manela joined in the ritual of the *ekedes*, the acolytes of possessed women who are under the care of the *orixas* who have revealed themselves. She took off her immaculate sash to wipe the sweat from Gildete's face; hands on hips, fists clenched, Oxala was muttering commands.

Manela began to sense the enormity of her transgression, the size of I her sin—it couldn't have been greater, alas, it couldn't! She'd have to invent a plausible explanation, figure out an acceptable excuse that would restrain Aunt Adalgisa's pitiless arm and shut her cursing mouth—some insults wound deeper than a couple of slaps. It was normally difficult for Manela to get around her aunt, who was mistrustful and speculative, but sometimes Manela managed to convince her and escape a sermon, a bawling out, and the leather strap. Not that she was deceitful by nature, but in times of panic and humiliation, there was nothing she could do but lie. Worse still was when nothing came to mind, and all that was left for her to do was confess her error and ask forgiveness: I'm sorry, Auntie, I won't do it again, ever again. I swear by God, by the soul of my mother. Today, Manela knew, such an entreaty for forgiveness couldn't

forestall punishment; the best it could do was soften it—and would that even be worthwhile?

Manela wiped Aunt Gildete's face, and without thinking, as if obeying orders—orders muttered by Oxala, perhaps—she followed Gildete through the entire triumphal dance of the enchanted one, commemorating his regained freedom—the end of his solitude and filth. She was getting dizzy, she felt a tingling in her arms and legs, she tried to keep her balance, was unable to, bent her body over, let herself go. As if in a dream, she saw herself as someone else, soaring in the air, and she realized that she didn't have to invent excuses or make up lies to tell her aunt because she wasn't committing any crime, misdemeanor, or error, any sin. There was nothing to confess, no reason to beg forgiveness and deserve punishment. With a leap of freedom, Manela danced in front of Oxala, *Baba Oke*, father of the Sacred Hill of Bomfim—she and Aunt Gildete went on in front of the church in the midst of the cadenced clapping of the Baianas. How did she know those steps, where had she learned that dance, acquired those fundamentals? Sprightly and light-footed, standing up against captivity, guilt and fear no longer weighed on her shoulders.

Oxolufa, or Oxala the elder, the greatest of all, the father, came for her and embraced her and held her, hugging her against his chest, trembling and making her tremble. As he went off, he shouted quite loud so they would know: *"Eparrei!"* and the Baianas repeated, bowing before Manela: *"Eparrei!"*

Once this change had come over Manela, Yansan, who had been present, left as suddenly as she had come. She carried away all the accumulated filth, all that dirt, to bury in the jungle: hesitation and submission, ignominy and pretense, the fear of threats and shouts, of slaps in the face, of the leather strap hanging on the wall, and worst of all, the pleas for forgiveness. Oya had cleansed Manela's body and straightened out her head.

So it was that the fright and mortification that had overcome Manela when the bells marked the hour of noon were followed by complete release: Filled with joy, in the rejection of yoke and harness, Manela was reborn. That was how the waters of Oxala flowed on that Bomfim Thursday. They had put out the fires of hell, *axé*.

## The *Coup de Foudre*

On that Bomfim Thursday, under the scalding and luminous January sun, at the end of the washing ceremony, Manela met Miro.

It was a *coup de foudre,* as Adalgisa's dear and esteemed neighbor, Professor Joao Batista de Lima e Silva, familiar with the French language and its literature, would have said upon learning about the case. But it was love at first sight only as far as Manela was concerned, because if one could believe Miro, he'd had his eye on her for some time and was only waiting for a chance to state his intentions.

Manela was busy on the steps of the church, scattering scented water over the delirious crowd—*filhas de santo* in trance were receiving *orixas;* seventeen Oxalas were hanging about the entrance, ten Oxolufas, and seven Oxaguinhas—when she heard someone say her name, calling her insistently:

"Manela! Manela! Look, here I am!"

She looked and she saw him, squeezed in along the steps, his pleading eyes fastened on her. His open mouth displayed white teeth against his black face, and unbelievable as it might seem in that horrible crush, his feet were dancing a *samba.* Manela leaned over and emptied the last drops from her clay jar over the big-mouth's kinky hair. His hair was combed out in an Afro, a symbol of the world struggle against racism made popular by American Black Panthers. Manela couldn't remember seeing him before, but what difference did that make?

Miro reached out his hand and said:

"Come."

# A Region in Denial

## Racial Discrimination and Racism in Latin America

By Ariel E. Dulitzky

## Editor's Introduction

Denials and a legacy of class struggle and revised history within imagined spaces are rampant in many Latin American nations, such as Cuba, Brazil, and Argentina, to name but a few. In this selection, readers will learn where and how racism and racial discrimination exist; the notion of "racial democracy" in Brazil is challenged as evidence reveals many imbalances in Brazilian society. This reading is a good place to start on this complex issue, and allows students to see that the United States is not unique with regard to race relations.

### References

Anderson, Benedict. *Imagined Communities: Reflections on the Origin and Spread of Nationalism*. New York: Verso, 2006.

Applebaum, Nancy P., Anne S. Macpherson, and Karin Alejandra Rosenblatt, eds. *Race and Nation in Modern Latin America*. Chapel Hill: University of North Carolina Press, 2001.

Dulitzky, Ariel E. "A Region in Denial: Racial Discrimination and Racism in Latin America." In *Neither Enemies Nor Friends: Latinos, Blacks, Afro-Latinos*, edited by Anani Dzidzienyo and Suzanne Oboler, 39–59. New York: Palgrave Macmillan, 2005.

acism (and racial discrimination) is, to a certain extent, alive and well in every society, country, and region of the world.[1] It can appear in a variety of forms depending on the culture or context in which it occurs and the period of history during which it rears its head. Nonetheless, one common thread that seems to be woven throughout almost every culture, country, and region is that people deny that racism even exists.

In this article we attempt to delve into the different forms of denying the existence of racial discrimination in Latin America. The crux of our argument is that the people of our region are prone to conceal, twist, and cover up the fact that racism and racial discrimination exists in our part of the world. This phenomenon of denial stands in the way of acknowledgment of the problem and, consequently, hampers effective measures that could be taken to eliminate and prevent racial discrimination. In order to identify the best strategies for combating racism, we must first take a close look at the different forms and manifestations of the phenomenon itself.

A kind of presumption of moral superiority vis-à-vis the United States of America is quite widespread throughout our region. Rarely does a conversation on this issue among Latin Americans take place without mentioning the serious incidence of racism and racial discrimination that exists in the land of our neighbors to the north, a claim that is altogether true. As the Brazilian scholar Antonio Sergio Guimaraes (1999:37; 2001) notes, we point out with nationalistic pride that racial segregation of the type that exists in the United States does not exist in our countries. We pompously tout our "racial democracies," "racial melting pots," "racial harmony," complete *mestizaje,* or mixing of races.

Nothing epitomizes Latin Americans' view on this issue as well as the declaration of the presidents and heads of state of South America that was issued in 2000 at a meeting in Brasilia. This statement reads: "The Presidents [of South America] view with concern the resurgence of racism and of discriminatory manifestations and expressions in *other parts of the world* and state their commitment to preserve South America from the propagation of said phenomenon."[2] Or as the Mexican government put it: "The government of Mexico opposes any form of discrimination, institutionalized or otherwise, as well as the new forms of discrimination, xenophobia and other forms of intolerance that have emerged in several parts of the world, particularly in the developed countries."[3]

In short, these leaders concur that racism and racial discrimination are practices that take place in other regions and that Latin Americans possess a moral fortitude that cannot and does not allow any discrimination to be practiced in their countries. Moreover, these statements echo the widespread sentiment of the region.

Our aim here is to encourage a debate on what we feel is a widespread and outright misrepresentation of Latin America as a region that is respectful of racial mobility and more tolerant toward racial identities than it really is. These misguided impressions are merely a reflection of the absence of a deep, sincere, and open political debate on the issue of race in our region. With regard to this point, the Mexican government is right when it states, "In Mexico, the indigenous issue is never approached as a problem of racial discrimination but as a matter related to the right to development and to their situation of economic and social marginalization (exclusion)."[4] This same government would also state that racial discrimination "is not even a issue of national debate."[5]

But to point out that this phenomenon is not part of the national debate, or that it is not viewed as racial discrimination, by no means erases or negates the fact that racism and racial discrimination do exist, and that the countries of the region refuse to admit and combat.

In reality, racial discrimination and racism, like the failure to recognize these phenomena and the absence of a debate on these issues in Latin America, are simply part and parcel of what could be dubbed the "democratic deficit" that we are experiencing in the region. Equality, as it relates to race, gender, ethnicity, or anything else, is still far from being viewed in the region as an essential and basic requirement for democracy. Equality cannot exist without democracy; nor can democracy exist without equality. Hence, the struggle to solidify democracy is a fundamental step in the struggle against racism and racial discrimination.

This article is partly based on a study conducted by Stanley Cohen (1996), which looked at different governments' responses to reports denouncing violations of human rights. In this study, three different types of denial are posited: literal denial (nothing has happened); interpretive denial (what is happening is actually something else); and justificatory denial (what's happening is justified).[6] Sometimes these types of denial appear in sequence; when one type is struck down, it is replaced by another type. For example, literal denial may prove ineffective because the facts may simply bear out that the black population is indeed more disadvantaged than the white population. Therefore, strategy shifts toward use of another type of denial such as a legalistic reinterpretation or a political justification (522).

Before delving into the subject at hand, we would first like to make a point of clarification. This article focuses primarily on the plight of the Black or Afro-Latin American population, with very little discussion on racial discrimination against indigenous peoples or other ethnic groups. It is by no means our intent to ignore or fail to recognize that indigenous peoples are victims of racial discrimination as well. We have chosen to center our analysis on this particular social group, for the most part, because Blacks have been the most low-visibility victims of racial discrimination in Latin American society today.

## A Look at the Current Situation in the Region

We must first make sure that readers understand what we mean by racism or racial discrimination. Even though it is true that forms, types, or definitions of "racism" or "racial discrimination" may vary widely, for the purposes of this article we use the definition provided by article 1(1) of the International Convention on the Elimination of All Forms of Racial Discrimination (referred to hereinafter as the "Convention against Racism" or the "Convention"):

> In this Convention the expression "racial discrimination" shall denote any distinction, exclusion, restriction or preference based on motives of race, color, lineage or national or ethnic origin whose purpose or result is to nullify or diminish the recognition, enjoyment or exercise, in equal conditions, of human rights and fundamental liberties in the political, economic, social, cultural or any other sphere of public life.

The true state of affairs in Latin American societies, nonetheless, stands in stark contrast with the objectives pursued by the International Convention. Although very few statistics are available on the phenomenon, the small amount of data we have at our disposal shows how racial discrimination permeates each and every realm of life in our region: from the social to the political, education,[7] labor,[8] cultural, and public health

sectors.[9] In countries like Colombia, the Afro-Colombian population is disproportionately a victim of political violence.[10] In other countries of Latin America, access to land has eluded the descendents of African peoples.[11] In many countries of the region, judicial (Adorno, 1999:123) and law-enforcement (Oliveira, 1998:50) systems provide less protection to Blacks and, at the same time, punish them more severely.

For example, a recent study by the UN Economic Council for Latin America shows that Afro-Latin Americans have little or no job security, which is proof of racial segregation throughout the region. Racial discrimination in the labor market stems from inequities in the education sector. Consequently, whites have more of a chance of successfully climbing the corporate ladder, so to speak, or making it to positions of power or upper management. Distribution of income in the region is revealed to be even more unfair when it is viewed by ethno-racial origin of the inhabitants. The Black population has a harder time gaining access to education; they are more likely to fall behind in their studies, to fail to make progress, to drop out of school, and to attend schools of inferior quality.[12]

The government of Colombia, one of the few governments that at least has clearly acknowledged, in written documents, the problem of discrimination, has described the plight of the Afro-Colombian population in the following terms:

> They are among the group of Colombians with the highest indices of unmet needs. Their health conditions are precarious, their sanitation conditions are the most deficient in the entire nation, and coverage of education services is poor. Housing in Afro-Colombian communities, in addition to [having] poor coverage of public utilities, shows problems in the legalization of property and lots, a high rate of overcrowding, and poor quality. It is estimated that the per capita income of [the members of] these communities is $500 per year, less than one-third of

the national average. Afro-Colombian women are facing conditions of poverty, high unemployment rates, low-quality jobs, deficient health care, and a high incidence of domestic violence. Afro-Colombian teens do not have optimal guarantees and opportunities to gain access to higher or vocational education, good jobs, and development in keeping with their world vision and with their sociocultural reality. The territorial entities where the Afro-Colombian population creates settlements are characterized by their poor ability to govern, plan, and manage.[13]

This scenario, which is identical to the situation in several countries of Latin America, makes it all the more necessary to take a closer and more honest look at our region in order to be able to adopt the necessary measures to overcome this crisis. Even so, there are still strong currents of thought in political, academic, and social circles, which deny that racial discrimination even exists or try to explain away these differences as a function of other variables, rather than as a function of race or ethnic origin. In the following section we look closely at some of these variables.

### "There Is No Racism or Racial Discrimination": Literal Denial

Literal denial is simply to say *"nothing has happened"* or *"nothing is happening"* What is of concern to us here is that this type of denial is synonymous with saying that there has never been any racial discrimination or racism in the past nor is there any at the present time. Over the past few years, different governments of Latin America have made statements to the Committee on the Elimination of Racial Discrimination (CERD) claiming, among other things, that "racial prejudice"[14] does not exist, "in our country problems of discrimination do not exist,"[15] "racial discrimination does not exist,"[16] "today racial problems practically do not exist any longer,"[17]

"this phenomenon does not appear in our country,"[18] or "in society at the present time racial prejudices are practically negligible."[19]

This type of discourse is typical not only of governments that have a well-known history of insensitivity to racial issues, but also of governments that have a track record of being committed, at least rhetorically, to racial equality. Paradoxically, these so-called racially sensitive governments are often the ones who most categorically deny the existence of the problem. It would not be entirely farfetched to hear the following argument brandished in discussing the issue with a Latin American: " *Our government would never allow something like that to happen, and therefore it could never have happened?*

A pseudo sophisticated way of denying that racial discrimination exists is to argue that it could not have taken place because discrimination is illegal in the countries of the region and the governments have even ratified every appropriate international instrument related to the subject. This legalistic version of denial of racial discrimination is based on the following specious claim: "Since racial discrimination is prohibited by law, our government would never allow it and, therefore, it could not have ever occurred" (Cohen, 1996:254).

The most syllogistic form of literal denial is the widespread myth that the region boasts a racial democracy because the concept of race has been officially rejected by government institutions. This type of denial has many variations but essentially amounts to saying that if races do not officially exist, then racism cannot exist either. Nevertheless, erasing the concept of race from laws and other official documents has by no means led to the end of race as a key factor in determining how the benefits of society are distributed, nor does it negate the fact that Latin American society is predicated upon a clearly pyramidal structure with Blacks and indigenous people at the bottom and whites at the top.

### "What Goes On in Latin America Is Not Racism or Racial Discrimination but Something Else":

At this point in time, it is hard, if not ludicrous, to categorically deny that racial discrimination and racism exist in Latin America. This is because groups that have been discriminated against have become more visible and have begun to engage in activism to address their plight. Additionally, a limited but growing number of studies and statistics, which bear out that racism and racial discrimination still exist in Latin America, are now available. Consequently, people resort to slightly more sophisticated explanations. Instead of denying that economic and social indicators show a wide gap between races, they commonly give reasons other than racism to account for the disparities among Blacks, indigenous peoples, and whites. These disparities, attitudes, and prejudices are framed in far less pejorative or stigmatizing theoretical terms than racism or racial discrimination.

The true story of the racial issue in Latin America is doctored in many different ways. In the following section we identify some of the ways in which the facts are distorted such that they do not fit the definition of racism or racial discrimination.

## Euphemisms

One of the most common ways of putting a spin on the facts is the use of euphemistic expressions to mask the phenomenon, confer a measure of respectability on the problem, or paint a picture of neutrality in the face of discriminatory practices. A variety of terms are used to negate or cloud the racist side of certain social conduct or government policies: "ethnic minority,"[20] "restrictions on immigration,"[21] "customer screening or selection" (*selección de clientes*),[22] "reservation of rights to refuse admission" (*reserva de admisión*),[23] "proper attire" (*Buena presencia*).[24]

Probably the most common euphemism attributes the differences among races to poverty. The syllogism goes something like this: People discriminate against Blacks or indigenous people *not* because they are black or indigenous, but because they are poor.

The government of Haiti, for example, cited economic reasons for the disparities between whites and other groups: "Even though it is true that in the private sphere prejudices related to color are sometimes expressed, in reality its origin lies in the social inequities that exist in Haitian society."[25] Similarly, the government of Peru claimed, "Today practically every Peruvian is of mixed blood and a racial problem no longer exists. Instead, there exists a problem of economic underdevelopment in certain sectors of the population."[26] Mexico has developed the most explicit arguments on this point: The indigenous issue is not "a problem of racial discrimination"; rather it has to do with "forms of discrimination derived from the socioeconomic reality."[27]

The myth of a *racial democracy*, which is defined as harmony between ethnic and racial groups and, therefore, the absence of racial discrimination, would lead people to believe that any display of racism and discrimination that may occur is usually a result of social and economic rather than racial prejudice. Once again we cite the official version of the Mexican government: "some forms of discrimination are a result of socioeconomic differences more than a distinction between ethnic groups, and they [the differences] have been addressed by means of a variety of government social development programs targeted toward the most vulnerable groups."[28] This way of thinking is so widespread and has endured for so long throughout Latin America that, regardless of a persons race, the population for the most part is unwilling to explain current social disparities among racial groups in terms of racial inequities. Yet, our societies quite readily accept explanations based on economic disparities (Minority Rights Group, 1999:23).

These interpretations are marred by faulty logic. First, they fail to explain why in our region even though not all people of color are poor, almost all poor people are colored.[29] One government did not have any problem acknowledging "a clear correlation between proportion of the indigenous population and poverty and marginalization indices."[30] Second, several statistical studies on economic disparities in Latin America have shown that even when all possible variables are factored out of the equation, including indicators of poverty, one variable, which can only be attributed to a persons race, always carries over.[31] Moreover, according to this specious argument, it would be lawful to discriminate against poor people. As far as we are aware, there is no provision of human rights law currently on the books that legitimizes unequal treatment of persons based on social class or economic status.[32] Justification of class-based over race-based discrimination, once again, is simply a corollary to the assumption that we live in racial democracies in Latin America. It is also a corollary to the ideological basis for that assumption, which is that societies in the region are monolithically mestizo or mixed raced and, therefore, allegedly free of prejudice and discrimination. If Latin America indeed lives in racial harmony and there is really only one race in our societies (the mestizo race), then it would follow that any disparities between population groups could never be explained by a persons race but rather would have to be explained as a function of poverty, social status, or education.

## Legalisms

Most interpretive denials of racism are laced with some sort of legalistic or diplomatic language to negate the existence of discriminatory practices. Many different legal defenses have been used to counter charges of racial discrimination. To take stock of every single one would far exceed the scope of this article, so in this section we offer only a few examples.

One form of legalistic argument is to maintain that racial discrimination is nonexistent in Latin America because the laws in the countries of the region do not establish rules of segregation or apartheid as is the case in certain other parts of the world. The claim is thus put forth that "never in history has any legal text been in effect that establishes racial discrimination even in a veiled way."[33] The implication of this statement is that discrimination can only exist when it is established by law, and not when sectors of the population are discriminated against by deed or when laws are applied or enforced in a discriminatory way.

Nevertheless, international conventions require our countries to do much more than simply erase discriminatory laws from the books. International treaties call for the adoption of specific laws in support of each provision of these conventions, egalitarian and nondiscriminatory enforcement of laws and conventions, and, particularly, the prevention, punishment, and elimination of discrimination in all its forms, whether by law or by deed. The CERD, therefore, has expressly mentioned the obligation of states to repeal any law or *practice* whose effect it is to create or perpetuate racial discrimination.[34]

The Convention against Racial Discrimination requires nations to adopt comprehensive legislation to prevent, eliminate, punish, and remedy racial discrimination. Such legislation does not exist at the present time in Latin American countries, as the CERD has been pointing out over the past two years.[35] Instead, the respective constitutions contain basic provisions that prohibit racial discrimination; yet the appropriate legislative structures to fully enforce those provisions are not in place.[36] Specifically, the Convention requires enactment of certain criminal laws, which prohibit and adequately penalize any act of racial discrimination that may be committed by individuals, organizations, public authorities, or institutions. To date, in many countries of the Americas, such laws are yet to be passed.[37] In other countries, even though legal provisions designed to eliminate unequal treatment based on racial factors may have already been enacted, express provisions making it unlawful to discriminate on the basis of national or ethnic origin have not been written into the laws.[38] Such specificity is necessary because these types of discrimination are the most prevalent forms of intolerance and bigotry in many nations of the region. In many countries in Latin America, there are no laws preventing racial discrimination in the private sector, despite the fact that section d, paragraph 1, of article 2 of the Convention provides that signatories shall prohibit any racial discrimination practiced not only by public authorities or institutions but also by private "groups or organizations."[39] Lastly, in many of our countries legislation currently in force has proven to be inadequate, either because the ban on discrimination does not go hand in hand with the appropriate punishments[40] or because punishments provided for by law are so lenient that they do not serve as an effective means to prevent, prohibit, and eradicate all practice of racial segregation.[41]

Another way people attempt to prove that racial discrimination does not exist in the region is to point to the fact that Latin American courts receive very few complaints of racial discrimination. As the government of Mexico stated, the absence of racial discrimination "can be corroborated by the absence of both domestic and international complaints"[42]—the logic being that an absence of court convictions for racial discrimination means that the phenomenon is non-existent. Nevertheless, this argument ignores important questions such as whether victims of racism are aware of the legal recourse available to them for their defense; whether laws are effective in combating racial discrimination; or whether the courts properly apply antidiscrimination laws. The low number of complaints may very well be attributable to "unawareness of existing legal remedies available for cases of racial discrimination, and to the public in general perhaps not being very aware of the protection against racial discrimination provided for in the Convention."[43] The small number of complaints and, consequently, convictions may also be due to a lack of confidence in law enforcement and judicial authorities.[44] Lastly, the low incidence of racial discrimination cases brought before the court may also stem from the fact that judicial or police officers do not rate this type of behavior as a display of racism or discrimination.[45]

In a variation of the argument that the absence of legislation making racial discrimination a crime is in itself proof that racial discrimination does not exist, the government of Venezuela stated: "Even though it is true that very few laws are in force against racial discrimination and any

defense or support *(apologia)* that may foment it, we can say that there is no practical need to legislate on this subject, given that problems of discrimination or defense thereof do not exist in our country.… [Such a] situation, fortunately unknown in our milieu, would be different if there were violent clashes between ethnic groups or if certain persons were alienated or left out on the basis of physical characteristics, since in explosive situations such as these would be, the Parliament, which cannot turn its back on the social reality, would issue laws on this subject. It has not done so because there has not been a need for it."[46]

In an extreme variation of this argument, governments respond to allegations of racism and racial discrimination by rattling off a long list of domestic laws enacted, international treaties ratified, and a host of legal mechanisms designed to punish those responsible for discrimination and racism. With such prohibitions in place, racial discrimination cannot possibly exist.

## Denials of Responsibility

Many times governments deny any type of state responsibility for racism and racial discrimination, although they acknowledge that such acts may indeed take place.

The argument is that even though some acts of racism and racial discrimination have occurred, such acts are events that cannot be attributed to the government, are out of its control, and are the product of deeply rooted social practices or private actors. The Dominican government, for example, has only accepted that "there exists the possibility that individually, someone in the country, with the utmost discretion supports racial discrimination."[47] Or as the government of Haiti has stated, in the event that there are incidents of racial discrimination, these "are in no case the work of the state."[48]

In any case, under the Convention against Racial Discrimination, these arguments are not a valid justification. Every state must guarantee effective application of the Convention. "Inasmuch as the practices of private institutions influence the exercise of rights or the availability of opportunities, the State Party must ensure that the result of these practices does not have as a purpose or effect the creation or perpetuation of racial discrimination."[49]

## Just Isolated Incidents

One of the most common ways in which governments respond to charges of racism or racial discrimination is to accept that a specific act has indeed taken place, but to deny that such acts are systematic, routine, or representative of a pattern of behavior. Typical responses in this category include:

> "Such acts arise in an isolated way and are the result of the motivation of individuals or very small groups."[50]
>
> Incidents of racial discrimination occur only "episodically and selectively."[51]
>
> "In present-day society racial prejudices are practically negligible and are manifested in the most intimate spheres of life."[52]
>
> What occurred was an *"isolated incident"*, such events never occurred in the past, and since they have not happened again, it is unfair to brand our government as racist on the basis of this single event.

## Justificatory Denial

*Justificatory denial* has countless variations, which, generally speaking, involve either an attempt to justify the argument that racism does not exist or an attempt to show that in some hypothetical situations, racism or racial discrimination is in fact justifiable. Some of these denials are offered in good faith; others are simply excuses, fabrications, ideological defenses, or attempts to neutralize allegations.

## Camouflaging Racism

We focus here on one of the most pernicious forms of denial—blaming the victim for his or her situation or making the victim of racism and racial discrimination invisible.

In perhaps its most extreme form, whole sectors of the population are simply said not to be victims of racism. Witness the popular Argentine saying: "We Argentines are not racist because we don't have any Blacks." The collective conscience in that country of the Southern Cone, however, refuses to ask key questions such as why today there is no Black population in Argentina, whereas in 1850, 30 percent of the population of Buenos Aires was Black.[53]

Governments throughout Latin America have engaged in a campaign to officially do away with any racial identification by claiming that the population is of mixed race *(mestizaje)*. This view is evident, for example, in the way censuses are conducted in the countries of the region. The census of almost every country in Latin America does not include any question on racial identity.[54] The exceptions are Brazil and a few other countries, which are halfheartedly beginning to inquire into these distinctions.[55] This practice only serves to camouflage a highly representative sector of Latin American populations. The absence of official statistics on the true makeup of the population has a most serious consequence: it prevents the true plight of sectors that are victims of discrimination from being known. This practice also makes it impossible to implement public policies to overcome these inequities.

This drastic negation of any racial distinctions within the population makes it impossible to question the prevailing norm in Latin America of a persons color being a decisive factor in determining chances and opportunities to succeed in society. In Latin America, the whiter you are, the better and greater your chances are; while the darker you are, the lesser and worse your chances are. The chromatic social scale is blatant throughout Latin America, and social surveys have begun to corroborate these disparities.[56]

While it is true that racial categories in Latin America differ from those of other parts of the world in that they are not exclusively of a dual nature, that is, Black and white,[57] this by no means does away with the disparities among races or with the fact that the darker the skin, the fewer the economic, cultural, educational, employment, and social opportunities. We could say that a "strong pigmentocracy" prevails throughout Latin America, in which a negative value is attached to darker skin color, thus relegating races other than the white race to the lower echelons of society (Casaus Arzu, 1998:138).

The idea that we are all mestizos,[58] we are all cafe-au-lait-colored, we all have some indigenous or black blood in us, is an obstacle to identifying and developing the concept of specific racial groups. This myth is used to prevent nonwhites from developing their own identity and demands; however, it is not used to attain a higher degree of equality and social integration for these sectors of the population. The official notion of a mixed race (*mestizaje*)[59] camouflages diversity and denies nonwhites the right to dissent, while making conditions ripe for excluding anyone who falls outside the "norm" of mestizo or mixed (Arocha Rodriguez, 1992:28).

Furthermore, the concept of a mixed race also undermines or weakens the political and social struggle against racial discrimination. If we are all mestizos, then there are no racial distinctions, and mere discussion of the racial issue is therefore viewed by many as foreign to the region. By raising such matters in Latin America, the thinking goes, people are only trying to bring problems into the region that belong to other countries.

Moreover, the mixed-race theory covers up the official racist policy of whitening or infusing white blood into society, which has been attempted in almost every single country of Latin America. Many Latin American countries made a concerted effort to bring down the number of Blacks and indigenous people in the population and, as a last resort, to camouflage these racial groups by encouraging miscegenation, or marriage between nonwhites and whites, to make the population whiter. For example, almost every country in the region has developed at one time or another immigration policies that restrict or deny entry to Black people while strongly promoting European immigration.

The mixed-race claim not only serves to camouflage or make the Black or indigenous population invisible but is also used as proof that racism does not exist. Mexico has explained the situation in the following way:

> Additionally, our historical experience and the makeup of the Mexican population—90 percent mestizo (mixed race), a product of the mix between Spaniards and indigenous people—give rise to an indisputable fact: the denial of either [one of these] origin[s] does not take place in our country, which is why there has been no need to legislate in this regard, unlike what goes on in other countries where the phenomenon of *mestizaje* did not occur.[60]

*Mestizaje* is also used as proof of harmony among different racial and ethnic groups. In other words, if there are mestizos, it is because there are mixed marriages between whites and Blacks or indigenous people. As the government of Cuba stated, the fact that there are a high number of racially mixed families on the island is a sign of how limited racial prejudice is.[61] Nonetheless, not even the magical force of *mestizaje* has managed to completely do away with racial prejudice when such marriages take place. Furthermore, many people in Latin America try to keep mixed marriages from ever taking place in their families.

The mixed raced/mixed marriage theory, however, is unable to conceal the fact that the Latin American population in general and the Black/indigenous population in particular feel that whitening ones lineage is the only route to improving ones standing on the social scale. This view is at the root of racism in Latin America; this attitude denies the Black or indigenous presence and identity and stresses the "white" side of the mixed race as the essential ingredient to obtain better social, employment, and education opportunities in a white-dominated world (Minority Rights Group, 1995:28). In reality, more than a democratizing force behind society, *mestizaje* constitutes, for the most part, one of the most masterful forms of racism in Latin America. In order to climb the social ladder, one must be as white as possible and the blending of races is the way to attain it.

In Latin America, as has been correctly pointed out, "the white/mestizo [person] forswears or abjures his or her indigenous [and, we add, Black] part and must constantly demonstrate his or her superiority," even when these displays only illustrate that it is impossible for mestizos to accept their white and Indian humanity" [or the Black side of their humanity, we add once again] (de la Torre, 1997:7).

Even though Latin American governments have officially denied or done away with the different racial identities that exist throughout the region, such an action has not done away with informal racial designations, which in fact have a decisive effect on the social structure in Latin America. Even at the risk of making a sweeping generalization, we feel compelled to call attention to a common fact that has persisted throughout Latin America independently of the social, political, historical, and cultural peculiarities of the different countries: there is discrimination based on skin color (Early, 1999).

Another way of saying that nonwhites are not victims of racism in Latin America is to reduce their sphere of action in society. Accordingly, it is socially acceptable to acknowledge that Blacks excel only in sports, music, and dance; indeed Black equates with soccer: to be Black is to be good at soccer or even to be a soccer player. In keeping with this same line of thinking, the victims of racism are excluded from other sectors, for example, the media, in order to "project the image of a racially white country" (Oscategui, 1998:31). For example, the CERD has stated its "concern for the information that the media provide regarding minority communities, including the consistent popularity of television programs in which stereotypes based on race or ethnic origin are promoted. The Committee states that those stereotypes contribute to reinforcing the cycle of violence and marginalization that has already had

serious repercussions on the rights of traditionally disadvantaged communities in Colombia."[62] The labor market is another place where there is a clear demarcation of the types of jobs that nonwhites may gain access to or not. Nonwhite populations in Latin America usually have access to the lowest-level and poorest-paid jobs.[63]

The last form of this type of denial involves turning the story around to pin the blame on the victims. This takes place when a Black or indigenous person denounces racially discriminatory practices. Many times, the person is branded a victim of unfounded complexes, without even the slightest consideration that he or she may instead be the victim of racial discrimination.

## Convenient Comparisons

One of the most common ways of attempting to justify the racial situation in Latin America is to compare the region with other countries of the world. Four countries, South Africa, the United States, Rwanda, and Bosnia, are old standbys that are often used for such comparisons. With regard to each instance, respectively, Latin Americans state, "we never had apartheid in our region"; "nor was there ever any legalized racial segregation";[64] and "we never had racially motivated, violent armed conflicts."[65]

In the report submitted by a government to the CERD, the only time the xenophobia, racism, and racial discrimination are mentioned is in reference to the plight of nationals from that country living in the United States.[66] Discrimination always takes place on the other side of the border.

The intellectual and political elite, in many ways, has made the United States the paragon of racial hatred against which all other societies must be measured. The specious claim goes something like this: since the segregationist laws and practices of the country to the north have not been applied in Latin America, there is no need to look at other forms of racial exclusion and alienation.

None of the above-mentioned comparisons are untrue and this ought to be a source of pride for Latin Americans. However, the people of the region, or anyone else for that matter, should not read anything more into these facts than what they say on the face of things. It is true that there has been no apartheid regime in the region; it is true that no racist legislation has ever existed in the region either; and it is also true that no Latin American government has implemented policies of ethnic cleansing.[67] Nonetheless, these are not the only manifestations of racism and racial discrimination. A myriad of phenomena can be found throughout Latin America that fits the definition of racial discrimination and racism.

## Conclusion: Is There a Future Without a Past?

A racist way of thinking has endured throughout our region over the years. Today it is not even entirely far-fetched to hear out of the mouths of Latin Americans such statements as: "The only solution for Guatemala is to improve the race, bring in Aryan studs to improve it. I had a German administrator on my farm for many years and for every Indian girl he got pregnant, I'd pay him an extra fifty dollars."[68]

The existence of racial discrimination and racism, however, continues to be denied or ignored by Latin American societies and governments alike. Very few studies have been conducted on the topic to date, very few statistics have been gathered, and no public debate on the issue is taking place. This grim picture constitutes a roadblock to the development of public policies to combat racial discrimination and racism on the national, regional, and international levels.

In recent years, the advent of democratically elected governments in the majority of the countries of Latin America has paved the way for the improvement of the human rights situation of the region in many ways. Most notably, most countries have no policies of serious state-planned violations. Nevertheless, our democracies still have not been successful at fulfilling their implicit promise and the basic tenet of ensuring full, formal, and effective equality for all segments of society. Consequently, the consolidation of democracy is looming over us both as an unavoidable challenge in Latin America

and as the path we must follow in order to combat racism and racial discrimination effectively.

The World Conference against Racism, Racial Discrimination, Xenophobia, and Related Forms of Intolerance (WCAR), which was convened by the United Nations in 2001, may yet spur on the inhabitants of the region to deal with an issue that has long been consigned to oblivion.

A regional meeting in preparation for the WCAR was held for the Americas in Santiago, Chile, from December 3 to December 7, 2000. Two parallel meetings were organized: the governmental conference, the Americas Preparatory Conference Against Racism, Racial Discrimination, Xenophobia and Related Forms of Intolerance (Regional PrepCom), and the parallel NGO forum, titled the Conference of Citizens Against Racism, Xenophobia, Intolerance and Discrimination (the Citizens Conference).

There were several positive outcomes from these meetings. The massive presence of civil society organizations should be highlighted. More than 1,700 people participated. There is still some hope that this significant mobilization could give birth to a strong regional movement to fight racism. The Santiago meetings also contributed to enhancing the dialogue among Afro-descendants throughout the region, bringing international attention to the challenges that they face. The Chile meetings represented a unique, and probably the first, opportunity for Afro-Latin Americans to appear as significant actors functioning in regional groups on the international level. Participating with a burgeoning collective identity that demonstrated enormous potential for bringing the fight against racism to the fore, they successfully heightened both their own visibility and that of the problems they face throughout the entire hemisphere.

On the governmental side, and at least in the declaratory documents, the Regional PrepCom allowed decisive actions to be taken to fight racial discrimination in the region. For the first time, all the governments of the Americas accepted that racial discrimination exists throughout the region and that it should be strongly combated. Some themes, which appeared in the Regional

PrepComs Final Declaration, deserve mention as they point to important changes in the official position of many states in the region highlighted through this article. The Final Declaration includes a clear recognition that the history of the hemisphere has often been characterized by racism and racial discrimination, and that these phenomena persist in the region (preamble). Moreover the governments of the region stated that the denial of the existence of racism and racial discrimination on the part of states and societies directly or indirectly contributes to their perpetuation (para. 2). The documents also included a positive call for governments to include ethnic or racial criteria in order to give visibility to diverse sectors of the population (para. 18).

It is important to note that the presidents and heads of state of the thirty-four countries of the hemisphere expressly endorsed this document. Similarly, the Inter-American Democratic Charter, adopted by the OAS General Assembly in Lima, Peru, on September 11, 2001, in its Article 9, established that "The elimination of all forms of discrimination, especially gender, ethnic and race discrimination, as well as diverse forms of intolerance, the promotion and protection of human rights of indigenous peoples and migrants, and respect for ethnic, cultural and religious diversity in the Americas contribute to strengthening democracy and citizen participation."

The WCAR was held shortly after the Regional PrepCom, during the first week of September 2001, in Durban, South Africa. While the objective of the WCAR was to address issues of discrimination and intolerance around the world and formulate recommendations and action-oriented measures to combat these evils in all their forms, most of the discussions focused on two issues: the conflict in the Middle East and the question of reparations. Notwithstanding the diplomatic hurdles, the event allowed Afro-Latin Americans to continue raising the level of public awareness on a number of important issues, thus replicating their Chilean success. For Latin America, the most important development is that the governments of the region did not retract their prior

recognition that the region faces important racial discrimination issues.

The mobilization of civil society groups was quite significant, resulting in a number of positive, tangible developments. Beyond highlighting the problems Afro-Latinos confront, the conference also acted as a welcome catalyst to put in motion the long-overdue debate on how to effectively address racial inequality. The progress here lies in the discussion itself. Perhaps for the first time in Latin America, governments and civil society began to debate racial inequality. At last, the debate over race seemed to have moved beyond the discrete circles of academics and activists to find an incipient place in the regions agenda. As an example, the OAS decided to start discussions on the adoption of an Inter-American convention against racism and any other form of discrimination and intolerance. For a region that, as the first part of this article suggests, denies the existence of racism and racial discrimination, this is an important development.

There have also been some promising institutional developments in the last couple of years in terms of creating public institutions charged specifically with addressing allegations of discrimination or helping in the definition and implementation of public policies for the prevention and combating of racial discrimination. Some examples of this trend are the creation of the National Institute against Discrimination, Xenophobia and Racism in Argentina,[69] the National Council for the Prevention of Discrimination in Mexico,[70] the Presidential Commission against Racism and Discrimination against Indigenous People in Guatemala[71] and the Special Secretariat on Policies for the Promotion of Racial Equality in Brazil[72] The creation of new institutions, in countries that traditionally did not officially address the problems of exclusion and marginalization in terms of discrimination, could signal a departure from some of the positions highlighted earlier in this article.

Perhaps the most important development in recent years is that the Brazilian government has begun imposing racial quotas for government jobs, contracts,[73] and university admissions.[74] As expected, these measures have unleashed an acrimonious debate in a country that has traditionally prided itself on being a "racial democracy." There is also a racial equality statute pending now before Congress that would make racial quotas obligatory at all levels of government and even in casting television programs and commercials. The debate is broad and very complex, covering questions such as the definition of who is black, a puzzling process in a country where more than 300 terms are used to designate skin color. It has also prompted a discussion on national identity where critics of the measures say the government is importing a solution from the United States, a country in which racial definitions and relations are very different.[75] Others say that racial quotas are not needed, since racism is not a feature of Brazilian society and conditions for Blacks will improve as poverty is gradually eliminated. The issue probably will be partially settled in the near future when the Brazilian Federal Supreme Court rules on the constitutionality of racial quotas being challenged by white applicants to federal universities. The decision could have an impact in Brazil and also in the rest of Latin America comparable to that of Brown v. Board of Education in the United States (Rohter, 2003).

In order to capitalize on the momentum created by the WCAR, it is indispensable to keep race and racial inequality in the forefront of Latin American political and legal debate. This is not an easy task and the region faces many challenges. While the Latin American governments took a crucial first step by formally acknowledging at the international level the existence of racial discrimination, this is just the beginning rather the end of the struggle. Despite some of the positive changes that have taken place in the last two years, it remains to be seen whether governments will start laying the groundwork for formulation of effective public policies, including legal reforms needed to address racial disparities. There are signs that officials in some Latin American governments are slowly incorporating diplomatic recognition of the existence of racism and racial discrimination into their official domestic discourse. But throughout the region whether Latin American governments will turn their rhetoric into action remains to be seen.

## Notes

1. The views expressed in this article are solely those of the author and do not reflect the official position of the Organization of American States or the Inter-American Commission on Human Rights. I wish to express my gratitude to Flavia Modell for her support in researching this article. I would also like to thank James Early and Ruthanne Deutsch for their input in an earlier version of this article,

2. Meeting of the presidents of South America, communique, Brazil, September 1, 2000.

3. 10th periodical report that the states parties were required to submit in 1994: Mexico. 30/03/95. CERD/C/260/Add. 1, paragraph 155.

4. 10th periodical report that the states parties were required to submit in 1994: Mexico. 30/03/95. CERD/C/260/Add. 1, paragraph 161.

5. 10th periodical report that the states parties were required to submit in 1994: Mexico. 30/03/95. CERD/C/260/Add. 1, paragraph 157. Nevertheless, there are authors who have begun to conduct studies on the situation of the indigenous peoples from a racial perspective. See Gall (1998 and 2000).

6. The method used in this study is somewhat limited, mainly because it is of a general nature and, therefore, does not cover specific aspects of racism or racial discrimination. The article is not meant to be a complete study of the significance of race in Latin America, the different manifestations of racial discrimination in the hemisphere, or all of the ways that the existence of racism is denied. We use the paper as a preliminary theoretical framework to draw out debate on the persistence of racism in our region.

7. For example, in Uruguay Black people have a lower level of education and a higher school dropout rate. 12th, 13th, and 14th Consolidated Report of Uruguay to the Committee on the Elimination of Racial Discrimination, &: 203 et seq.

8. In Brazil, the Black population shows a higher level of unemployment than the white population, earns at least 40% less salary, and holds the lowest-grade and most unstable jobs on the labor market, which

also provide the least benefits. See Inter-American Trade Union Institute for Racial Equality (2000).

9. In Nicaragua, for example, even though 32.3% of the nations population has access to potable water, the percentage drops off sharply to 8.8% for the population living on the Atlantic coast, where the majority of the indigenous and Afro-Caribbean populations in the country are concentrated. See International Human Rights Law Group (2000).

10. See chapter 11 of the English version of Inter-American Commission on Human Rights (1999).

11. As is the case of the remaining survivors of the Quilombos in Brazil, the Garifunas in Honduras, or the Afro-Caribbean peoples in Nicaragua.

12. CEPAL, Etnicidad, Raza y Equidad en America Latina y el Caribe, LC/R. 1967, March 8, 2000, 36 et seq.

13. 9th periodical report that the states parties were required to submit in 1998: Colombia. 17/11/98. CERD/C332/Add. I (State Party Report). See on this same topic, Plan Nacional de Desarrollo de la Poblacion Afrocolombiana, Departamento Nacional de Planeacion, 1998.

14. CERD/C331/Add. 1, 02/11/99, and 6 (Dominican Republic).

15. 13th periodical report that the signatories were required to submit in 1994: Venezuela. 13/05/96. CERD/C263/Add. 8/Rev 1, 77.

16. 13th periodical report that the signatories were required to submit in 1998: Haiti. 25/05/99. CERD/C/336/Add. 1 and 15 and 17.

17. Summary of the minutes of the 1317th session: Peru. 16/03/99. CERD/C/SR. 1317, 78.

18. 10th periodical report that the signatories were required to submit in 1994: Mexico. 30/03/95. CERD/C/260/Add. 1, paragraph 157.

19. 13th periodical report that the signatories were required to submit in 1997: Cuba. 07/10/97. CERD/C/319/Add. 4 and 16.

20. In order to cover up exclusion of minorities such as indigenous people in Guatemala or the Black population in Brazil.

21. Immigration policies in our region are highly racist. Uruguay, Paraguay, Honduras, Costa Rica, and Panama prohibited people of African origin from immigrating. Venezuela and the Dominican Republic placed restrictions on the immigration of

individuals of African extraction. Quoted in Carlos Hasenbalg (1998:168).

22. *For* example, this was the criterion used by dance clubs or discos in Peru to discriminate. See Law 27049, Un Gesto Politico contra la Discrimination Racial, Ideele. Lima, February 1999, *no.* 115, p. 57.

23. This is the criterion that is used in Uruguay to prevent entry into certain establishments or clubs. See Mundo Afro (1999:12, 35).

24. One of the most widely used devices in Brazil to keep Afro-Brazilians out of the labor market or to make access difficult for them.

25. 13th periodical report that the signatories were required to submit in 1998: Haiti. 25/05/99. CERD/C336/Add. 1.

26. Summary proceedings of the 1317th session: Peru. 16/03/99. CERD/C/SR. 1317, 78.

27. Final Observations of the Committee on the Elimination of Racial Discrimination: Mexico. 22/09/95. A/50/18, paragraphs 353–398.

28. Summary proceedings of the 12306th session: Mexico. 21/10/97. CERD/C/SR. 1206, paragraph 5. The following day, the same representative of the government would admit that when certain practices act as an obstacle to the application of Articles 2 to 5 of the Convention, that constitutes ethnic, if not racial, discrimination. Summary proceedings of the 1207th session: Bulgaria, Mexico. 21/10/97. CERD/C/SR. 1207, paragraph 3.

29. "In Peru, not every *cholo* (mestizo, mixed race, black, or Indian) is poor, but almost every poor person is *cholo*" (Oscatequi, 1998:31).

30. 10th periodical report that the signatories were required to submit in 1994: Mexico. 20/03/95. CERD/C/260/Add. I, paragraph 40. In response to this argument, the CERD stated its "particular concern for the fact that the signatory does not seem to realize that the latent discrimination that the 56 indigenous groups that live in Mexico are experiencing is covered by the definition of racial discrimination that appears in Article 1 of the Convention. The description of the difficult situation of those groups as mere unequal participants in socioeconomic development is inadequate." Final Observations of the Committee on the Elimination of Racial Discrimination: Mexico. 22/09/95. A/50/18, paragraphs 353–398.

31. See Telles and Lim (1998:465–474) and Lovell (2000:85), showing how equally qualified Afro-Brazilians who are defined as both Black and brown Brazilians earn less than white Brazilians.

32. The American Convention of Human Rights states: "The States Parties to this Convention pledge to respect the rights and liberties [that are] recognized therein and to guarantee their free and full exercise to any person who may be subject to their jurisdiction, without any discrimination whatsoever due to reasons of origin, social and economic position or any other social condition" (Article 1.1). The International Covenant on Civil and Political Rights states: "Each one of the States Parties to this Covenant pledge to respect and guarantee all individuals who may be found in their territory and may be subject to their jurisdiction, the rights [that are] recognized in this Covenant, without any distinction whatsoever of social origin, economic position, any other social condition" (Article 2.1).

33. 8th periodical report that the signatories were required to submit in 1998. Addition, Dominican Republic, CERD/C/331/Add. 1, 02/11/99 and 27.

34. Compilation of General Recommendations: 11/02/99. CERD/C/365, General Recommendation XIV pertaining to paragraph 1 of Article 1 of the Convention (42nd Period of Sessions. El enfasis nos pertenece).

35. See, for example, Final Observations of the Committee on the Elimination of Racial Discrimination: Chile. 20/08/99. A/54/18, paragraphs 365–383.

36. See, for example, Final Observations of the Committee on the Elimination of Racial Discrimination: Colombia. 20/08/99. A/54/18, paragraphs 454–481.

37. See, for example, Final Observations of the Committee on the Elimination of Racial Discrimination: Uruguay. 19/08/99. A/54/18, paragraphs 454–435.

38. See, for example, Final Observations of the Committee on the Elimination of Racial Discrimination: Costa Rica. 07/04/99. CERD/C/304/Add. 71 and CERD/C/SR/1317, (Peru), 03/16/99, paragraph 35.

39. See, for example, Final Observations of the Committee on the Elimination of Racial Discrimination: Costa Rica. 07/04/99. CERD/C/304/Add. 71.

40. Final Observations of the Committee on the Elimination of Racial Discrimination: Peru. 12/04/99. CERD/C/304/Add. 69 (hereafter referred to as CERD, Peru).

41. CERD, Costa Rica.

42. 10th periodical report that the signatories were required to submit in 1994: Mexico. 30/03/95. CERD/C260/Add. 1, paragraph 157.

43. Final Observations of the Committee on the Elimination of Racial Discrimination: Haiti. A/54/18, paragraphs 253–271.

44. A point made in Brazils report, CERD/C/SR.1157, 10/23/96, paragraph 55.

45. For example, in Brazil most complaints alleging the crime recognized as racism according to the Constitution, as well as Law 7716/89, amended by Law 9459/97, are described as "crimes against honor."

46. 13th periodical report that the signatories were required to submit in 1994: Venezuela. 13/05/96. CERD/C/263/Add. 8/Rev. 1, paragraph 77.

47. 8th periodical report that the signatories were required to submit in 1998: Dominican Republic. 02/11/99. CERD/C331/Add. 1, paragraph 6.

48. 13th periodical report that the signatories were required to submit in 1998: Haiti. 25/05/99. CERD/C/336/Add.1.

49. Compilation of General Recommendations: 11/02/99. CERD/C/365, General Recommendation 20 (48th period of sessions, 1996).

50. 12th, 13th, and 14th Consolidated Report of the Oriental Republic of Uruguay to the Committee on the Elimination of Racial Discrimination, paragraph 56.

51. Ibid., paragraph 34.

52. 13th periodical report that the signatories were required to submit in 1997: Cuba. 07/10/97. CERD/C/319/Add. 4, paragraph 16.

53. Someone once called Afro-Argentines the first *"desaparecidos"* in the history of the country. See Goldberg (2000:36).

54. There is a widespread sentiment that data collection on racial makeup constitutes a form of discrimination. The government of Uruguay, for example, recognized this practice as being discriminatory in its 12th, 13th, and 14th Consolidated Report to the Committee on the Elimination of Racial Discrimination, paragraph 3. To cite examples, Argentina has not included questions on race or color since 1914; Bolivia, since 1900; Peru, since 1961; Ecuador, since 1950; Venezuela, since 1876; Nicaragua, since 1920; Honduras, since 1945; and the Dominican Republic, since 1950. (Quoted in Hasenbalg, 1998:166.)

55. For example, Bolivia.

56. See Telles and Lim (1998) in which the authors look at how *pardos* (brown people) are closer in terms of social status to the *pretos* (Blacks) than to *brancos* (whites) in Brazil.

57. In fact, there are over 100 different categories in Brazil. See an interesting article by Eugene Robinson (1999), recounting the experience of an African American in Brazil in terms of racial identity.

58. For example, an article that appeared in Peru states that "there is a broad spectrum of interpretive possibilities on the origin, function, and destiny of Black people in Peru, but none of them separates their future from the mixed race *{mestizo}* complex that characterizes the nation" (Millones, 1996:16).

59. In this article, we shall not analyze how the origin of *mestizaje* in Latin America hearkens back to the sexual violence perpetrated by the Spanish and Portuguese conquistadors against indigenous women and later by slave traders against women brought from Africa as slaves.

60. 10th periodical report that the signatories were required to submit in 1994: Mexico. 30/03/95. CERD/C/260/Add. 1, paragraph 157.

61. CERD/C/319/Add. 4, 10.07.97, paragraph 16.

62. Final Observations of the Committee on the Elimination of Racial Discrimination: Colombia. 20/08/99. A/54/18, paragraphs 454–481.

63. Santiago Bastos y Manuela Camus, La exclusion y el desafio. Estudios sobre segregacion etnica y empleo en la ciudad de Guatemala (1998).

64. "To speak of racism in Venezuela is somewhat complex, since it is not a very accepted topic, especially if we use the forms of racism that exist in the United States, Germany or in the Republic of South Africa as a point of reference" (Mijares, 1996:52),

65. It would be possible to take exception to this statement by considering the cases of the *politica de tierra arrasada* (scorched earth policy) in Guatemala or the many policies of extermination that were implemented against indigenous populations in different countries of Latin America.

66. 10th periodical report that the signatories were required to submit in 1996: Mexico. 30/09/96. CERD/C/296/Add. 1, paragraph 73 ("feeling of xenophobia and racial discrimination in some sectors of American society") and paragraph 75 ("at the present time, it is relatively easy to inflame racist and xenophobic sentiments in some sectors of American

society against the streams of migrant labor or refugees"). The report only mentioned the indigenous people as constituting one of the most vulnerable groups to violations of human rights (paragraph 5) or migrant workers on the southern border who face the prospects of fear and uncertainty, and on a few occasions it mentioned the situations of violence, corruption, and vulnerability (paragraph 59), but never did it mention discrimination (within its borders).

67. Of course, with the exceptions noted in the footnote above.

68. Response given in a survey conducted in Guatemala among traditional families in that country, in Casaus Arzu (1998:130).

69. Ley creation del IN AD I Instituto Nacional contra la Discriminacion y la Xenofobia y el Racismo, 23.515, promulgada de hecho, July 28, 1995, Ley 24.515.

70. Decreto por el que se expide la Ley Federal para Prevenir y Eliminar la Discriminacion, June 11, 2003, Diario Oficial de la Federacion.

71. Acuerdo Gubernativo 390–2002 de creacion de la Comision Presidencial contra el Racismo y la Discriminacion contra los Pueblos Indigenas.

72. Law 10.678, May 23, 2003, Cria a Secretaria Especial de Politicas de Promocao da Igualdade Racial, da Presidencia da Republica, e da outras providencias.

73. Presidential decree 4.228 of May 13, 2002, establishing a national program of affirmative action.

74. Law 3.708 of Rio de Janeiro, September 11, 2001 (establishes a quota system of 40% of all the admissions slots for "Black and brown" students in the local universities of Rio de Janeiro).

75. See Carneiro (2003), arguing for the examples from the United States that can be helpful for the Brazilian experience.

## References

Adorno, Sergio. 1999. Racial discrimination and criminal justice in Sao Paulo. In *Race in Contemporary Brazil: From Indifference to Inequality*, ed. Rebecca Reichmann. University Park: Pennsylvania State University Press.

Arocha Rodriguez, Carlos. 1992. Afro-Colombia denied. In *NACLA Report on the Americas: The Black Americas, 1492–1992* 25, no. 4 (February).

Bastos, Santiago, and Manuela Camus. 1998. La exclusion y el desafio: Estudios sobre segregacion etnica y empleo en el area metropolitana de Guatemala. *FLACSO* 43.

Carneiro, Sueli. 2003. Amicus curiae. *Correio Braziliense,* January 8.

Casaus Arzu, Marta Elena. 1998. *La metamorfosis del racismo en Guatemala.* Guatemala City: Cholsamaj.

Cohen, Stanley. 1996. Government responses to human rights reports: Claims, denials and counterclaims. *Human Rights Quarterly* 18:3.

de la Torre, Carlos. 1997. La letra con sangre entra: Racismo, escuela y vida cotidiana en Ecuador, Paper presented at the 20th Congress of the Latin American Studies Association.

Early, James. 1999. Reflections on Cuba, race, and politics. *Souls: A Critical Journal of Black Politics, Culture,, and Society* 1, no. 2 (Spring).

Economic Commission on Latin America and the Caribbean (ECLAC). 2000. Etnicidad, raza y equidad en America Latina y el Caribe, August.

Gall, Olivia. 1998. Racism, interethnic war and peace in Chiapas. Paper presented at the 21st Congress of the Latin American Studies Association.

———. 2000. Mestizaje-indigenismo and racism in the Mexican state's ideology of national integration. Paper presented at the 23rd Congress of the Latin American Studies Association.

Goldberg, Marta Beatriz. 2000. Nuestros negros, desaparecidos o ignorados? *Todo es Historia* 393 (April).

Guimaraes, Antonio Sergio. 1999. *Racismo e antiracismo no Brasil.* Sao Paulo: Editora 34, Ltda.

——— 2001. The misadventures of nonracialism in Brazil. In *Beyond Racism,* ed. Charles V. Hamilton, Lynn Huntley, Neville Alexander, Antonio Sergio Guimaraes, and Wilmot James. Boulder, CO: Lynne Rienner Publishers.

Hasenbalg, Carlos. 1998. Racial inequalities in Brazil and throughout Latin America: Timid responses to disguised racism. In *Constructing Democracy: Human Rights, Citizenship, and Society in Latin America,* ed. Elizabeth Jelin and Eric Hershberg. New York: Perseus Books.

Inter-American Commission on Human Rights. 1999. Third Report on the Human Rights Situation in Colombia. OAS/ser. L/V; II. 102, doc. 9, rev. 1, February 26.

Inter-American Trade Union Institute for Racial Equality. 2000. Map of the Black population in the Brazilian labor market.

International Human Rights Law Group. 2000. Submission to the Inter-American Commission on Human Rights, March 3.

Lovell, Peggy A. 2000. Gender, race, and the struggle for social justice in Brazil. *Latin American Perspectives* 27:85–102.

Millones, Luis. 1996–1997. Peruanos de Eban. *Bienvenida Lima,* December-February.

Minority Rights Group. 1995. *No Longer Invisible: Afro-Latin Americans Today.* London: Minority Rights Group.

———. 1999. *Afro-Brazilians: Time fir Recognition.* London: Minority Rights Group.

*Mijares, Maria Marta.* 1996. Racismo y endoracismo en Barlovento: Presencia y ausencia en Rio Chico: Autoimagen de una poblacidn barloventena. *Caracas: Fundacidn Afroamerica.*

*Mundo Afro.* 1999. Situacidn de discriminacion y racismo en el Uruguay.

Oliveira, Barbosa e dos Santos. 1998. *A cor do medo: O medo da cor.*

Oscategui, Jose. 1998. Poblacion, crecimiento economico y racismo en el Peru. *Actualidad Economica* (Lima), May.

Robinson, Eugene. 1999. On the beach at Ipanema. *Washington Post Magazine,* August 1.

Rodriguez, Romero Jorge. 2000. La discrimination racial en la epoca de la globalizacion economica. *Mundo Afro.*

Rohter, Larry. 2003. Racial quotas in Brazil touch off fierce debate. *New York Times,* April 5.

Telles, Edward, and Nelson Lim. 1998. Does it matter who answers the race question?: Racial classification and Income inequality in Brazil. *Demography* 35 (4):465–474.

UNITED NATIONS. 1995. Committee on the Elimination of Racial Discrimination. 10th periodical report that the signatories were required to submit in 1994: Mexico. March 30, CERD/C/260/Add. 1.

———. Committee on the Elimination of Racial Discrimination. 12th, 13th, and 14th Consolidated

Report of Uruguay to the Committee on the Elimination of Racial Discrimination.

———. 1998. Committee on the Elimination of Racial Discrimination. 9th periodical report that the signatories were required to submit in 1998: Colombia. November 17, '98. CERD/C332/Add. 1 (State Party Report).

———. 1999. Committee on the Elimination of Racial Discrimination. Dominican Republic CERD/C331 /Add. 1, November 3 and 6.

———. 1996. Committee on the Elimination of Racial Discrimination. 13th periodical report that the signatories were required to submit in 1994: Venezuela. May 13, CERD/C263/Add. 8/Rev. 1.

———. 1999. Committee on the Elimination of Racial Discrimination. 13th periodical report that the signatories were required to submit in 1998: Haiti. May 25, CERD/C/336/Add. 1.

———. 1999. Committee on the Elimination of Racial Discrimination Summary of the minutes of the 1317th session: Peru. March 16. CERD/C/SR, 1317, &78.

———. 1997. Committee on the Elimination of Racial Discrimination 13th periodical report that the signatories were required to submit in 1997: Cuba. October 7. CERD/C/319/Add. 4, & 16.

———. 1995. Committee on the Elimination of Racial Discrimination. Final observations of the Committee on the Elimination of Racial Discrimination: Mexico. September 22, A/50/18.

———. 1995. Committee on the Elimination of Racial Discrimination. Final observations of the Committee on the Elimination of Racial Discrimination: Mexico. September 22, A/50/18, paragraphs 353–398.

———. 1997. Committee on the Elimination of Racial Discrimination. Summary proceedings of the 12306th session: Mexico. October 21, CERD/C/SR. 1206, paragraph 5.

———. 1997. Committee on the Elimination of Racial Discrimination. Summary proceedings of the 1207th session: Bulgaria, Mexico. October 21, CERD/C/SR. 1207, paragraph 3.

———. 1999. Committee on the Elimination of Racial Discrimination. 8th periodical report that the signatories were required to submit in 1998. Addition: Dominican Republic, CERD/C/331 / Add. 1, November 2.

———. 1999. Committee on the Elimination of Racial Discrimination. Final observations of the Committee on the Elimination of Racial Discrimination: Chile. August 20, A/54/18.

———. 1999. Committee on the Elimination of Racial Discrimination. Final observations of the Committee on the Elimination of Racial Discrimination: Colombia. August 20, A/54/18.

———. 1999. Committee on the Elimination of Racial Discrimination. Final observations of the Committee on the Elimination of Racial Discrimination: Uruguay. August 19, A/54/18.

———. 1999. Committee on the Elimination of Racial Discrimination. Final observations of the Committee on the Elimination of Racial Discrimination: Costa Rica. April 7, CERD/C/ 304/ Add. 71.

———. 1999. Committee on the Elimination of Racial Discrimination. Final observations of the Committee on the Elimination of Racial Discrimination: Peru. April 12, CERD/C/304/Add. 69.

———. 1999. Committee on the Elimination of Racial Discrimination. Final observations of the Committee on the Elimination of Racial Discrimination: Haiti. A/54/18, paragraphs 253–271.

———. 1999. Committee on the Elimination of Racial Discrimination. Final observations of the Committee on the Elimination of Racial Discrimination: Colombia. August 20, A/54/18.

# Humor and Culture

# Freud Goes to *South Park*

## Teaching Against Postmodern Prejudices and Equal Opportunity Hatred

### By Robert Samuels

● ● ● ● ● ● ● ● ● ● ● ● ● ● ● ● ● ● ● ● ● ● ● ● ● ● ● ● ● ● ● ● ● ● ● ● ● ●

## Editor's Introduction

Although the author discusses the role of humor with regard to matters of race and intolerance, he also weaves important considerations on how reverse psychology can also invert meanings. Early in the selection, Robert Samuels makes it clear that minorities are frequently "seen as victimizers and abusers of the welfare system, whereas the wealthy majority is positioned to be the victim of excessive taxes and reversed racism."[1] Students should reflect on and perhaps even keep a diary to document when and where they hear about these issues in the media or in conversation.

While the popular and often controversial show *South Park* frequently lampoons and satirizes contemporary issues, it also may "knowingly or unknowingly" play into the current trend of using stereotypes and ethnic humor to address cultural assimilation and internalization of self-hatred according to Samuels.[2]

### Notes

1. Robert Samuels. "Freud Goes to South Park: Teaching Against Postmodern Prejudices and Equal Opportunity Hatred." In *Taking South Park Seriously*, edited by Jeffrey Andrew. New York: State University of New York Press, 2008.

Like many other television shows and movies, *South Park* gains a great deal of its popularity by proclaiming itself to be politically incorrect and intolerant of all forms of tolerance. Moreover, through a common rhetorical reversal, the creators of this show often present themselves as being tolerant of intolerance; in other words, as my students often report, its humor is generated by "saying what you are not supposed to say." This chapter argues that this rhetorical reversal, where one is taught to be intolerant of tolerance and tolerant of intolerance, is part of a larger social effort to challenge and reverse progressive efforts to fight stereotypes and prejudices in American culture. Furthermore, this rhetorical reversal can also be seen in the political and cultural process of undermining the popular support for the welfare state while calling for tax breaks for the wealthy. In this upside-down world, minorities are now often seen as victimizers and abusers of the welfare system, whereas the wealthy majority is positioned to be the victim of excessive taxes and reversed racism.

Knowingly or unknowingly, shows such as *South Park* feed this rhetorical reversal that influences so many students and makes teaching about critical thinking and social change in higher education even more difficult. One reason why pop culture humor plays such a major role in this attempt to reverse the cultural representation of minorities and dominant groups is that comedy itself often works by reversing values and social positions. Thus, in the classic structure of humor, a man acts like a woman or a pauper acts like a king. Moreover, much of popular comedy today is based on the use of ethnic stereotypes and prejudices that are allowed to be recycled because the victims of these negative depictions are the ones making these destructive self-representations. In fact, this chapter argues that the very structure of cultural assimilation and immigration calls for the internalization of negative self-representations.

### Assimilated Stereotypes in *South Park*

The assimilation and internalization of self-hatred in the film *South Park: Bigger Longer & Uncut (1999)* is represented through the character of Kyle Broslovski who is attacked in a humorous way for being Jewish.[1] Furthermore, the representation of his character and his family play off of the most basic stereotypes concerning Jewish people. Importantly, one of the two main writers of this show is Jewish and thus we are forced to ask the question of why Jews in our culture often participate in the recirculation of anti-Semitic stereotypes.

This question of internalized anti-Semitism offers us one of the keys to understanding contemporary prejudices. Most systems of prejudice go through three major stages. At first, prejudices are brutally applied through real acts of dehumanization and enslavement. The next stage of prejudice often involves legal segregation and state-sponsored discrimination. Finally, in a third stage, the objects of prejudice internalize the

stereotypes by which they have been victimized.[2] In this postmodern stage, negative and positive stereotypes provide a ground for self-recognition and identity.[3] Moreover, the mass culture industry reinforces these negative self-representations by basing characters on the largest available cultural generalizations. Internalized anti-Semitism thus plays into this logic by basing Jewish identity on cultural assimilation, victimhood, and self-deprecating humor.

However, when the various stereotypes and prejudices in the show and movie are pointed out, some students are quick to argue that every group is equally attacked and no one takes the attacks seriously. Here, we see strong examples of the rhetoric of reversal and universalization: From a globalizing perspective, these students claim that equal opportunity hatred is not intolerance and that popular culture has no meaning or effect anyway. In fact, students often feel that the teacher who points to prejudice in culture and society is really the one with the problem. In this version of "shooting the messenger," the teacher who tries to get students to become aware of the destructive nature of prejudice in our society is seen as a highly sensitive person who does not know how to take a joke and does not accept the universalized notion of equal opportunity intolerance.

Teachers must recognize this cultural reversal and not try to challenge directly these deeply held unconscious social beliefs. However, students can learn how to detect and move beyond the various rhetorical mechanisms that our culture uses to reinforce and recirculate prejudices and stereotypes. The trick is to analyze destructive rhetorical figures in a safe transitional place that is neither too personal nor too alien. Popular culture comedies such as *South Park* can offer us this transitional space, but providing students with the critical tools and concepts that can be employed to stop the flow of information and examine the specific cultural elements used to construct humor and identity in our society is important.

One rhetorical strategy that popular culture employs is the use of extreme exaggeration both to circulate prejudices and to deny the import of these negative self-representations. For example, in the *South Park* movie, one of the main stereotypes is the relationship between the aggressive Jewish mother and the oppressed Jewish son. In fact, the main plot of the movie is that Kyle's Jewish and politically correct mother wants to attack Canada because two Canadian filmmakers have made a foul-mouthed film that has affected her son and his friends. In this narrative, the stereotype of the overly protective Jewish mother is exaggerated to the point that this maternal superego threatens to cause an international war. Furthermore, this extreme depiction of a Jewish mother is presented along with a series of de-contextualized references to the Holocaust and World War II: There is a Canadian Death Camp, children join La Resistance, there are charges of "crimes against humanity," and various representations of concentration camps.

An important idea in this pop culture example is the notion that what in part links the internalization of anti-Semitic stereotypes to the subtle and not-so-subtle reminders of the Holocaust is the strategy of taking serious issues concerning prejudice and trying to empty them of their initial meaning and value. For instance, in one scene that takes place in Hell, we see a morphing between images of Gandhi, George Burns, Hitler, Saddam Hussein, and Satan. From the postmodern perspective of the filmmakers, little difference exists between someone who played God in a movie (George Bums), someone who was a leader of his people (Gandhi), a former totalitarian leader (Hitler), a hated former leader (Hussein), and the Christian representation of Evil (Satan). Because these figures are only images without any historical and cultural context, they seem to have lost all inherent value or significance. In fact, these images have become secondary texts that can be assimilated into new contexts for our humor and entertainment. Furthermore, the fate of these de-contextualized images parallels the fate of immigrating people who must assimilate to a new cultural context by shedding the value of their previous cultural and historical traditions and beliefs.[4]

We can find a strong incidence of this logic of assimilation and internalized anti-Semitism in the title of the movie: *South Park: Bigger Longer & Uncut* This title combines allusions to censorship, the uncircumcised penis, and a sense of phallic power. Moreover, because the Jewish mother becomes the main proponent of politically correct censorship in the movie, we discover an interesting equation between the circumcision of the Jewish male, the dominance of the Jewish mother, and the censorship of free speech. Here, the Jewish ritual of circumcision is blamed on the mother and attached to a loss of freedom. In fact, what is idealized is the non-Jewish, uncircumcised exercise of phallic power and free speech.[5] The assimilation and internalization of anti-Semitism thus results in the idea that the root of all evil in the world is derived from the Jewish tradition of circumcising men and cutting them off from their free and manly expression of aggression and sexuality.[6]

Because the movie declares itself to be bigger, longer, and uncut, we can assume that true phallic power comes from the ability to deny circumcision and censorship by identifying with the idealized free and non-Jewish male member.[7] The movie therefore subtly plays on the standard stereotypical opposition between the powerful Christian male and the feminized Jew. In turn, this opposition is projected onto a political fight where the Jewish mother becomes the source for feminizing and censoring the victimized Jewish male. Furthermore, this demonization of the Jewish mother and the feminized Jewish male is hidden behind the general rhetorical defensive strategy of mocking the idea that the media influences children in a negative way. According to the film's logic, the problems with our children do not stem from the fact that they copy the obscene and prejudicial representations that they see in the media; rather, the problem is that the Jewish maternal superego wants to censor and castrate the naughty boys for expressing their true desires. Importantly, some students are often quick to buy this conservative rhetoric positing that the true cause of intolerance in our society is the politically correct people who are trying to fight intolerance.

One reason why some students may equate political correctness with intolerance and prejudicial intolerance with tolerance is that that they have grown up in a culture shaped by a successful conservative campaign to reverse our understandings of prejudice and tolerance. A key aspect of this rhetorical reversal is the universalized notion that our society no longer has any prejudices and therefore anyone who points out prejudices must be the cause of prejudice. In the case of teaching about prejudices, this reversed rhetoric cannot help but to enter into the room, and teachers can deal with this conservative ideology in an indirect way. Because a direct attack on the conservative effort to reverse racism may serve to reinforce students' political ideologies and investments, examining this rhetoric in a nonpolarizing way is important. Furthermore, the first step in this process of educating against the rhetorical reversal is to critique the notion of universal tolerance and then show examples of intolerance in popular culture. Teachers can also work to change the popular view of political correctness by critiquing its excesses and affirming the positive aspects of treating others with respect.

Although many students will claim that *South Park* is a liberal, anticonservative show, for the writers of the film and television program, political correctness is clearly the primary evil they fight against.[8] Like the incorrigible children that they portray and like many contemporary Americans, Matt Stone and Trey Parker feel strongly that censorship is worse than hate speech and that free speech is the ultimate good that should be celebrated. This desire to endorse a universal message of free speech coupled with their idealization of the unrestrained individual is apparent in the many interviews in which they defend their usage of bathroom humor and politically incorrect stereotypes. For instance, in response to the question of why he stresses the Jewishness of the character Kyle, Stone, whose mother is Jewish, proclaims, "It just creates more opportunity for comedy. It gives us more things to make fun of and we just think it's funny."[9] What Stone does not say is why Kyle's Jewish identity is funny and how this humor relates to Stone's own secular upbringing in Texas and Colorado.

To help my students think about the culture of political incorrectness and internalized racism, getting them to reflect on how humor and comedy function is important. One of the first ideas I posit is the notion that humor often derives its source from real feelings of pain and anxiety that are then turned into a "positive" experience by entertaining others. In fact, in Freud's highly misunderstood work, *Jokes and Their Relation to the Unconscious*, he posits the true goal of a joke is to bond with a third party and to bribe this social other not to analyze or criticize one's humor (119). Thus, jokes not only release repressed urges and desires, but they also constitute a social act of bonding.

Importantly, Freud's theory of humor is dominated by references to Jewish jokes.[10] One reason Freud gives for this choice is the debatable idea that Jews are more self-critical than other people and thus they make better comics (133). However, as many people insist, in our culture, all types of social groups are the target of humor and, in most cases, the comic is from the same group that is being attacked. Central to this structure of in-group comedy is the idea that attacking someone in your own group is okay, but someone from another group cannot attack your group. In many cases, I have found this logic of the inner group attacking itself functions to circulate prejudice under a safe cover. Furthermore, one of Freud's central ideas about humor is his notion that the ethnic group member performs an act of self-mockery for a neutral party and, therefore, even when a person of an in-group mocks his or her own group, that presentation of intolerance is performed for the social and cultural other.

In this structure of humor, we find the basic process of assimilation as the appeal of the minority to the dominant culture's definitions and values. Furthermore, Freud insists that the object and second party of the joke plays the role of the social censor who must be avoided (116). In fact, for Freud, the primary example of humor is a dirty joke that is meant to seduce a woman, but due to her high moral standing, the joke must be redirected toward a male third party. In this structure, the third party becomes the ally of the first party joke teller against the second party female object and social censor. If we now apply this structure to the general framework of the film *South Park*, we see that the Jewish mother represents the object of the joke and the source of social censorship.[11] To overcome the Jewish mother's resistance to the pure expression of sexual aggression (the desire of the joke teller), the mother must be attacked for the benefit and the enjoyment of the third party or audience. The joke teller and the audience thus bond over the attack on the Jewish mother.

Through this theory, we can begin to see how so much of our popular culture is often centered on a process of male bonding through the tragic or comedic stigmatization of minority groups. Even if the audience is not comprised entirely of men, this theory argues that the viewer is placed in the third-party position of being the one who accepts or rejects the presentations of the first-party joke teller. Here, the third party represents the dominant culture that must be bribed by the first party's victimization of the second party. In the case of *South Park*, we can say that Matt Stone (a Jew) victimizes his Jewish mother and identity to bond with his audience. Internalized anti-Semitism thus serves the processes of assimilation by sacrificing a part of the subject's own ethnic identity in the goal of bonding with the dominant culture.

## The Myth of Free Speech

In response to this theory of assimilation and prejudice in popular culture, some may argue that we have a society built on tolerance and equal opportunity prejudice and, therefore, no one group is ever really being singled out. Although I would not deny aspects of this argument, I respond by pointing out that the rhetoric of universal equality can work to veil important inequalities in our society. In fact, teachers can reveal to students how the agenda of conservative politics helps to explode the myth of the neutral realm of universal free speech and tolerance. As Stanley Fish argues in his book *There's No Such Thing as Free Speech*,

the claim for a universal tolerance of all expression is always grounded on a hidden agenda of particular vested interests (7). Moreover, Fish posits that all universal claims are invalid because they do not take into account the context and history of their own formulations (viii). Therefore, Fish affirms that we must always contextualize every universal claim to see what interests lie behind it. In the case of *South Park*, the universal claim of free speech relies on the unstated idea that words have no real effect on people and thus they should never be constrained. However, this idea is itself challenged by the notion that the words of the politically correct do actively constrain the freedoms of the politically incorrect. Yet the way out of this conflict is to argue that, unlike the words and actions of the proponents of political correctness, the politically incorrect makers of this movie do not believe that their representations have any meaning or context.

With regard to *South Park*, by making references to the Holocaust without any concern for the original context of these representations, the writers are able to claim that these depictions are not harmful to any particular group. Likewise, the representation of Kyle's Jewishness is seen as being purely entertaining and not anti-Semitic because the writers believe that their representations have no value or effect. One reason they can make this claim is that they do not believe that ethnic identity itself has any value or meaning other than its ability to make people stand out from the dominant crowd and be laughed at. Within the context of *South Park* and the ideologies affecting student subjectivities, this strategy of denying the value or import of ethnic identity and other cultural influences is a key to the idea that popular culture is really about nothing. In this sense, what Americans seem to value the most is the idea that our culture is meaningless and our words and representations have no real effect. From this perspective, there is no such thing as hate speech and what is really wrong about politically correct people and teachers in general is that they take words and representations too seriously. In this way the United States uncannily is the most Zen-like culture around because what we value the most is our ability to spend a great deal of time experiencing nothingness and nonmeaning.

## It's Only a Joke

In the teaching of popular culture, this Zen-like philosophy represents one of the strongest convictions of the audience.[12] Students often steadfastly cling to their right to meaningless entertainment and interpret any attempt to contextualize or interpret popular culture as a horrible act threatening to rob them of their most cherished value. How do we then reconcile these two opposing claims? On one side, we have the argument that popular culture has no meaning or value and, on the other side, we find the argument that nothing has more value than the defense of popular culture and the freedom of expression.

Freud's theory of jokes helps us to reconcile this conflict by positing that the main function of jokes is to present serious issues in a manner that shields them from any type of criticism and analysis. As with free speech, humor thus creates a responsibility-free zone where people are given the opportunity to state anything they like without fear of censor or restraint. Yet humor itself needs restraint because it is generated out of the conflict between infantile desires (pure sex and aggression) and social norms. To hide this conflict, the first-person joke teller must rely on the third-party audience's ability to process the information of the joke while denying the value of the same information. For example, ethnic jokes rely on cultural stereotypes that the audience must recognize and understand but not acknowledge as being meaningful or valuable.

This Freudian theory of humor helps to define the relations among assimilation, popular culture, and internalized prejudices. In the context of assimilation, one first reduces one's ethnic identity to the level of a stereotype, and then one tells the dominant culture that this representation means nothing. Thus, Matt Stone says that people like to laugh at the stereotypical representations of Jewish characters and, at the same time, he claims that these representations are only entertainment and have no real meaning. Freud is able to account for this contradiction between the value and the meaninglessness of stereotypes through his notion of preconscious representations. This theory is one of the most misunderstood and neglected aspects of his work because it breaks down the simple opposition between unconscious and conscious ideas. By saying that stereotypes are preconscious, Freud indicates that we use them without our conscious awareness of them, and so they take on an automatic quality as if they were coming from some foreign place. Therefore, we feel that we are not responsible for these preconscious representations because we are barely aware of them and we do not use them intentionally. Yet in popular culture these types of preconscious prejudices are the most prevalent because people assimilate and circulate ideas that they claim are not their own and have no meaning. Furthermore, saying that people have no prejudices because our culture itself is predicated on the ability of a mass audience to recognize generalized traits of characters and ethnic groups is ridiculous. What we often assimilate in our culture are serious preconscious representations and generalizations that are placed in an unserious responsibility-free zone.

## The Rhetoric of Denial

One reason why a film like _South Park_ is such an effective pedagogical tool is that it helps to reveal the popular rhetorical methods employed for both assimilating stereotypes and denying their value and responsibility. The way that the writers accomplish this task of removing themselves from any responsibility for their representation of prejudices is to make the scapegoating process itself a ridiculous aspect of the film. Thus, the movie includes a song that openly anticipates the critics of the movie and the movie within the movie:

Off to the movie we shall go

Where we learn everything that we know
'cause the movies teach us
What our parents don't have time to say
And this movie's gonna make our lives complete

Although these lyrics indicate that children are highly influenced by the media, the words present this argument in such a stupid-sounding song that people are signaled not to take this idea seriously. In fact, this blaming of the media is then transformed into the humorous technique of using Canada as a scapegoat:

Blame Canada
Shame on Canada for—
The smut we must cut
The trash we must smash
The laughter and fun
Must all be undone
We must blame them and cause a fuss
Before somebody thinks of blaming us

Like the song about the influence of the media, this song posits that parents blame other people, such as Canadians, to avoid their own responsibilities. The film sends important messages, but it then undercuts these same messages by placing them in contexts where the audience is told not to take them seriously. Therefore, by making fun of the way that people blame the media and other people for their own problems, the movie is able to remove all responsibility from its own representations.

Within this context of scapegoating and the denying of responsibility in the movie, we find several references to the Holocaust. For example, as the war between the United States and Canada heats up, we see a news anchor deliver the following address:

A full-scale attack has been launched on Toronto, after the Canadians' last bombing, which took a horrible toll on the Arquette family. For security measures, our great American government

is rounding up all citizens that have any Canadian blood, and putting them into camps. All Canadian-American citizens are to report to one of these Death Camps right away. Did I say, "Death Camps"? I meant, "Happy Camps," where you will eat the finest meals, have access to fabulous doctors, and be able to exercise regularly. Meanwhile, the war criminals, Terrance and Phillip, are prepped for their execution. Their execution will take place during a fabulous USO show, with special guest celebrities.

The mention here of "Death Camps," "fabulous doctors," and the execution of "war criminals" refers to and mocks aspects of the Holocaust. Once again, we must ask why would these writers do this? Are these references made because they are so recognizable, or does the humor set out to make light of the true traumatic nature of the Holocaust?

One possible way of responding to these questions is to look at the way the Holocaust is tied to Jewish identity in our culture and the way that this identity is both affirmed and denied in the film. In the case of the Jewish boy, Kyle, one of the running jokes on the show and in the movie is that it is not his fault for being Jewish. We find this sentiment stated in one of the final scenes of the movie where Kyle's friend Cartman tries to bond with Kyle as they face potential death:

CARTMAN: [hunkering down, with Kyle, in the trench] Kyle? All those times I said you were a big, dumb Jew? I didn't mean it. You're not a Jew.
KYLE: Yes, I am. I am a Jew, Cartman!
CARTMAN: No, no, Kyle. Don't be so hard on yourself.

The anxiety that causes this joke to be funny is the idea that being Jewish is inherently bad and a constant source of self-hatred; thus, Cartman can only bond with his friend by trying to tell him not to take his Jewish self-hatred so seriously. What may tie this question of Jewish self-hatred to the Holocaust is the idea that Jews hate themselves for being victims and their victim status comes from the Holocaust.

This topic of ethnic self-hatred is one of the most difficult issues for students. Because so much of popular culture seems to be about self-love, thinking about the roles self-negation plays in our society does not make sense to many students. Yet this type of self-conflict is exactly what needs to be explored in a class dedicated to positive social change because the inability of people to acknowledge the multiple parts of their own identities results in limiting self-knowledge and demonizing others who are connected with the rejected parts of the self.

## On Jewish Self-Hatred

To explore further this question of ethnic self-hatred, I look to Sandor Oilman's work on anti-Semitism. In his book, *Jewish Self-Hatred,* Oilman argues that a central driving force behind internalized anti-Semitism is the Jewish desire to assimilate into the dominant culture. He claims that for Jewish people to fit into the society in which they live, they must not only accept the values and mores of the dominant reference group, but they must also accept chat group's fantasies about Jews (2). Yet the dominant group sends a double message to Jews: You should be like us, and thus lose all of your ethnic differences, and you will never be like us because of the differences that we have attached to you (2). Assimilation therefore offers a double bind for the Jewish person and all other minority groups, and Gilman posits that this double bind is then internalized (2–3). Self-hatred is in this sense based on the minority group's identification with the dominant group's hatred of any type of ethnic difference.

Gilman adds to this argument the idea that the assimilated person always knows that he or she has not completely assimilated, and thus a lingering sense of failure and rejection is always either internalized or projected onto other members of one's own group. For instance, Gilman argues that most of Freud's Jewish jokes that he discusses in his theory of humor are based on demonizing

Eastern European Jews (264). Oilman posits that Freud makes fun of these other Jews so that he can split off the good Jew from the bad Jew and differentiate between his own assimilation as a good German scientist and the failure of other (Eastern European) Jews to assimilate. Moreover, Gilman thinks that one reason Freud wanted to conduct a scientific study of Jewish jokes was that Freud believed science offered a universal non-Jewish language (268). Freud's turn to "objective science" is therefore itself an attempt at assimilating into a universalizing discourse; however, this act of assimilation constantly fails, and so he must perpetually return to the question of Jewish identity.

The irony of Freud's attempt to create a non-Jewish universal science of the mind was made apparent when the Nazis and other people labeled psychoanalysis the "Jewish Science." From one perspective, this term is accurate because the question of Jewish identity has often haunted the ability of psychoanalysis to be considered a modern universal science of the mind; Judaism has always represented a challenge to universalizing discourses, be it the universalizing discourse of Christianity, American assimilation, modern science, or Fascism. Not only do the Jewish people often consider themselves to be God's chosen people, but they have also been labeled as different from the dominant cultures in which they live. Jewish particularity has therefore often come into conflict with the universalizing tendencies of Western culture. Yet, in this age of identity politics, one would think that this particularizing ethnic identity formation would be a source of power and self-affirmation. However, as my analysis of *South Park* shows, ethnic identity has become a major form of debasement and entertainment for the general public.

To understand why Jewishness and other forms of ethnic identity represent sources of humiliation and self-hatred in culture today, we can take into account the link between the universalizing global economy and the popular culture of assimilation. Because capitalism, like modern science, is ideally a universal discourse that treats every participant in the same way, it tends to take on an air of being tolerant of everyone and everything. As Jean-Paul Sartre argues,

we will accept you as long as... but not really...

a price theoretically does not change when a Jew or a Muslim approaches the price tag, just like a scientific experiment does not change if a Jew or a non-Jew does it.[13] Jews and other minority groups thus turn to science and capitalism to escape their own particular identities and to enter into a discourse where they can be treated as equals. This equality is the ideal of modern universal tolerance: Everyone should be treated equally regardless of race, creed, or gender. However, postmodern culture turns this modern ideology on its head and, instead of preaching universal tolerance, it often preaches universal intolerance. Thus, what becomes circulated and distributed is not some purely abstract science experiment or price tag but a system of prejudices and generalizations in the form of the mass media.

In revealing and critiquing the use of prejudice in the movie *South Park,* I have shown how popular culture often circulates the intolerance of ethnic difference under the safe protection of meaningless humor and equal opportunity racism. However, humor is never completely meaningless and racism and intolerance are never universal or equal. In fact, we can affirm that pop culture representations have helped to provide the rhetorical foundation for a political reversal of victims and victimizers. In this cultural context, revealing these reversals and teaching against equal opportunity hatred becomes important.

## Notes

1. This chapter deals with the movie *South Park: Bigger Longer & Uncut* (1999) and not with the television show. However, I hope that the reader and avid watcher of the television program will be able to see connections and differences between the movie and the show.

2. Elisabeth Young-Bruehl's *The Anatomy of Prejudice* offers a broad analysis of the history of prejudice in Western culture.

3. Although Jewish people have often internalized stereotypes, this mode of self-representation only begins to dominate the use of prejudices in contemporary culture.

4. This chapter uses the notion of assimilation to account for the central defining process of postmodern culture. Assimilation not only refers to the ways that minority cultures are asked to fit into the dominant cultures, but also the technological methods that allow for the reconstruction of history and narrative discourses,

5. For a discussion of the multiple meanings of circumcision in Western culture and Judaism, see Daniel Boyarin's A *Radical Jew: Paul and the Politics of Identity* (67–68, 230–31, 112–13, 225–26).

6. Sandor Oilman's *Jewish Self-Hatred* provides a detailed discussion of the history of internalized anti-Semitism.

7. In the movie, one of the young characters confuses Jesus with the clitoris as the key to making a female happy.

8. While political correctness is often associated in popular culture with the supposedly oppressive power of minority groups and academic liberals, this film reveals some of the hidden anti-Semitic sources for the condemnation of these groups.

9. This interview with Matt Stone and Trey Parker can be found on the online version of the Jewish Student Press Service, at http://www.jsps.com/stories/south-park.shtml.

10. For an extended analysis of the Jewish aspects of Freud's jokes, see Sandor Oilman's *Jewish Self Hatred* (261–69).

11. Whereas Freud distinguishes among the first, second, and third parties of the joke, he does not differentiate between the object of the joke and the object's relation to the social censor.

12. Most teachers shy away from being critical of students; however, the ways that students and other people resist interpreting many aspects of popular culture is necessary to note.

13. See Sartre's *Anti-Semite and Jew* (110–1).

## Works Cited

Boyarin, Daniel. A *Radical Jew: Paul and the Politics of Identity*. Berkeley: University of California Press, 1994.

Fish, Stanley. *There's No Such Thing as Free Speech*. New York: Oxford University Press, 1994.

Freud, Sigmund. *Jokes and Their Relation to the Unconscious*. New York: Norton, 1960.

Oilman, Sandor. *Freud, Race, and Gender*. Princeton, NJ: Princeton University Press, 1993.

———. *Jewish Self Hatred: Anti-Semitism and the Hidden Language of the Jews*. Baltimore, MD: Johns Hopkins University Press, 1986.

Sartre, Jean-Paul. *Anti-Semite and Jew*. New York: Shocken, 1948.

Young-Bruehl, Elisabeth. *The Anatomy of Prejudices*. Cambridge, MA: Harvard University Press, 1996.

#thisis2016 : Asian-Americans respond     10/13/16

  - Asians considered people of color?

- Chinese firm apologizes after racist detergent ad
  (CNN world)
    - large pop. of black people in South Provience of
    guangdong, China
      - say they experience racism, ad is an
      example

* New York Times Article ((atherine Porter 11/7/18)
  └ Trudeau Apologizes for Canada's Turning Away Ship of Jews
  Fleeing Nazis

  - St. Louis 1939, More then 250 Killed in Nazi death camps
      ↗
    Steamliner

  - Justin Trudeau (Prime Minister): years of anti-semitic foreign
    policy

  - more than 900 passagers, 4 months before WWII began

  - U.S. also refused pleas for asylum